SHOOTERS

VERTIGO

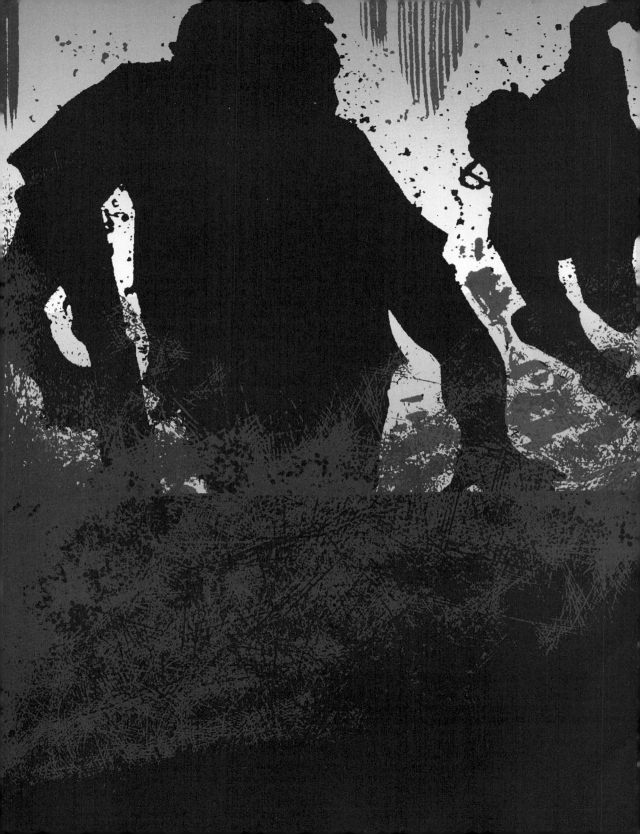

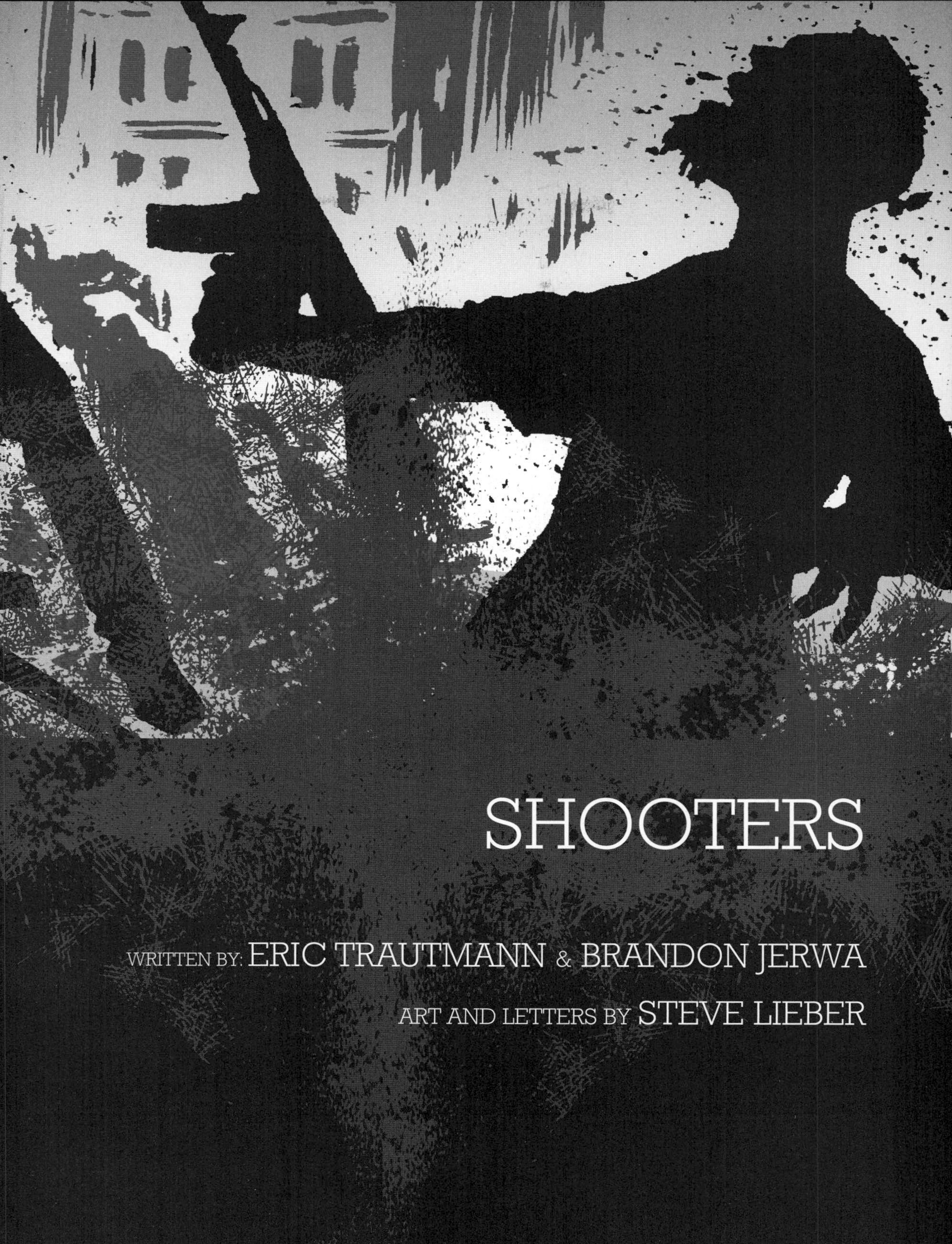

SHOOTERS

WRITTEN BY: ERIC TRAUTMANN & BRANDON JERWA

ART AND LETTERS BY STEVE LIEBER

7/2/12 13it 22.98

Joan Hilty Editor
Sarah Litt Assistant Editor
Robbin Brosterman Design Director – Books
Louis Prandi Publication Design

Karen Berger Senior VP – Executive Editor, Vertigo
Bob Harras VP – Editor-In-Chief

Diane Nelson President
Dan DiDio and **Jim Lee** Co-Publishers
Geoff Johns Chief Creative Officer
John Rood Executive VP – Sales, Marketing and Business Development
Amy Genkins Senior VP – Business and Legal Affairs
Nairi Gardiner Senior VP – Finance
Jeff Boison VP – Publishing Operations
Mark Chiarello VP – Art Direction and Design
John Cunningham VP – Marketing
Terri Cunningham VP – Talent Relations and Services
Alison Gill Senior VP – Manufacturing and Operations
David Hyde VP – Publicity
Hank Kanalz Senior VP – Digital
Jay Kogan VP – Business and Legal Affairs, Publishing
Jack Mahan VP – Business Affairs, Talent
Nick Napolitano VP – Manufacturing Administration
Sue Pohja VP – Book Sales
Courtney Simmons Senior VP – Publicity
Bob Wayne Senior VP – Sales

SUSTAINABLE
FORESTRY
INITIATIVE

Certified Chain of Custody
At Least 25% Certified Forest Content
www.sfiprogram.org
SFI-01042
APPLIES TO TEXT STOCK ONLY

PULLING THE TRIGGER

It's a cool, spring Sunday evening, and my wife and I are eating dinner when we get the news that Osama Bin Laden has been killed by U.S. forces in Pakistan.

There's shock, amazement, and inevitably sadness, as my wife bursts into tears.

She's missing her brother Dave, you see.

****

There's a sense of—not accomplishment, but a kind of "done-ness" about it all, a feeling of closure. That fire in my gut still burns every time I think of that horrible day in September, 2001, when Bin Laden loaded a bunch of fanatics into his ideological gun and fired them at the Pentagon, the World Trade Center, and that heartbreaking stray round that ended in a field in Pennsylvania. Sure, that fire still burns, it's still there, but it has cooled a bit.

Rationally, I know that nothing is ever as clean or as simple as this. The whitehats gunning down the bad man only works in fiction. I know that the death of one old man, long relegated to the role of charismatic figurehead, doesn't really solve any of the problems our nation has been struggling through since the Towers fell.

But there is that feeling of closure.

I pour us each a stiff glass of Glenlivet; my wife hates whiskey, but she takes some anyway.

It's about fifteen years old, and a little sweet for my taste—I prefer something smokier, with a nastier bite—but I put it down anyway and pour again.

Dave was always a single-malt kind of guy, you see.

****

It was sometime in 2003 that I began researching the rise of the private military corporation. I was a licensing wonk in the game division at Microsoft, and was in the middle of building a story bible for a near-future, cyber-punky corporate espionage property, and, on such projects, I tend to look at the current state of affairs and try to extrapolate outward. (And on this particular property, we were eerily prescient. Catch Greg Rucka at a convention sometime and ask him about superflu and corporate military forces. We were ahead of the curve to a *scary* degree.)

I became fascinated with these private armies, poring through tales of companies with names like "Executive Outcomes" quelling rebellions in Africa through a thoroughly effective application of brutal, deadly force. At that point, Blackwater wasn't long removed from being a couple of shooting ranges and the manufacturer of steel targets for firearms training. Firms like Triple Canopy were redefining for-hire military services for the 21st century, not quite mercenaries, and certainly not traditional combat forces, either.

It was spooky stuff, but interesting, and I idly jotted down a notion: "Someone should write a thriller or series of thrillers with a contractor as a protagonist."

That was it, really, just a note jotted down on a notepad I've long ago discarded, thinking I'd try my hand at it. A potboiler, heavy on action and tech, fun to write, easy to forget.

That was not to last.

****

My long-suffering wife, Gabrielle, is from a Hawaiian family: close-knit, occasionally squabbling, highly demonstrative folks. (This came as an icewater splash of culture shock to me, an only child from a German family; my people certainly love each other, but it's a quieter, less chaotic bond we share.)

Gabrielle's family is also quite large (more culture shock for me), and has a longstanding military tradition. Her father is an infantryman, a retired Lt. Colonel in the United States Army, who fought in Viet Nam, and has the Combat Infantryman's Badge and Purple Heart to prove it. Her eldest brother? A West Pointer. And then there was Dave.

Dave was an infantryman as well, like his father, who was a Reservist and Green Beret (in one of, if not *the*, largest National Guard Special Forces units). When I first met Gabrielle, David was "away on business"—serving something ridiculous like two tours in Iraq and a tour in Afghanistan (along the way earning a Combat Infantryman's Badge of his own).

He'd been gone for months, but we managed to schedule our wedding for Dave's leave.

The first time I met him was at Seattle-Tacoma International Airport, returning with his unit to a room full of wives, children waving "Welcome Home, Daddy!" signs, proud parents, and me. I've never been sized up as a non-threat so fast in my life.

Dave was, to me, soft-spoken and laconic, with occasional flashes of sly wit and good humor. Clearly tough as nails, he nonetheless doted on his baby sister, and let me know in no uncertain terms (and with a glint in his eye) that, should I fail to take adequate care of her, that would be unfortunate for me.

I loved him immensely, almost immediately.

****

Dave's unit was not scheduled to return to Iraq any time soon, and—after some initial rest, he embarked on an aggressive program of physical and martial fitness: exercise, running, pistol work.

After honing himself into the best shape he'd been in years, he hired on with a private military company, Blackwater, determined to go back to Iraq as soon as possible. Why? we asked him. His wife, Cindy, supported him but clearly had some trepidation, and Gabrielle fretted about it from time to time. His answer was typical: "My work there isn't done yet."

Dave's occasional letters home were filled with stories about how he'd connected with the locals, particularly the children he met. He spoke at length about working to improve things at the ground level — building schools, repairing infrastructure, and so on. (No doubt, this appealed to him from his civilian profession as a master carpenter and contractor.) Often, his team would be called upon to supply medical assistance to locals in crisis; leave it to Dave to have a story about an emergency field amputation that was both horrifying and hysterically funny.

Why'd he go back? Dave's work just wasn't done yet, you see.

****

At the same time, media reports of Blackwater "mercenaries" (security contractors of a certain type bristle at that term, I quickly learned) on the streets of New Orleans after Katrina, and several stories of excessive and unnecessary gunplay overseas were starting to become commonplace. Before long, Blackwater was the face of what was wrong in the conflicts in the Middle East.

I found it very hard to reconcile the reports with the character of the man I knew.

And at that point, the notion of my little potboiler action novel went out the window.

I started researching more, talking to people I know in the business and in the military, and learned as much as I could. Others had started to do the same, and a series of excellent books on the subject (notably P.W. Singer's *Corporate Warriors* and Gerald Schumacher's *A Bloody Business*) had begun to surface.

It became clear to me that, as in any large organization—be it corporate, or military, or law enforcement — there was good and bad; people like Dave, trying to do what they saw as necessary for the greater good, and bad apples letting money and the power of being weapons-free and more-or-less autonomous go to their heads.

Certainly the Marine unit in Baghdad—pinned down by insurgent fire until Blackwater Little Bird helos responded and pulled them out of harm's way— saw plenty of good in Blackwater's presence in the area.

An entire book could be written on the "Iron Horse Express": private contractors, under command of U.S. forces, who drove tractor-trailers loaded with mail and equipment during Operation Iraqi Freedom. These contractors, most unarmed, drove what were essentially giant, slow-moving targets through one of the deadliest regions on the planet, simply to make sure the mail got through.

For all the bad being reported, you didn't see a lot of coverage of the good, I decided, and the book I'd been planning changed.

****

Dave worked a protective detail, serving as personal security. (In practical terms: the bodyguard who has to soak up the bullets meant for the principal.)

He'd once said to me that he'd be protecting the people who would be bringing peace to the region; the dichotomy of the modern soldier (be it military or private military) is the recognition that peace and stability often require the application of violence. If you can stop something bad from happening by pulling the trigger at the right time, then you damn well pull the trigger.

On 19 September 2005, Dave, three other Blackwater operators, and a State Department security officer were killed by a vehicle-borne improvised explosive device in Mosul, Iraq. The published report indicated that, while protecting a State Department official (we have never been told who), an insurgent attempted to collide with the vehicle containing the team's "principal." Dave's vehicle intercepted the insurgent, rammed it, and triggered the detonation.

The State Department official was unharmed.

I had no trouble reconciling *that* action—protecting someone he felt was necessary to bring peace to the troubled region—with Dave's character.

****

For many months after Dave's death, the book sat in a drawer. When I did finally dust it off, I'd become paralyzed. The fictional "hero" of the story had certain surface similarities to Dave (though they differed in several crucial respects), but I was terrified that I'd get something wrong, write the wrong thing, and somehow cause more pain to my wife, my family, Dave's widow. That they'd see, for example, a scene where the military bureaucracy, enmeshed in the business of a multifront war, is less than protective of one of its own and think it was me casting aspersions on the "family business."

And so it sat.

And sat.

And sat.

****

When Joan Hilty asked me to pitch something to Vertigo, asking for something military themed, I dusted the novel off, reexamined it...

...and put it right back in the drawer. There was no way I could do it, I thought. It was too raw, too personal, and even though my protagonist was *not* intended as an avatar for Dave I still had fears of harming a family still struggling to patch itself back together after a terrible, inconsolable loss. If I did it wrong, then I would have turned a story into a weapon pointed at my family, and then pulled the trigger.

We pitched a dozen other ideas, and of course, none of them stuck.

****

A digression here. Bear with me.

Brandon Jerwa.

The book you're holding in your hands absolutely would never have seen the light of day if not for him. There's a certain perception among the team that created *Shooters* that this is "my" story.

My story is sitting in a drawer, unfinished, and it's going to stay there.

I don't make friends easily. Like I said: only child, emotionally reserved (a.k.a. emotionally *stunted*), and, if I'm being honest, a combative prick on most days.

It wasn't until I saw the way my wife's family interacted that I really felt I *understood* family. Had I not been so warmly embraced by my wife's family, I wouldn't have friends like Brandon. One of the lessons Dave and his siblings, parents, and wife taught me was opening up to the people closest to you.

So Brandon, like Dave, is my brother, in the truest sense, and we'd each take a bullet for the other.

****

Brandon and I had been developing ideas for a co-writing project for some time, and finally, as pitch after pitch flopped with Joan, we reexamined the novel.

Brandon brought much-needed emotional remove from some of the stuff I was too fearful to touch, while simultaneously keeping me honest, and delivering what I believe is the most emotional, from-the-heart material of his considerable career.

And here we are.

Without Brandon, there's no *Shooters*. Period.

Add to the mix Steve Lieber.

We'd been hunting for just the right artist, someone who could handle both the emotional beats of the story, make us care about these people and the wreckage of their lives *and* the challenge of handling realistic action, military hardware and so on.

Amazingly either through karma, or kismet, or just blind good fortune he actually said yes, and, speaking for both Brandon and myself, we couldn't have been happier.

Steve's skill and genius at illustrating characters that live, breathe, *feel*, and his prodigious gift for the arcane juju that is graphic storytelling was the final piece of the puzzle, and it's been a privilege watching the pages roll into the inbox.

Without Steve, there's no *Shooters*. Period.

Good friends, all, for whom I'd take a bullet, and—thanks to them—this stopped being "my" story a long time ago.

****

Osama Bin Laden is dead, and so is my brother-in-law, the victims of 9/11, and the countless dead and wounded in insurgent bombings and military actions since 2001. Someone pulled the trigger, and the bullets tore paths through millions of lives.

And that's what the book is about: the consequences of pulling the trigger, and the cost of accepting that responsibility.

With any luck? Mission accomplished.

Eric Trautmann
Raymond, Washington

Iraq, just outside of Baghdad
International Airport (BIA).
Now.

This is what it all comes down to.

All of the bullshit about God and
Country, about duty, and honor.
About *money*.

It's just this: **men with guns,**
doing their best to kill *other*
men with guns.

You can try to justify
it all you want.

Rationalize it to your
heart's content.

When the chips are
down, you fight for
one reason only.

You tell yourself You fight because
it's what you're trained to do. It's
your **profession**.

It's a lie, of course.

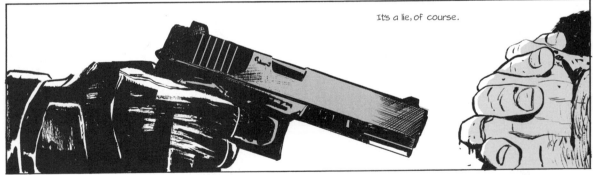

The truth is this: You
fight because war is
who you are.

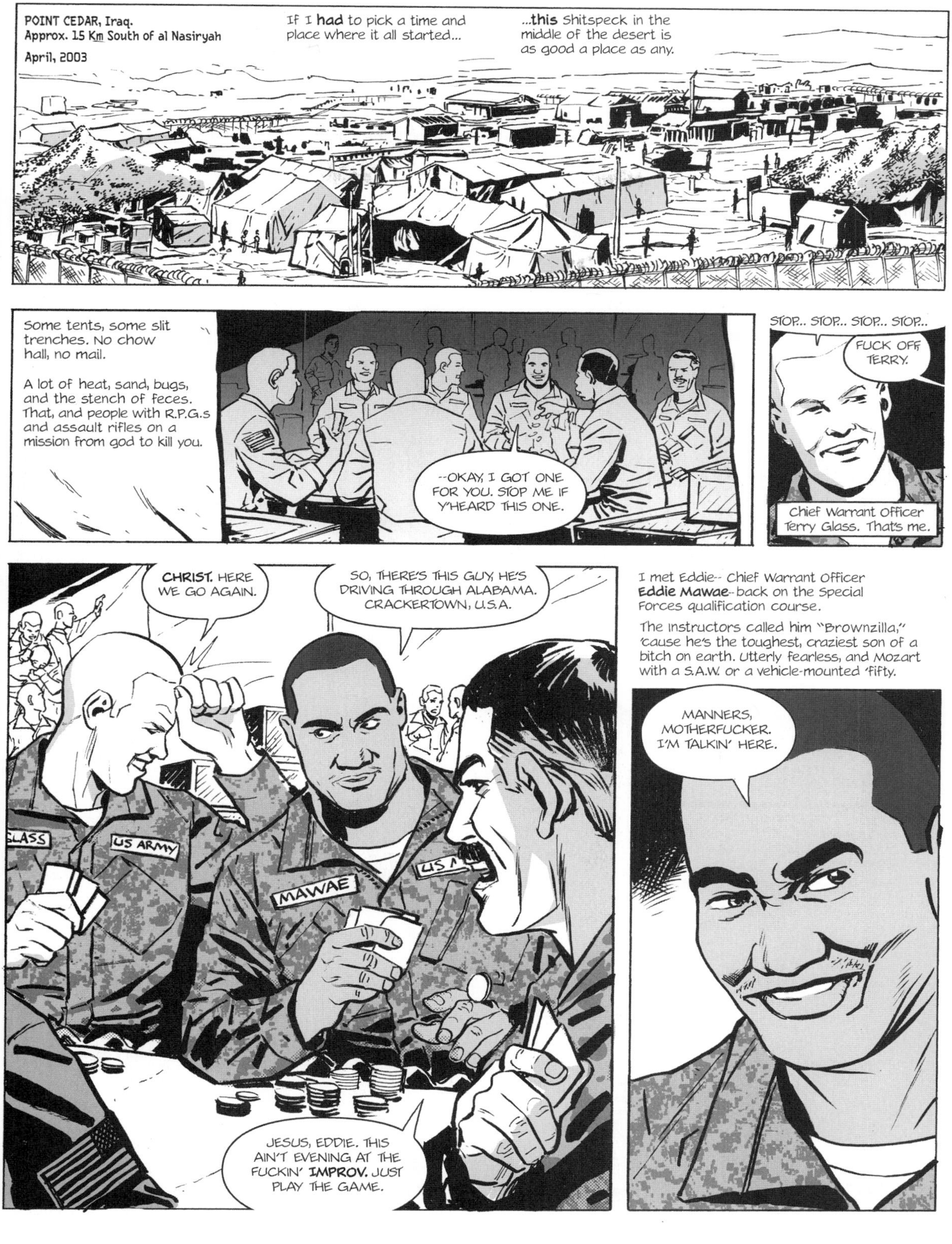
POINT CEDAR, Iraq.
Approx. 15 Km South of al Nasiryah
April, 2003
If I **had** to pick a time and place where it all started...
...**this** shitspeck in the middle of the desert is as good a place as any.
Some tents, some slit trenches. No chow hall, no mail.
A lot of heat, sand, bugs, and the stench of feces. That, and people with R.P.G.s and assault rifles on a mission from god to kill you.
--OKAY, I GOT ONE FOR YOU. STOP ME IF Y'HEARD THIS ONE.
STOP... STOP... STOP... STOP...
FUCK OFF, TERRY.
Chief Warrant Officer Terry Glass. That's me.
CHRIST. HERE WE GO AGAIN.
SO, THERE'S THIS GUY, HE'S DRIVING THROUGH ALABAMA. CRACKERTOWN, U.S.A.
GLASS
US ARMY
MAWAE
US A
JESUS, EDDIE. THIS AIN'T EVENING AT THE FUCKIN' **IMPROV.** JUST PLAY THE GAME.
I met Eddie-- Chief Warrant Officer **Eddie Mawae**--back on the Special Forces qualification course.
The instructors called him "Brownzilla," 'cause he's the toughest, craziest son of a bitch on earth. Utterly fearless, and Mozart with a S.A.W. or a vehicle-mounted 'fifty.
MANNERS, MOTHERFUCKER. I'M TALKIN' HERE.

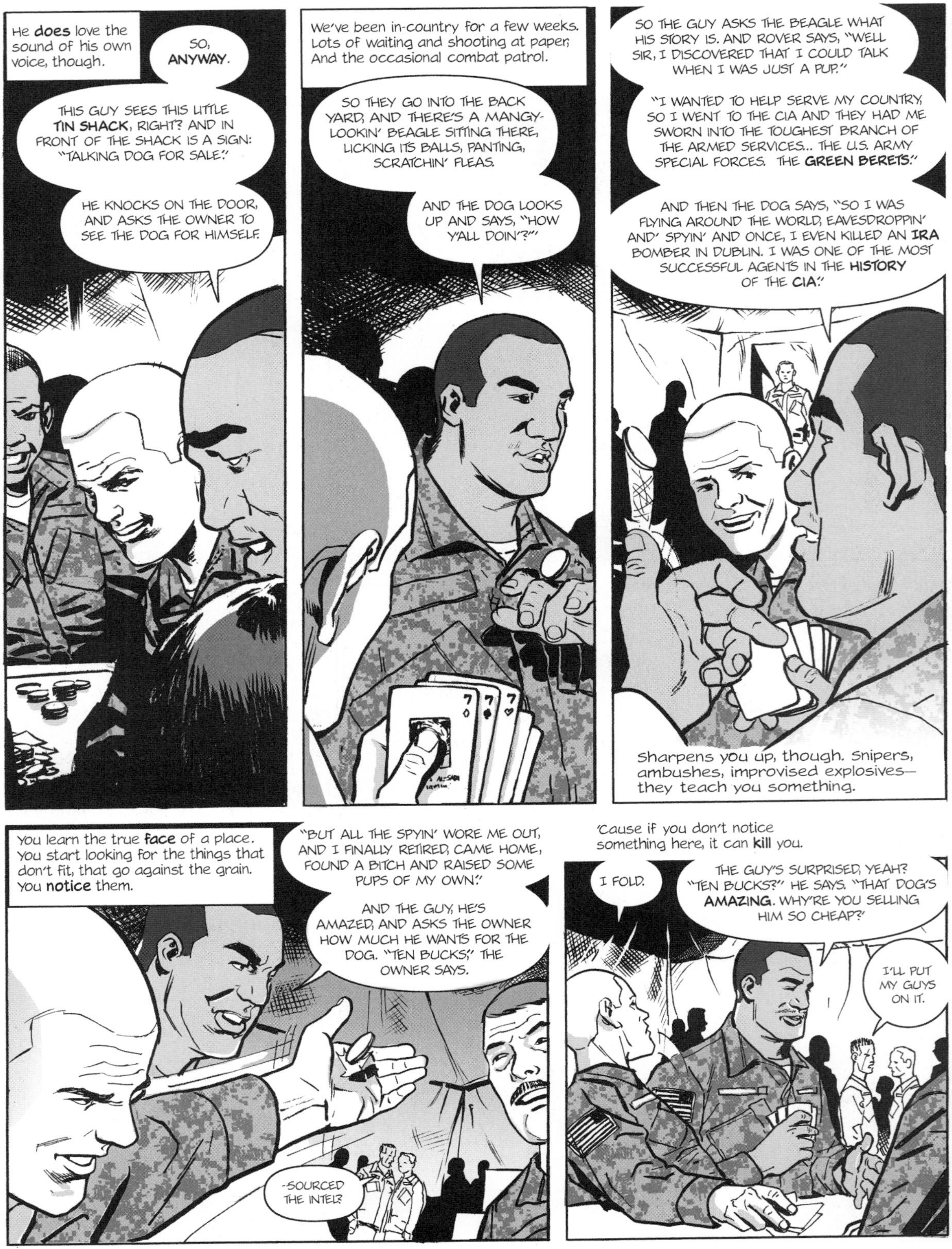
He **does** love the sound of his own voice, though.
SO, **ANYWAY**.
THIS GUY SEES THIS LITTLE **TIN SHACK**, RIGHT? AND IN FRONT OF THE SHACK IS A SIGN: "TALKING DOG FOR SALE."
HE KNOCKS ON THE DOOR, AND ASKS THE OWNER TO SEE THE DOG FOR HIMSELF.
We've been in-country for a few weeks. Lots of waiting and shooting at paper; And the occasional combat patrol.
SO THEY GO INTO THE BACK YARD, AND THERE'S A MANGY-LOOKIN' BEAGLE SITTING THERE, LICKING ITS BALLS, PANTING, SCRATCHIN' FLEAS.
AND THE DOG LOOKS UP AND SAYS, "HOW Y'ALL DOIN'?"
SO THE GUY ASKS THE BEAGLE WHAT HIS STORY IS. AND ROVER SAYS, "WELL SIR, I DISCOVERED THAT I COULD TALK WHEN I WAS JUST A PUP."
"I WANTED TO HELP SERVE MY COUNTRY, SO I WENT TO THE CIA AND THEY HAD ME SWORN INTO THE TOUGHEST BRANCH OF THE ARMED SERVICES... THE U.S. ARMY SPECIAL FORCES. THE **GREEN BERETS**."
AND THEN THE DOG SAYS, "SO I WAS FLYING AROUND THE WORLD, EAVESDROPPIN' AND' SPYIN' AND ONCE, I EVEN KILLED AN **IRA** BOMBER IN DUBLIN. I WAS ONE OF THE MOST SUCCESSFUL AGENTS IN THE **HISTORY** OF THE **CIA**."
Sharpens you up, though. Snipers, ambushes, improvised explosives— they teach you something.
You learn the true **face** of a place. You start looking for the things that don't fit, that go against the grain. You **notice** them.
"BUT ALL THE SPYIN' WORE ME OUT, AND I FINALLY RETIRED, CAME HOME, FOUND A BITCH AND RAISED SOME PUPS OF MY OWN."
AND THE GUY, HE'S AMAZED, AND ASKS THE OWNER HOW MUCH HE WANTS FOR THE DOG. "TEN BUCKS," THE OWNER SAYS.
-SOURCED THE INTEL?
'Cause if you don't notice something here, it can **kill** you.
I FOLD.
THE GUY'S SURPRISED, YEAH? "TEN BUCKS?" HE SAYS. "THAT DOG'S **AMAZING**. WHY'RE YOU SELLING HIM SO CHEAP?"
I'LL PUT MY GUYS ON IT.

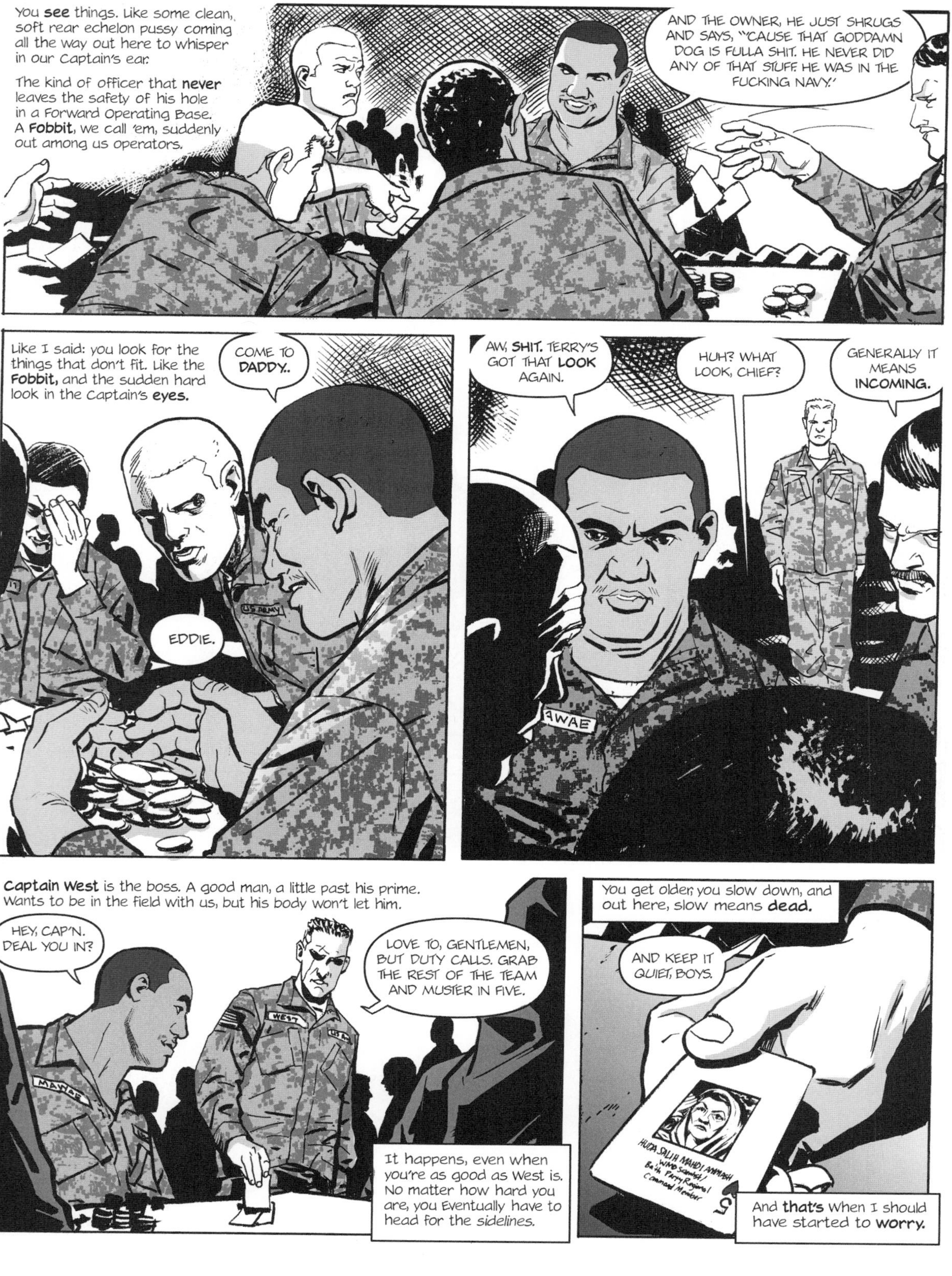

You **see** things. Like some clean, soft rear echelon pussy coming all the way out here to whisper in our Captain's ear.
The kind of officer that **never** leaves the safety of his hole in a Forward Operating Base. A **Fobbit**, we call 'em, suddenly out among us operators.
AND THE OWNER, HE JUST SHRUGS AND SAYS, "'CAUSE THAT GODDAMN DOG IS FULLA SHIT. HE NEVER DID ANY OF THAT STUFF. HE WAS IN THE FUCKING NAVY.'
Like I said: you look for the things that don't fit. Like the **Fobbit,** and the sudden hard look in the Captain's **eyes.**
COME TO **DADDY**..
EDDIE.
AW, **SHIT.** TERRY'S GOT THAT **LOOK** AGAIN.
HUH? WHAT LOOK, CHIEF?
GENERALLY IT MEANS **INCOMING.**
Captain West is the boss. A good man, a little past his prime. Wants to be in the field with us, but his body won't let him.
HEY, CAP'N. DEAL YOU IN?
LOVE TO, GENTLEMEN, BUT DUTY CALLS. GRAB THE REST OF THE TEAM AND MUSTER IN FIVE.
It happens, even when you're as good as West is. No matter how hard you are, you eventually have to head for the sidelines.
You get older, you slow down, and out here, slow means **dead.**
AND KEEP IT QUIET, BOYS.
HUDA SALIH MAHDI AMMASH
WMD Scientist/ Ba'th Party Regional Command Member
And **that's** when I should have started to **worry.**

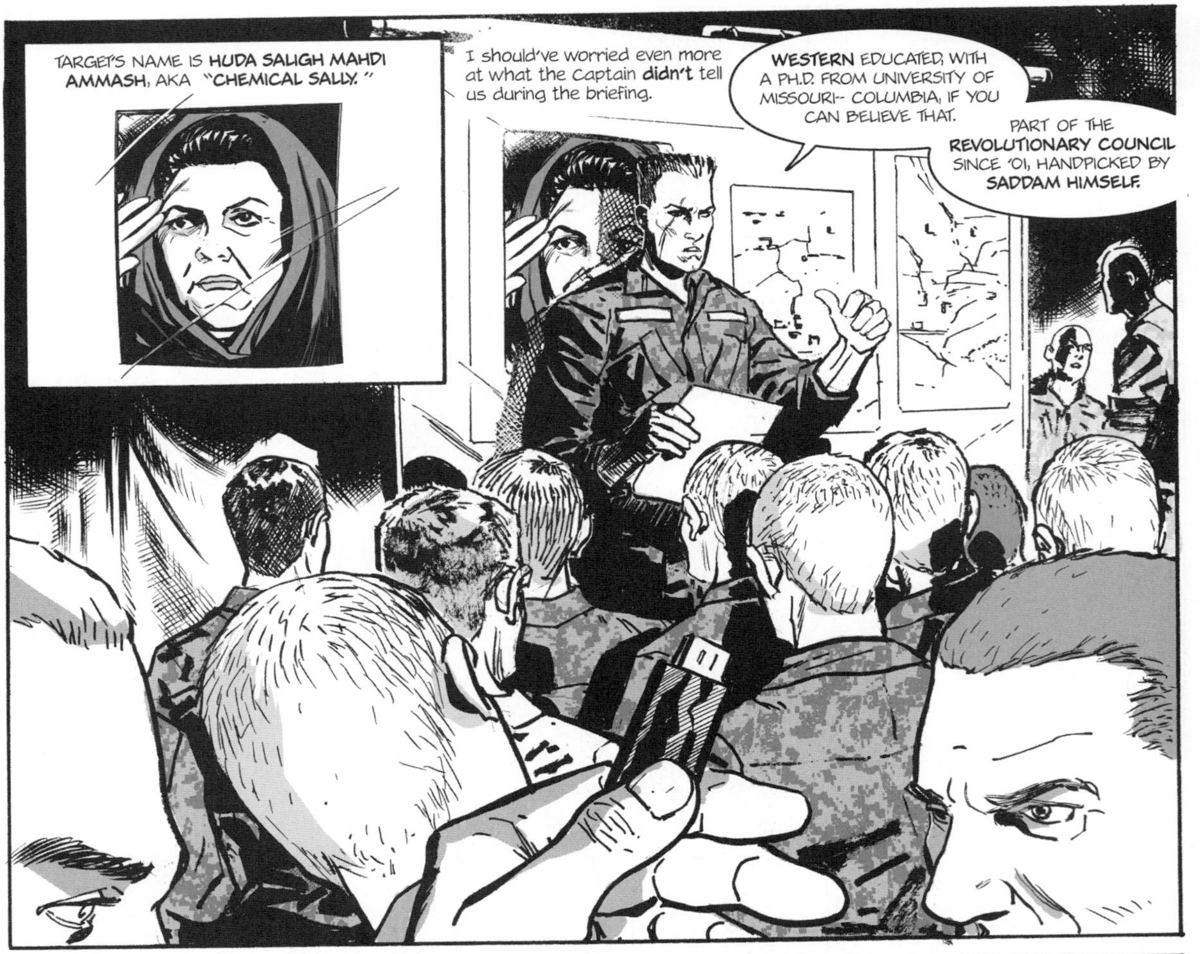

TARGET'S NAME IS **HUDA SALIGH MAHDI AMMASH**, AKA **"CHEMICAL SALLY."**
I should've worried even more at what the Captain **didn't** tell us during the briefing.
WESTERN EDUCATED, WITH A PH.D. FROM UNIVERSITY OF MISSOURI-- COLUMBIA, IF YOU CAN BELIEVE THAT.
PART OF THE **REVOLUTIONARY COUNCIL** SINCE '01, HANDPICKED BY **SADDAM HIMSELF.**

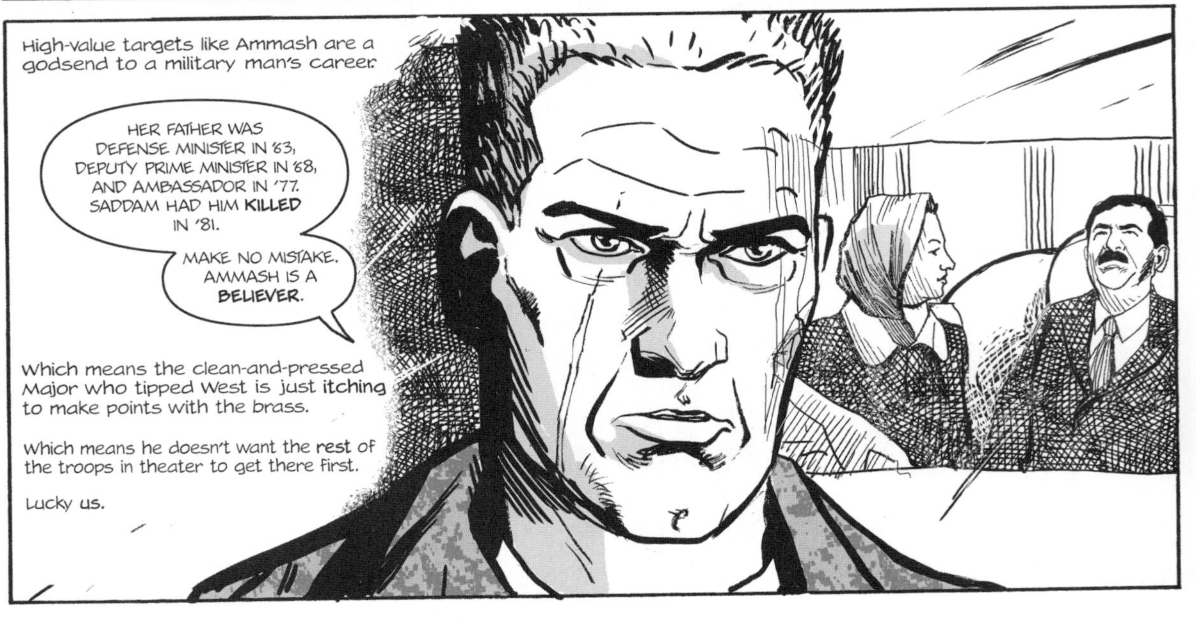

High-value targets like Ammash are a godsend to a military man's career.
HER FATHER WAS DEFENSE MINISTER IN '63, DEPUTY PRIME MINISTER IN '68, AND AMBASSADOR IN '77. SADDAM HAD HIM **KILLED** IN '81.
MAKE NO MISTAKE. AMMASH IS A **BELIEVER**.
Which means the clean-and-pressed Major who tipped West is just **itching** to make points with the brass.
Which means he doesn't want the **rest** of the troops in theater to get there first.
Lucky **us**.

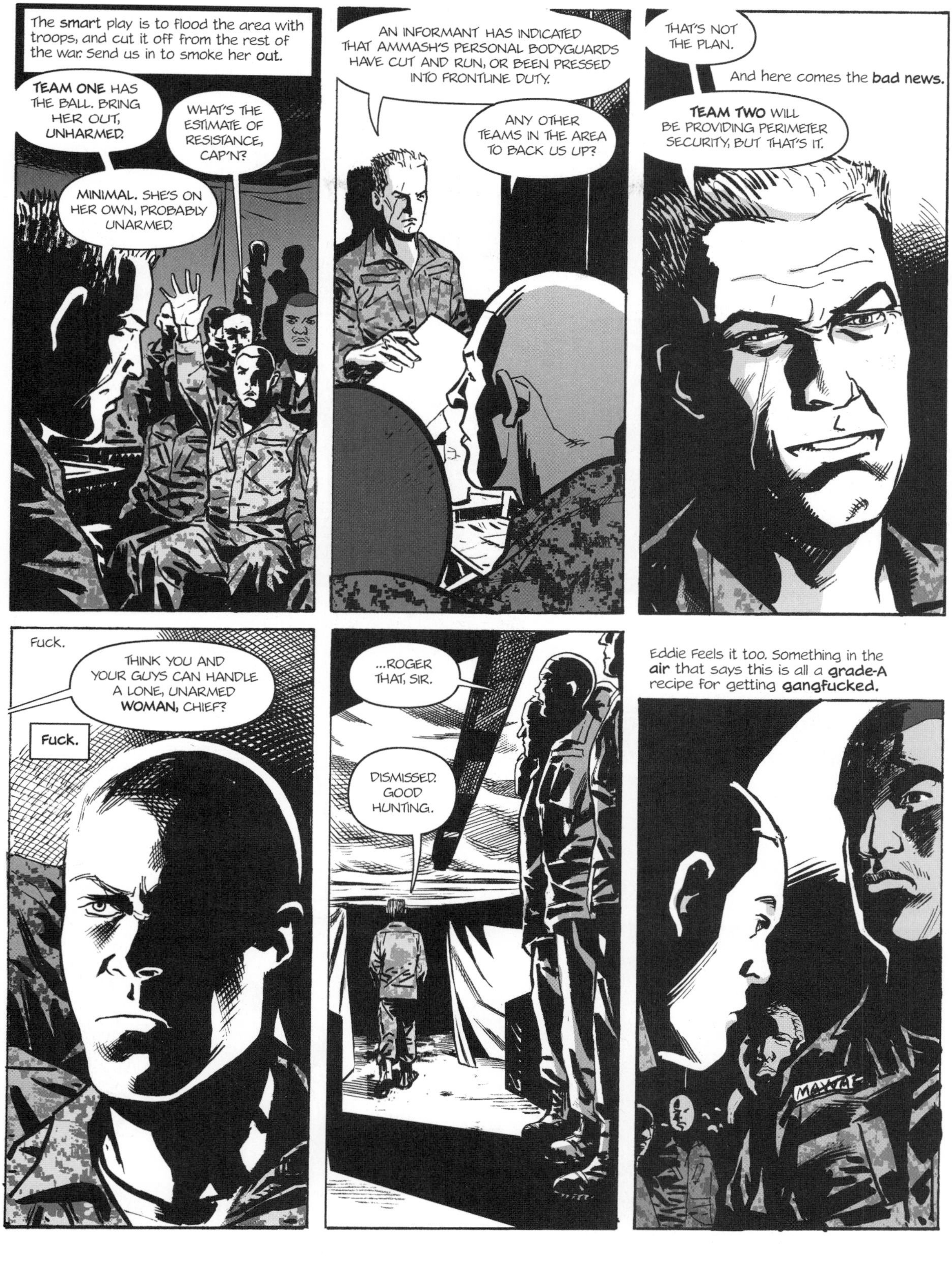

The smart play is to flood the area with troops, and cut it off from the rest of the war. Send us in to smoke her out.
TEAM ONE HAS THE BALL. BRING HER OUT, UNHARMED.
WHAT'S THE ESTIMATE OF RESISTANCE, CAP'N?
MINIMAL. SHE'S ON HER OWN, PROBABLY UNARMED.
AN INFORMANT HAS INDICATED THAT AMMASH'S PERSONAL BODYGUARDS HAVE CUT AND RUN, OR BEEN PRESSED INTO FRONTLINE DUTY.
ANY OTHER TEAMS IN THE AREA TO BACK US UP?
THAT'S NOT THE PLAN.
And here comes the bad news.
TEAM TWO WILL BE PROVIDING PERIMETER SECURITY, BUT THAT'S IT.
Fuck.
THINK YOU AND YOUR GUYS CAN HANDLE A LONE, UNARMED WOMAN, CHIEF?
Fuck.
...ROGER THAT, SIR.
DISMISSED. GOOD HUNTING.
Eddie Feels it too. Something in the air that says this is all a grade-A recipe for getting gangfucked.

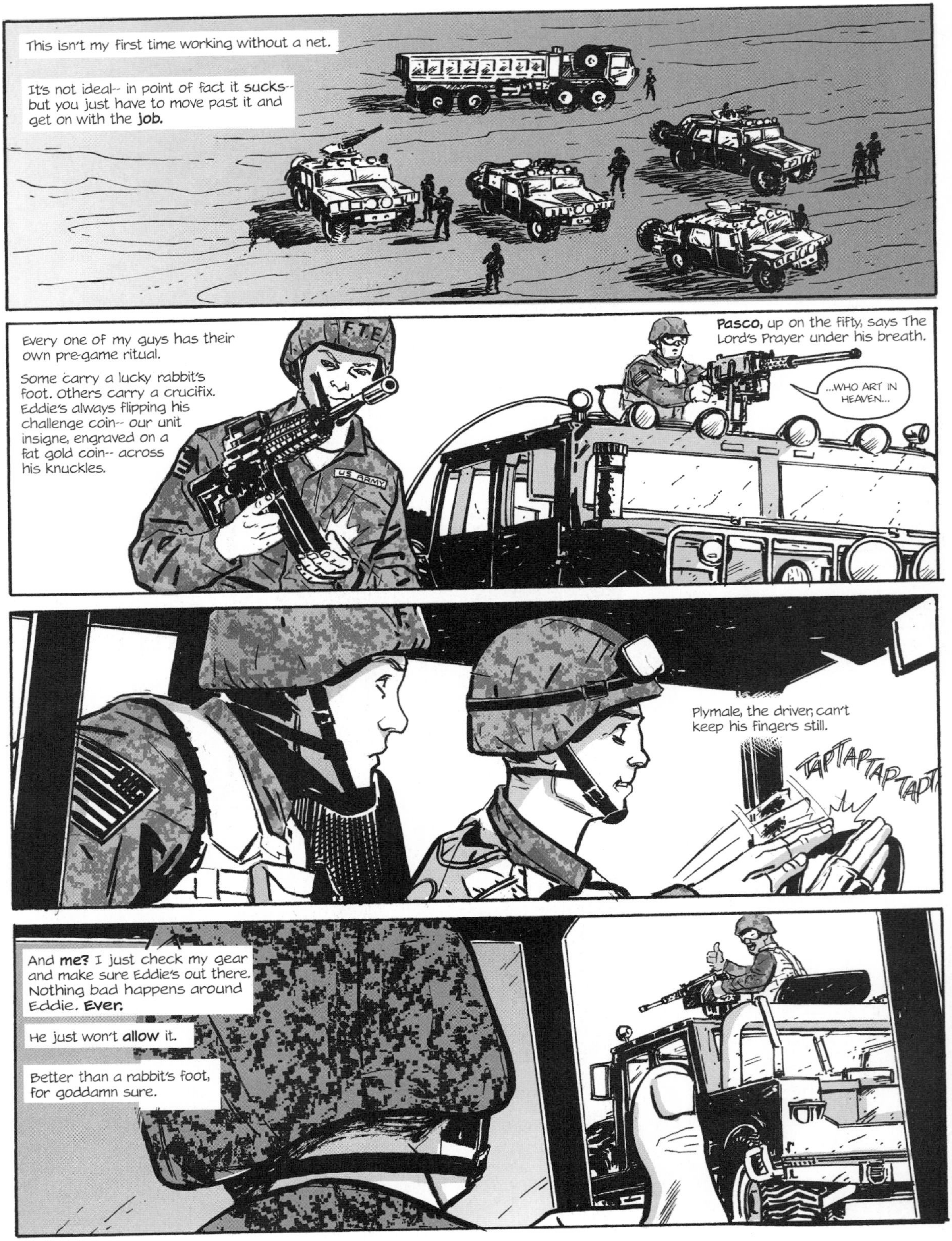

This isn't my first time working without a net.
It's not ideal-- in point of fact it sucks-- but you just have to move past it and get on with the job.
Every one of my guys has their own pre-game ritual.
Some carry a lucky rabbit's foot. Others carry a crucifix. Eddie's always flipping his challenge coin-- our unit insigne, engraved on a fat gold coin-- across his knuckles.
F.T.E
US ARMY
Pasco, up on the fifty, says The Lord's Prayer under his breath.
...WHO ART IN HEAVEN...
Plymale, the driver, can't keep his fingers still.
TAPTAPTAPTAPT
And me? I just check my gear and make sure Eddie's out there. Nothing bad happens around Eddie. Ever.
He just won't allow it.
Better than a rabbit's foot, for goddamn sure.

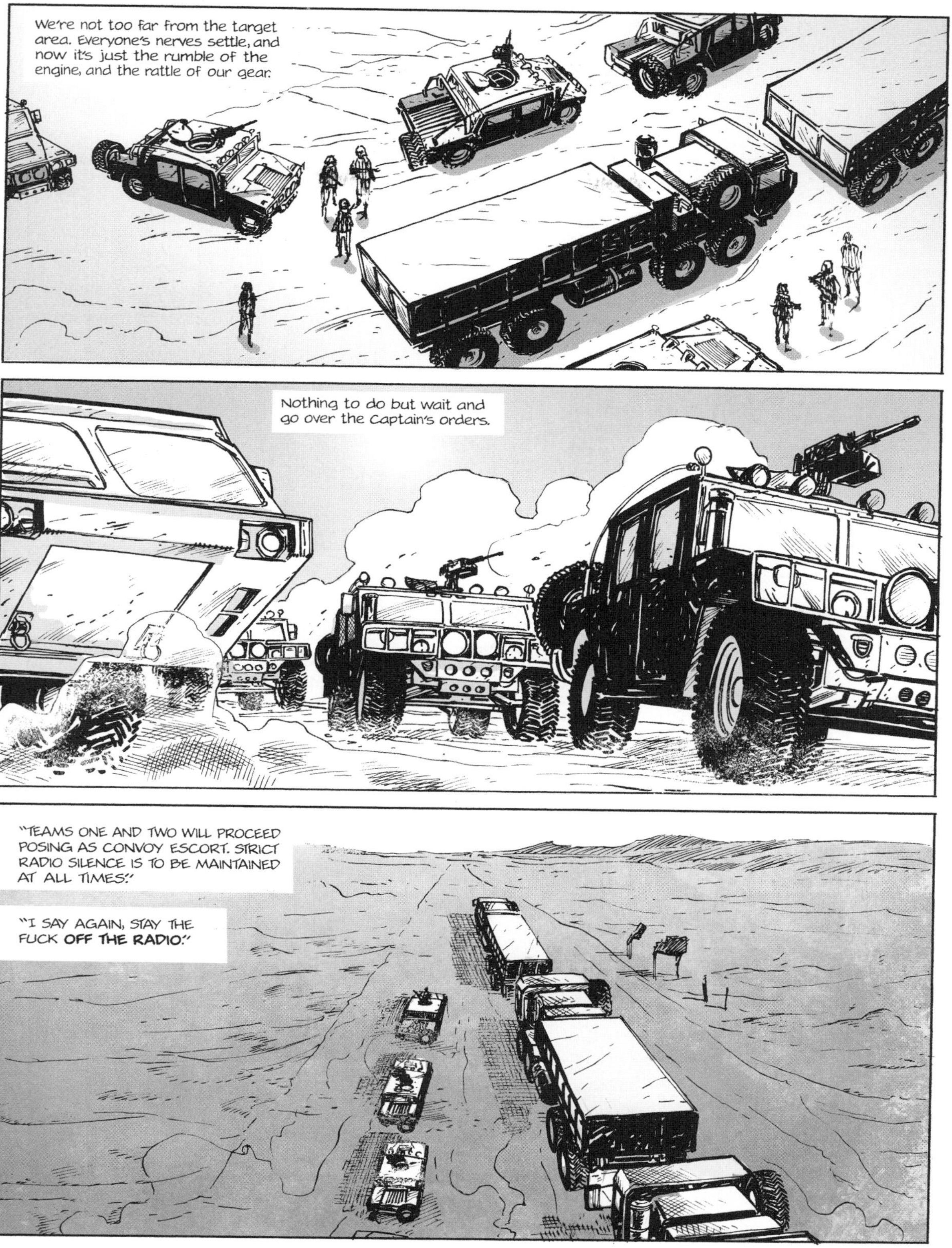
We're not too far from the target area. Everyone's nerves settle, and now it's just the rumble of the engine, and the rattle of our gear.
Nothing to do but wait and go over the Captain's orders.
"TEAMS ONE AND TWO WILL PROCEED POSING AS CONVOY ESCORT. STRICT RADIO SILENCE IS TO BE MAINTAINED AT ALL TIMES."
"I SAY AGAIN, STAY THE FUCK **OFF THE RADIO**."

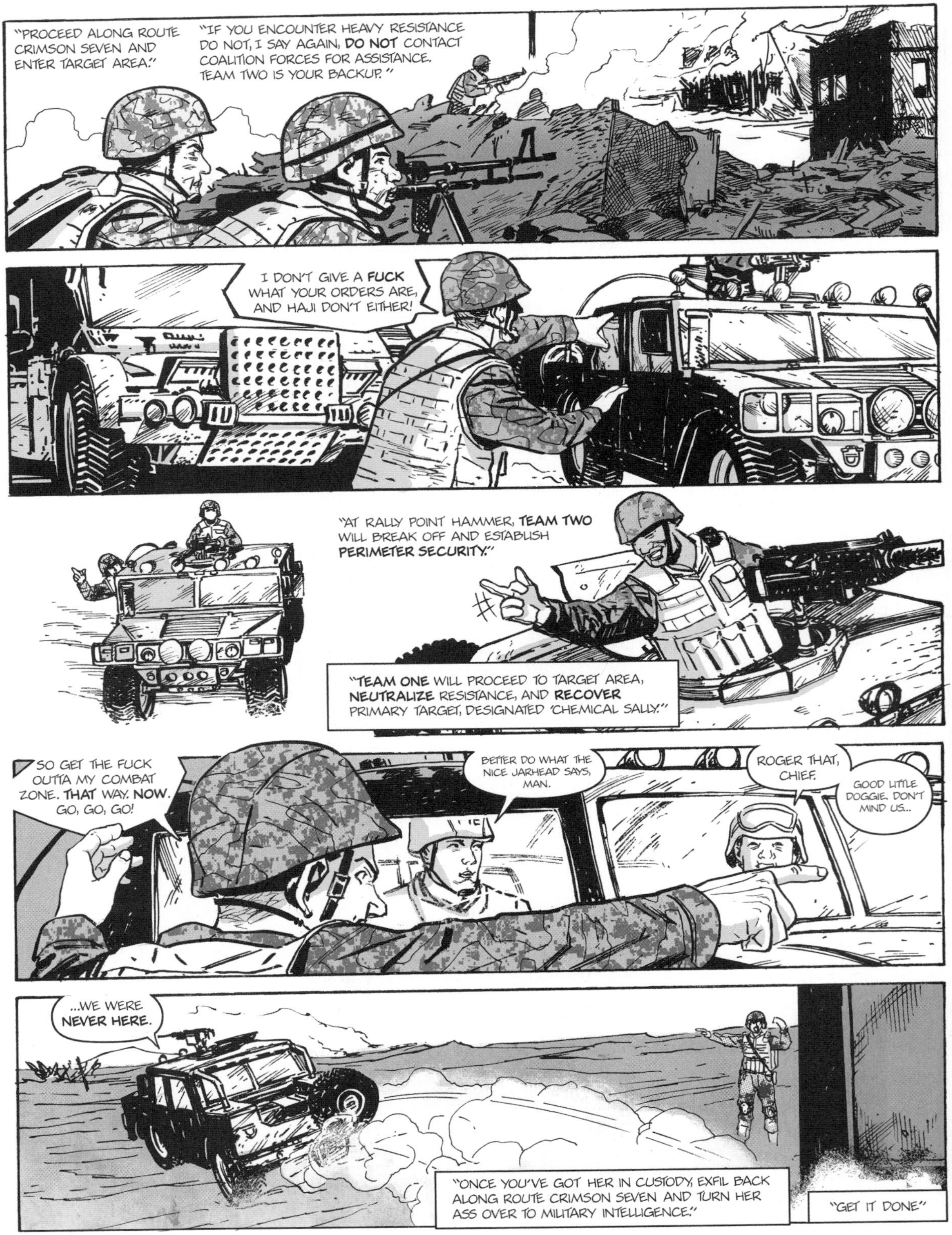

"PROCEED ALONG ROUTE CRIMSON SEVEN AND ENTER TARGET AREA."
"IF YOU ENCOUNTER HEAVY RESISTANCE DO NOT, I SAY AGAIN, DO NOT CONTACT COALITION FORCES FOR ASSISTANCE. TEAM TWO IS YOUR BACKUP."
I DON'T GIVE A FUCK WHAT YOUR ORDERS ARE, AND HAJI DON'T EITHER!
"AT RALLY POINT HAMMER, TEAM TWO WILL BREAK OFF AND ESTABLISH PERIMETER SECURITY."
"TEAM ONE WILL PROCEED TO TARGET AREA, NEUTRALIZE RESISTANCE, AND RECOVER PRIMARY TARGET, DESIGNATED 'CHEMICAL SALLY.'"
SO GET THE FUCK OUTTA MY COMBAT ZONE. THAT WAY. NOW. GO, GO, GO!
BETTER DO WHAT THE NICE JARHEAD SAYS, MAN.
ROGER THAT, CHIEF.
GOOD LITTLE DOGGIE. DON'T MIND US...
...WE WERE NEVER HERE.
"ONCE YOU'VE GOT HER IN CUSTODY, EXFIL BACK ALONG ROUTE CRIMSON SEVEN AND TURN HER ASS OVER TO MILITARY INTELLIGENCE."
"GET IT DONE"

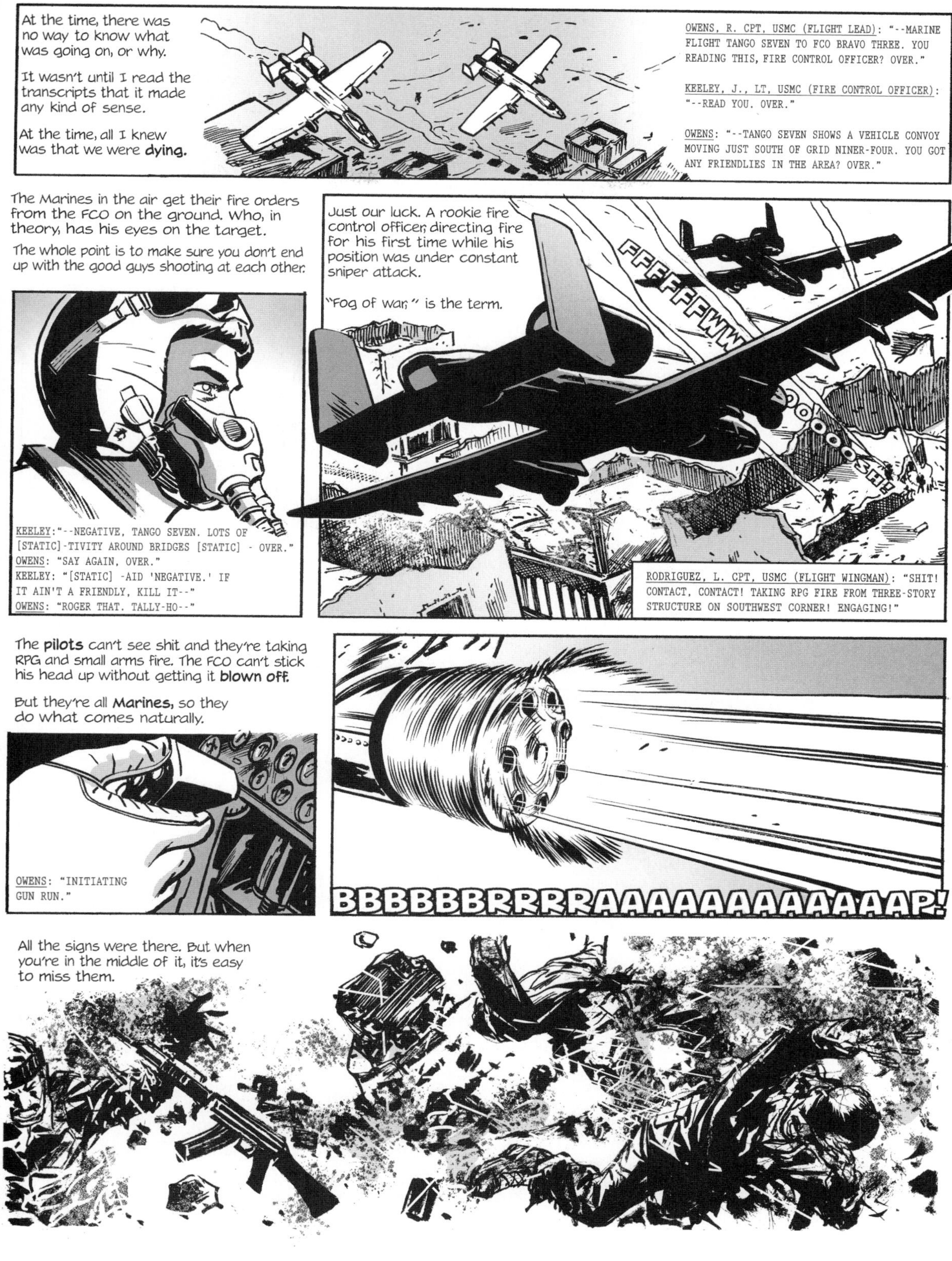
At the time, there was no way to know what was going on, or why.
It wasn't until I read the transcripts that it made any kind of sense.
At the time, all I knew was that we were **dying.**
OWENS, R. CPT, USMC (FLIGHT LEAD): "--MARINE FLIGHT TANGO SEVEN TO FCO BRAVO THREE. YOU READING THIS, FIRE CONTROL OFFICER? OVER."
KEELEY, J., LT, USMC (FIRE CONTROL OFFICER): "--READ YOU. OVER."
OWENS: "--TANGO SEVEN SHOWS A VEHICLE CONVOY MOVING JUST SOUTH OF GRID NINER-FOUR. YOU GOT ANY FRIENDLIES IN THE AREA? OVER."
The Marines in the air get their fire orders from the FCO on the ground. Who, in theory, has his eyes on the target.
The whole point is to make sure you don't end up with the good guys shooting at each other.
KEELEY: "--NEGATIVE, TANGO SEVEN. LOTS OF [STATIC]-TIVITY AROUND BRIDGES [STATIC] - OVER."
OWENS: "SAY AGAIN, OVER."
KEELEY: "[STATIC] -AID 'NEGATIVE.' IF IT AIN'T A FRIENDLY, KILL IT--"
OWENS: "ROGER THAT. TALLY-HO--"
Just our luck. A rookie fire control officer, directing fire for his first time while his position was under constant sniper attack.
"Fog of war," is the term.
FFFFFFWW
OOOOOSH!
RODRIGUEZ, L. CPT, USMC (FLIGHT WINGMAN): "SHIT! CONTACT, CONTACT! TAKING RPG FIRE FROM THREE-STORY STRUCTURE ON SOUTHWEST CORNER! ENGAGING!"
The **pilots** can't see shit and they're taking RPG and small arms fire. The FCO can't stick his head up without getting it **blown off.**
But they're all **Marines,** so they do what comes naturally.
OWENS: "INITIATING GUN RUN."
BBBBBBRRRRRAAAAAAAAAAAAAP!
All the signs were there. But when you're in the middle of it, it's easy to miss them.

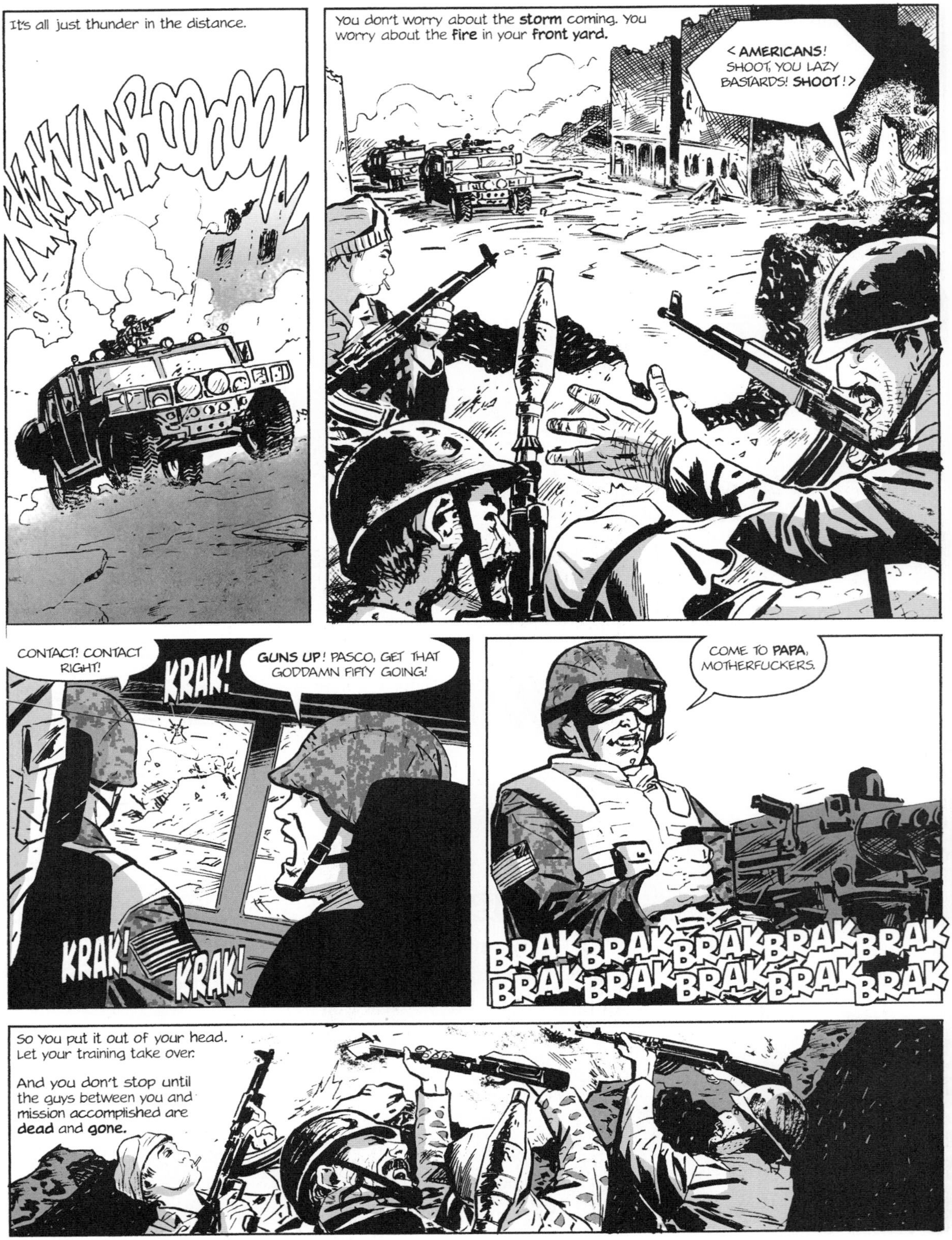

It's all just thunder in the distance.
You don't worry about the **storm** coming. You worry about the **fire** in your **front yard.**
< **AMERICANS**! SHOOT, YOU LAZY BASTARDS! **SHOOT**! >
CONTACT! CONTACT RIGHT!
KRAK!
GUNS UP! PASCO, GET THAT GODDAMN FIFTY GOING!
KRAK!
KRAK!
COME TO **PAPA**, MOTHERFUCKERS.
BRAK BRAK BRAK BRAK BRAK
BRAK BRAK BRAK BRAK BRAK
So You put it out of your head. Let your training take over.
And you don't stop until the guys between you and mission accomplished are **dead** and **gone.**

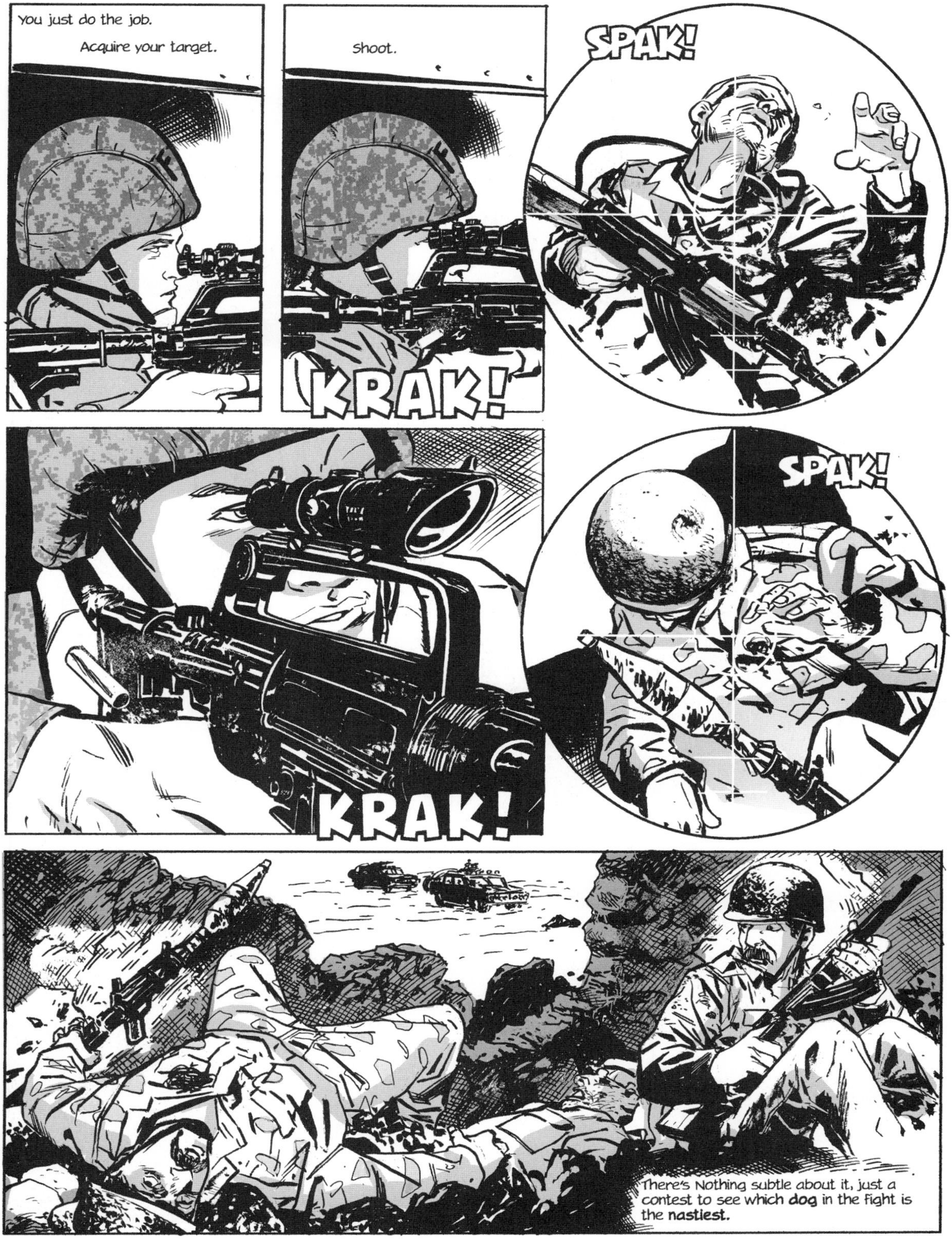

You just do the job.
Acquire your target.
Shoot.
KRAK!
SPAK!
KRAK!
SPAK!
There's Nothing subtle about it, just a contest to see which **dog** in the fight is the **nastiest.**

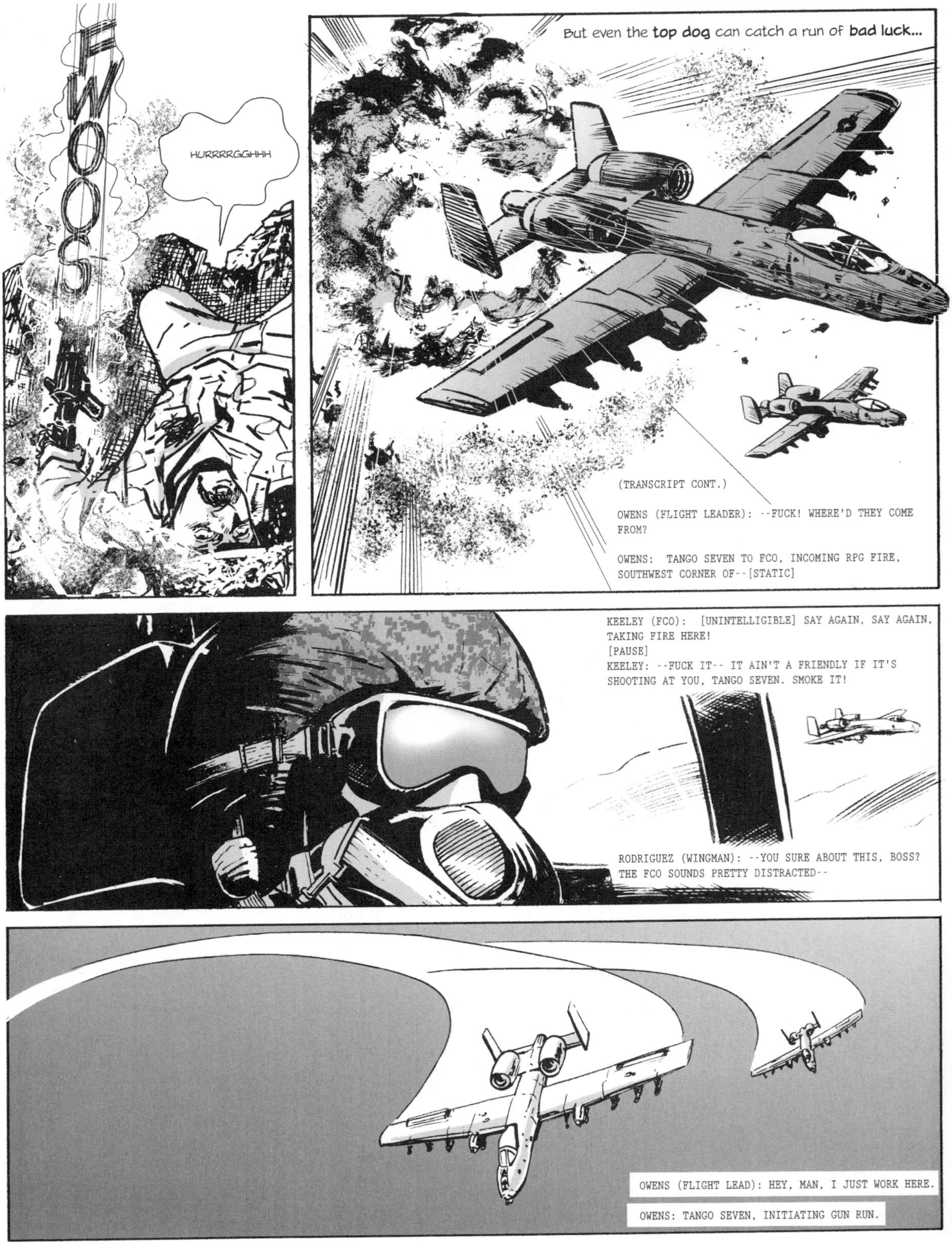
FWOOOS
HURRRRGGHHH
But even the **top dog** can catch a run of **bad luck...**
(TRANSCRIPT CONT.)
OWENS (FLIGHT LEADER): --FUCK! WHERE'D THEY COME FROM?
OWENS: TANGO SEVEN TO FCO, INCOMING RPG FIRE, SOUTHWEST CORNER OF--[STATIC]
KEELEY (FCO): [UNINTELLIGIBLE] SAY AGAIN, SAY AGAIN, TAKING FIRE HERE!
[PAUSE]
KEELEY: --FUCK IT-- IT AIN'T A FRIENDLY IF IT'S SHOOTING AT YOU, TANGO SEVEN. SMOKE IT!
RODRIGUEZ (WINGMAN): --YOU SURE ABOUT THIS, BOSS? THE FCO SOUNDS PRETTY DISTRACTED--
OWENS (FLIGHT LEAD): HEY, MAN, I JUST WORK HERE.
OWENS: TANGO SEVEN, INITIATING GUN RUN.

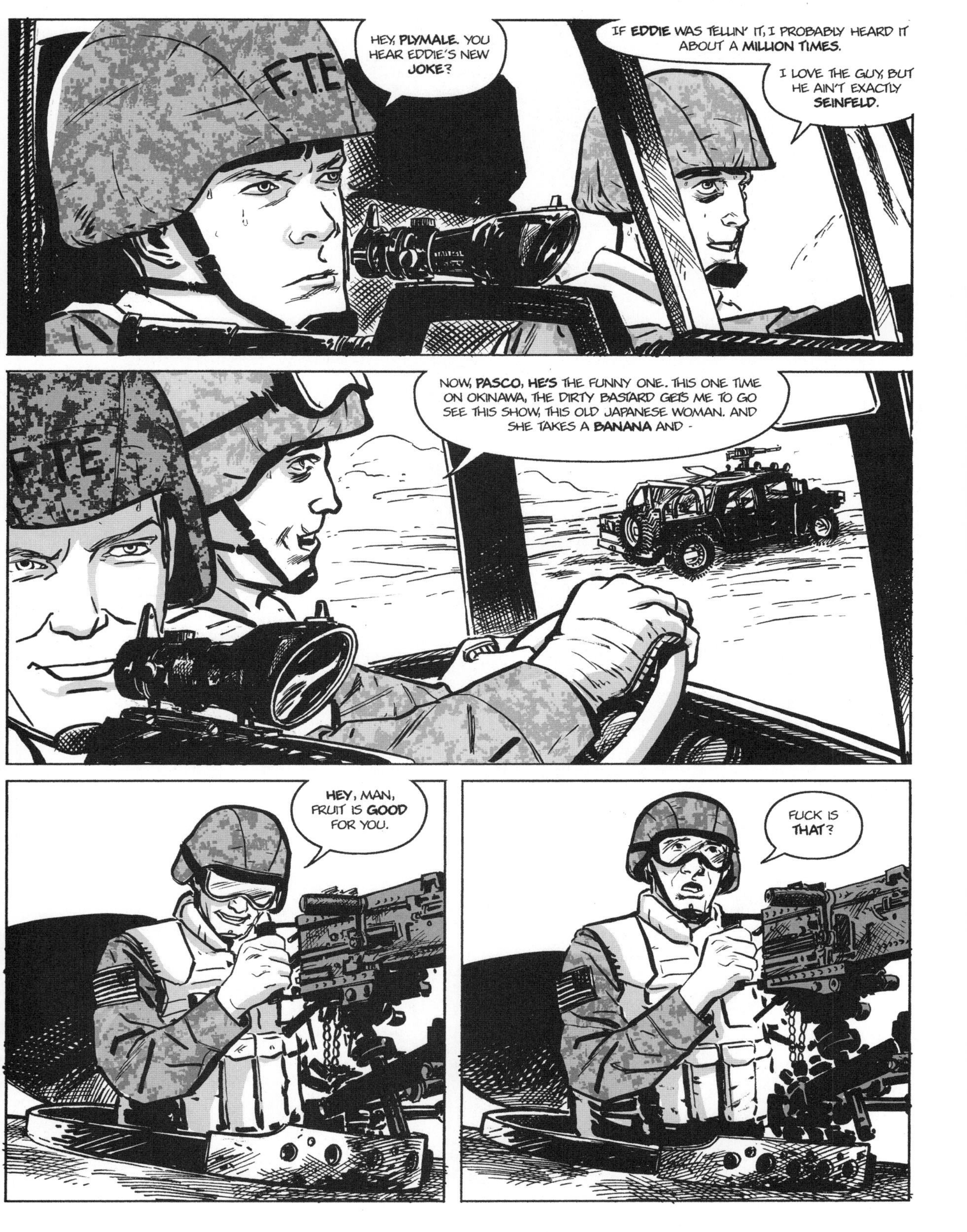
HEY, PLYMALE. YOU HEAR EDDIE'S NEW JOKE?
IF EDDIE WAS TELLIN' IT, I PROBABLY HEARD IT ABOUT A MILLION TIMES.
I LOVE THE GUY, BUT HE AIN'T EXACTLY SEINFELD.
NOW, PASCO, HE'S THE FUNNY ONE. THIS ONE TIME ON OKINAWA, THE DIRTY BASTARD GETS ME TO GO SEE THIS SHOW, THIS OLD JAPANESE WOMAN. AND SHE TAKES A BANANA AND -
HEY, MAN, FRUIT IS GOOD FOR YOU.
FUCK IS THAT?

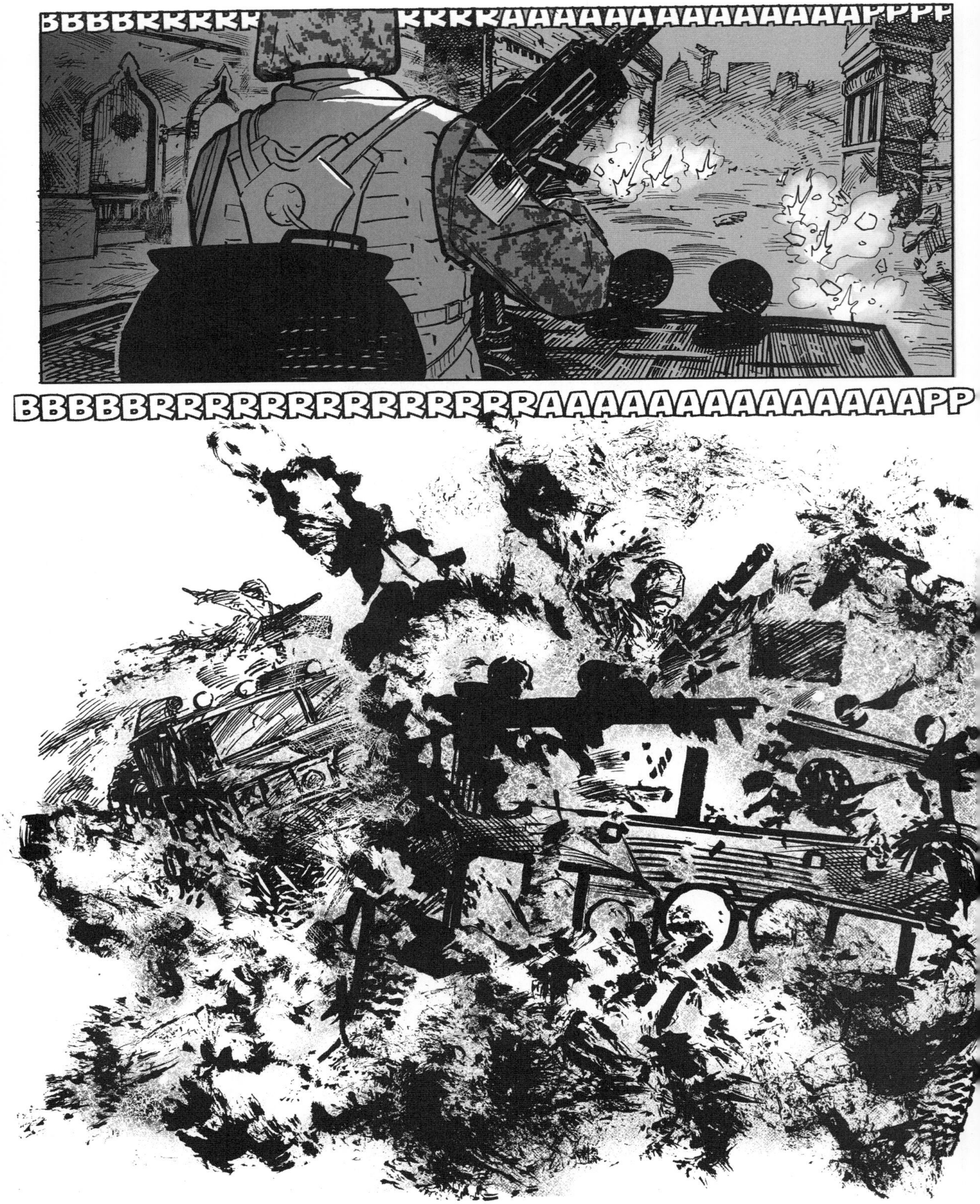
BBBBRRRRR
RRRRAAAAAAAAAAAAAAPPPP
BBBBBRRRRRRRRRRRRRAAAAAAAAAAAAAAPP

The **A-10 Warthog** was built to shatter tanks like fine **crystal.**

The 30mm rotary cannon on its nose fires depleted uranium slugs at a rate of about 3900 rounds. Per **minute.**

BBRRAAAAAAAAAAAAAAAAAAAI

SHIT--

Imagine being caught in a tornado. Only, instead of wind, the tornado is made up of **gunfire.**

Or imagine being struck by the wrath of **God.**

NOW imagine something ten times **worse.**

That's what being hit by an A-10 is like.

FUCK. FUCK. **FUCK.**

They call this **fratricide.** Or, more colorfully, a **"blue on blue."**

More commonly, it's referred to as **"friendly fire."**

Sure **looks** friendly, doesn't it?

17

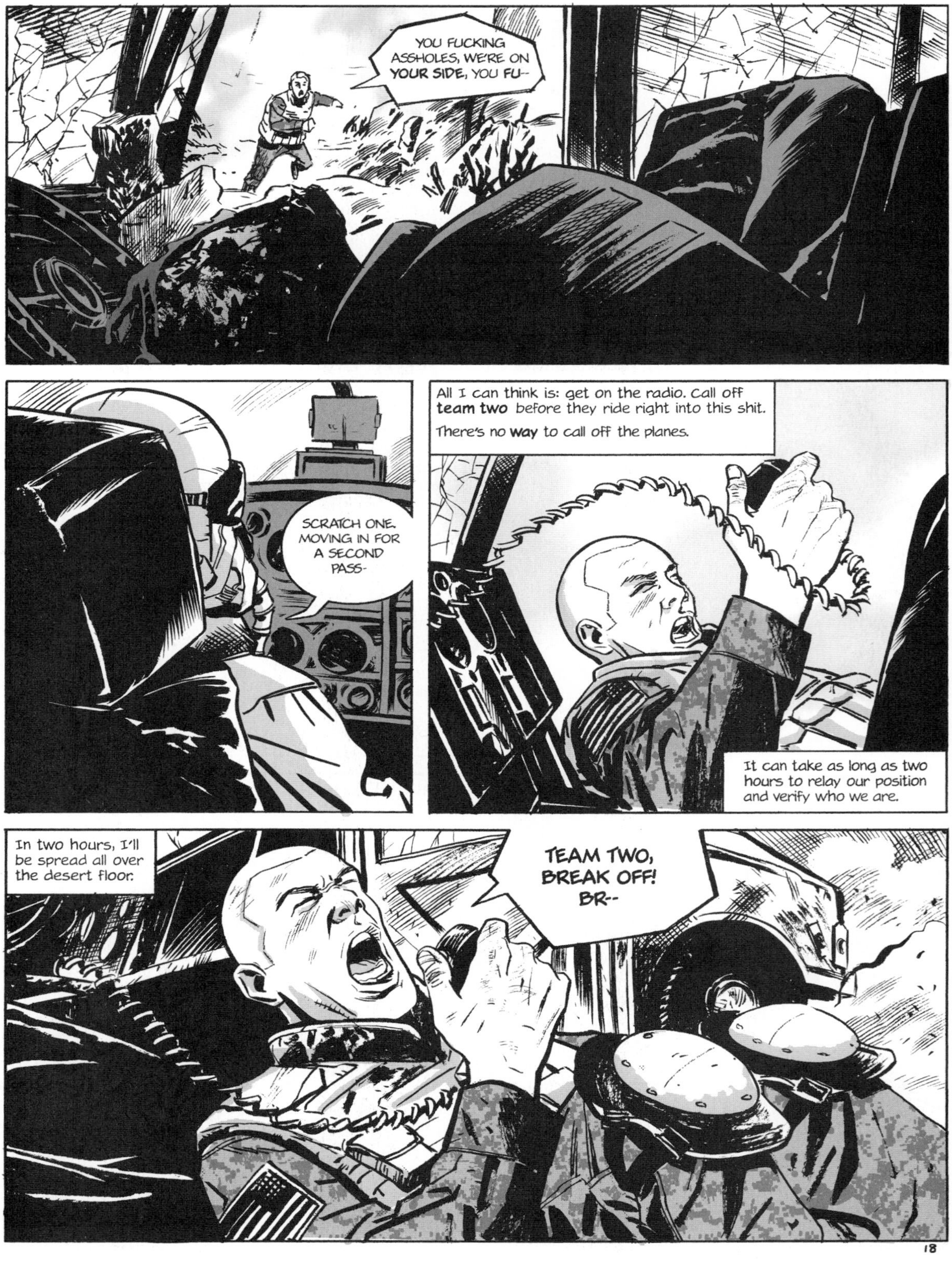

YOU FUCKING ASSHOLES, WE'RE ON **YOUR SIDE**, YOU FU--
SCRATCH ONE. MOVING IN FOR A SECOND PASS-
All I can think is: get on the radio. Call off **team two** before they ride right into this shit.
There's no **way** to call off the planes.
It can take as long as two hours to relay our position and verify who we are.
In two hours, I'll be spread all over the desert floor.
TEAM TWO, BREAK OFF! BR--

And then **God** hits me again, and this time he's not pulling his punches.

--UUUUUNH

WHUZZAT?

Can't see.

Can't hear anything, except ringing. Like a church bell that never fades.

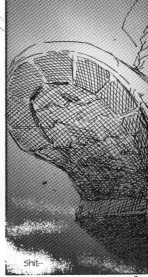
Shit--

19

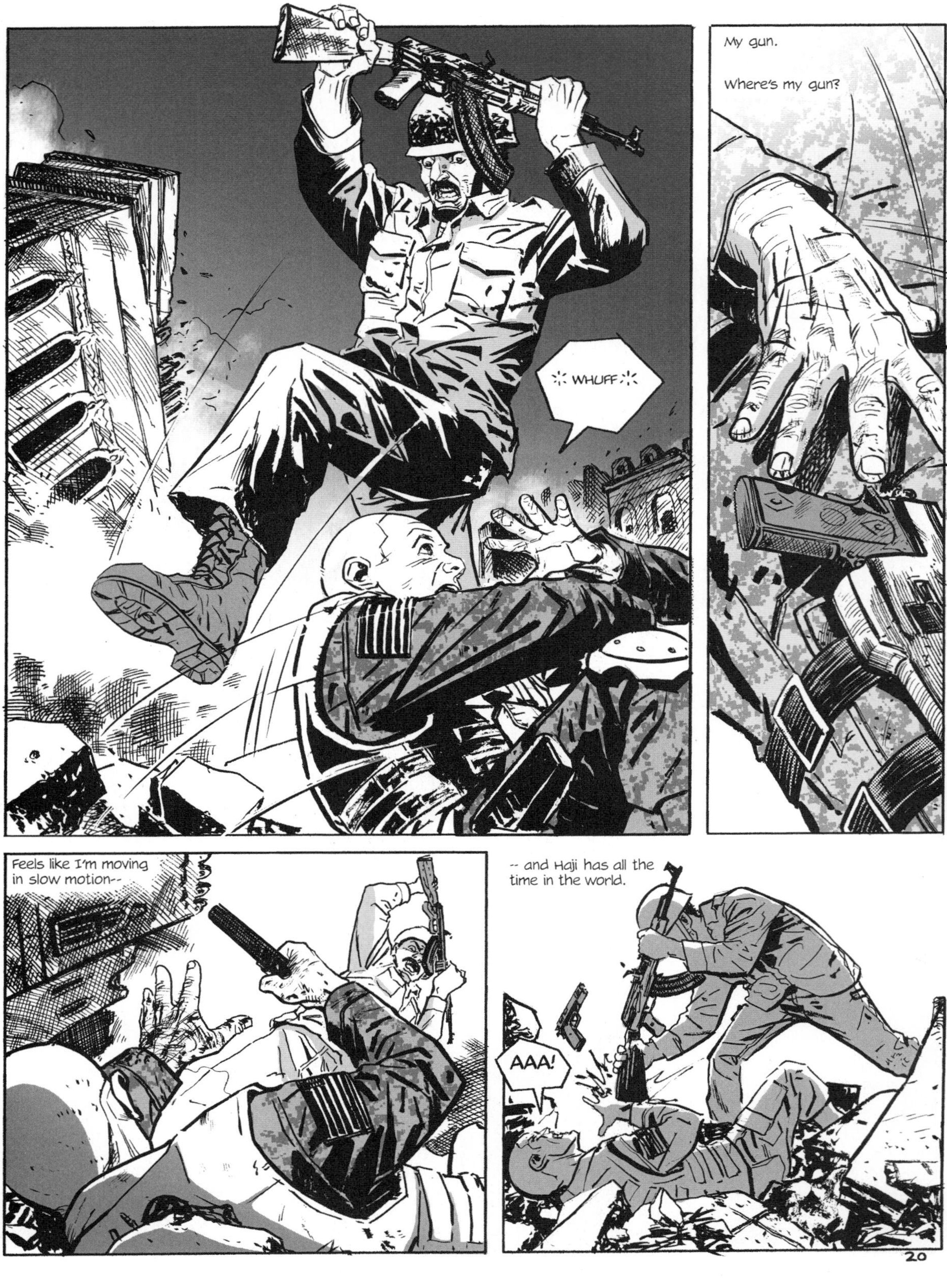

WHUFF
My gun.
Where's my gun?
Feels like I'm moving in slow motion--
-- and Haji has all the time in the world.
AAA!

HELLO, AMERICAN!

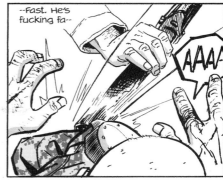

--Fast. He's fucking fa--

AAAA

-- Get to the pistol-- my only chance--

Almost got it. **Almost** g--

NNNNYYAAAAHHHH!

< STILL WANT TO **FIGHT**, YEAH? >

< THAT'S **GOOD**. THAT'S **GOOD**, AMERICAN. >

< YOU GO ON AND **FIGHT**-- >

<-- IT WILL **ALL** BE OVER IN A MINUTE--- >

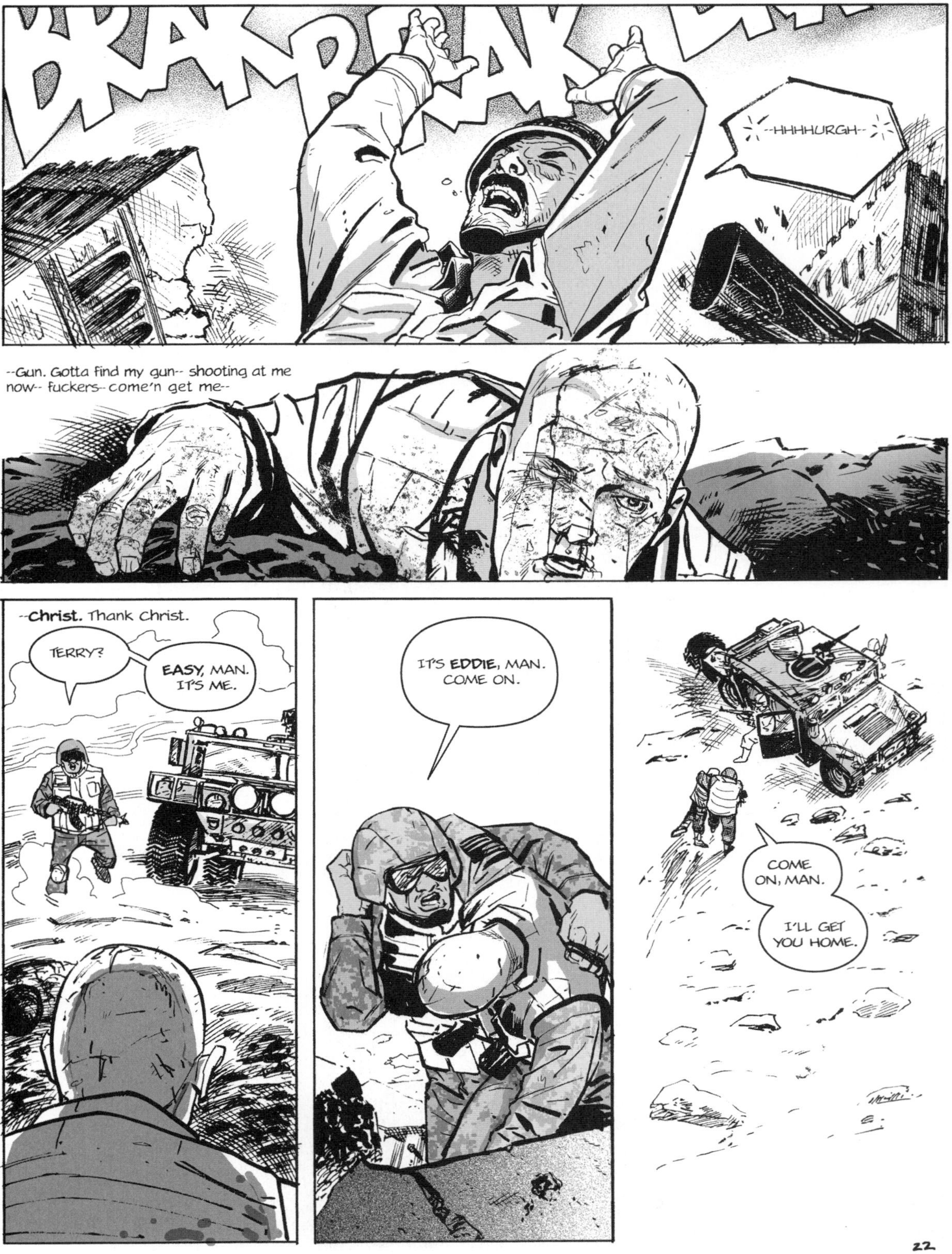
--HHHHURGH--
--Gun. Gotta find my gun-- shooting at me now-- fuckers--come'n get me--
--Christ. Thank Christ.
TERRY?
EASY, MAN. IT'S ME.
IT'S EDDIE, MAN. COME ON.
COME ON, MAN.
I'LL GET YOU HOME.

And he does. Halfway home, at least.
LANDSTUHL REGIONAL MEDICAL CENTER (LRMC)
LANDSTUHL, GERMANY
MAY 1, 2003

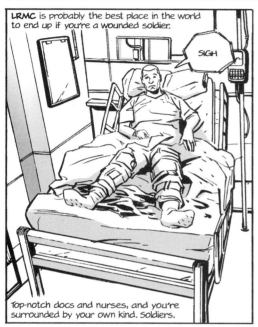

LRMC is probably the best place in the world to end up if you're a wounded soldier.

SIGH

Top-notch docs and nurses, and you're surrounded by your own kind. Soldiers.

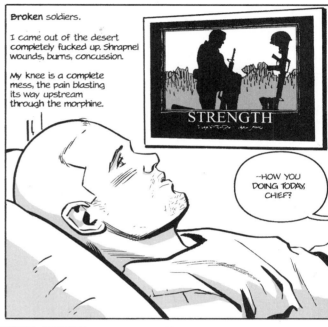

Broken soldiers.

I came out of the desert completely fucked up. Shrapnel wounds, burns, concussion.

My knee is a complete mess, the pain blasting its way upstream through the morphine.

STRENGTH

--HOW YOU DOING TODAY, CHIEF?

MORNING, SARN'T.

IT'S **AFTERNOON**, CHIEF.

HOW'S THE **KNEE**?

SAME AS YESTERDAY. HURTS LIKE A **BASTARD**.

I EXPECT IT DOES--

--OL' **HAJI** WHACKED IT PRETTY **GOOD**.

CHIEF?

YOU GOT A VISITOR, IF YOU'RE UP TO IT.

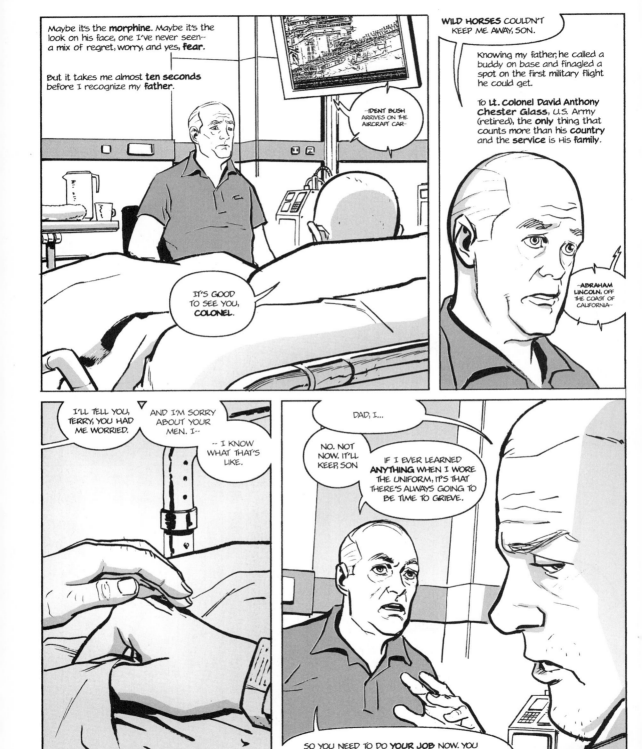

Maybe it's the **morphine**. Maybe it's the look on his face, one I've never seen-- a mix of regret, worry, and yes, **fear**.

But it takes me almost **ten seconds** before I recognize my **father**.

-IDENT BUSH ARRIVES ON THE AIRCRAFT CAR-

IT'S GOOD TO SEE YOU, **COLONEL**.

WILD HORSES COULDN'T KEEP ME AWAY, SON.

Knowing my father, he called a buddy on base and finagled a spot on the first military flight he could get.

To **Lt. Colonel David Anthony Chester Glass**, U.S. Army (retired), the **only** thing that counts more than his **country** and the **service** is **His family**.

-ABRAHAM LINCOLN, OFF THE COAST OF CALIFORNIA-

I'LL TELL YOU, TERRY, YOU HAD ME WORRIED.

AND I'M SORRY ABOUT YOUR MEN. I--

-- I KNOW WHAT THAT'S LIKE.

DAD, I...

NO. NOT NOW. IT'LL KEEP, SON

IF I EVER LEARNED **ANYTHING** WHEN I WORE THE UNIFORM, IT'S THAT THERE'S ALWAYS GOING TO BE TIME TO GRIEVE.

SO YOU NEED TO DO **YOUR JOB** NOW. YOU NEED TO CONCENTRATE ON GETTING YOUR ASS **OUT** OF **THAT** BED, AND OUT OF **THIS** HOSPITAL.

24

AND ALL YOU NEED TO KNOW RIGHT NOW IS THAT I'M VERY PROUD OF YOU.
AND I'M PROUD TO BE ABLE TO PRESENT THIS.
The old man had to pull some serious strings to do this. It's just not how this is usually done.
The Badge of Military Merit-- the Purple Heart-- is one of the oldest honors still awarded by the military, dating back to the Revolutionary War.
The award nobody really wants.
WAIT. YOU SAID SOMETHING ABOUT MY TEAM-- DID ANYONE--
--THEY DIDN'T MAKE IT, TERRY.
I'M SO SORRY, SON. I'M SO SORRY.
NO. NO.
I want to scream. At him. At the ceiling. At the world.
But the words catch in my throat. To say it out loud means it's real.
And it can't be. It can't be real.

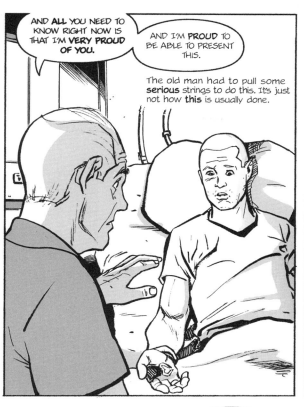

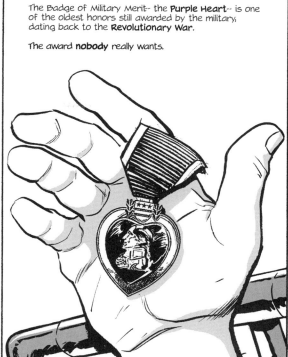

He keeps talking, in that same low, calm voice that I've known all my life.

I can barely hear him. Of all the **first team** guys, only **Doyle, Sanz, Amherst** and I made it out of **Nasiriyah.**

Doyle died on the way to the medevac. **Sanz** and **Amherst** made it to the field hospital before **they** lost the fight.

Leaving me--**just me**-- to remember how they all died.

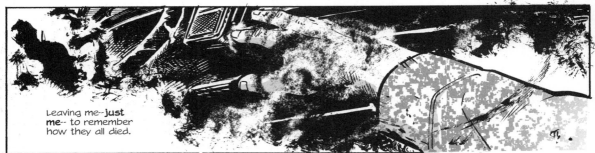

To remember good men turned into ruined meat in an instant.

The one who **survived.**

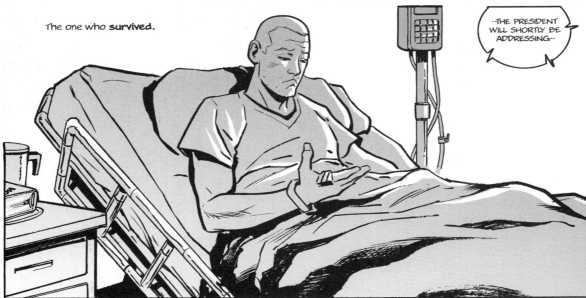

--THE PRESIDENT WILL SHORTLY BE ADDRESSING--

--THERE'S SOMETHING ELSE, SON. I'M NOT SURE IF I SHOULD EVEN--

--THAT IS TO SAY, IT'S, IT'S NOT--

In my entire life, I've **never** seen my father **speechless**.

JUST SPIT IT OUT, DAD.

JUST GET IT OVER WITH.

I **already** know what he's going to say. The "incident" that landed me here, and my brothers in body bags, is **embarrassing** to the Army.

And if there's one thing the military can't abide, it's **embarrassment**.

--LOW AMERICANS: MAJOR COMBAT OPERATIONS IN IRAQ HAVE **ENDED**. IN THE BATTLE OF IRAQ, THE **UNITED STATES** AND OUR **ALLIES** HAVE PREVAILED.

THE OTHER MEN IN YOUR UNIT. THEY --

--**YOURS** IS THE ONLY CITATION BEING AWARDED, SON.

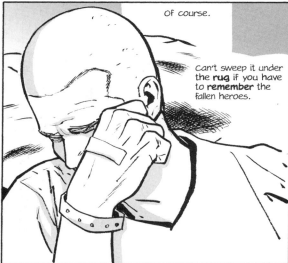

Of course.

Can't sweep it under the **rug** if you have to **remember** the fallen heroes.

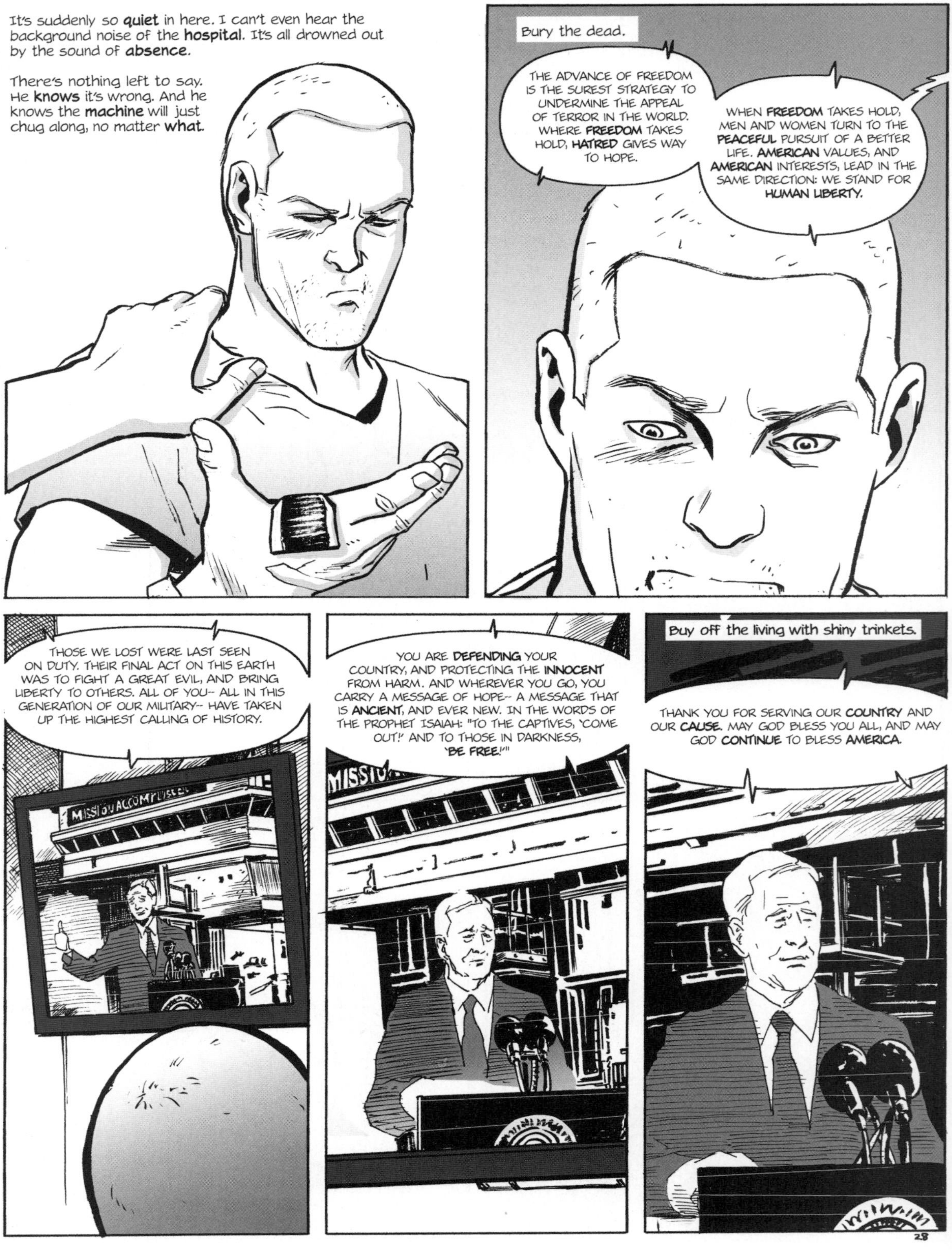
It's suddenly so **quiet** in here. I can't even hear the background noise of the **hospital**. It's all drowned out by the sound of **absence**.
There's nothing left to say. He **knows** it's wrong. And he knows the **machine** will just chug along, no matter **what**.
Bury the dead.
THE ADVANCE OF FREEDOM IS THE SUREST STRATEGY TO UNDERMINE THE APPEAL OF TERROR IN THE WORLD. WHERE **FREEDOM** TAKES HOLD, **HATRED** GIVES WAY TO HOPE.
WHEN **FREEDOM** TAKES HOLD, MEN AND WOMEN TURN TO THE **PEACEFUL** PURSUIT OF A BETTER LIFE. **AMERICAN** VALUES, AND **AMERICAN** INTERESTS, LEAD IN THE SAME DIRECTION: WE STAND FOR **HUMAN LIBERTY.**
THOSE WE LOST WERE LAST SEEN ON DUTY. THEIR FINAL ACT ON THIS EARTH WAS TO FIGHT A GREAT EVIL, AND BRING LIBERTY TO OTHERS. ALL OF YOU-- ALL IN THIS GENERATION OF OUR MILITARY-- HAVE TAKEN UP THE HIGHEST CALLING OF HISTORY.
YOU ARE **DEFENDING** YOUR COUNTRY, AND PROTECTING THE **INNOCENT** FROM HARM. AND WHEREVER YOU GO, YOU CARRY A MESSAGE OF HOPE-- A MESSAGE THAT IS **ANCIENT**, AND EVER NEW. IN THE WORDS OF THE PROPHET ISAIAH: "TO THE CAPTIVES, 'COME OUT!' AND TO THOSE IN DARKNESS, **'BE FREE!'**"
Buy off the living with shiny trinkets.
THANK YOU FOR SERVING OUR **COUNTRY** AND OUR **CAUSE.** MAY GOD BLESS YOU ALL, AND MAY GOD **CONTINUE** TO BLESS **AMERICA.**

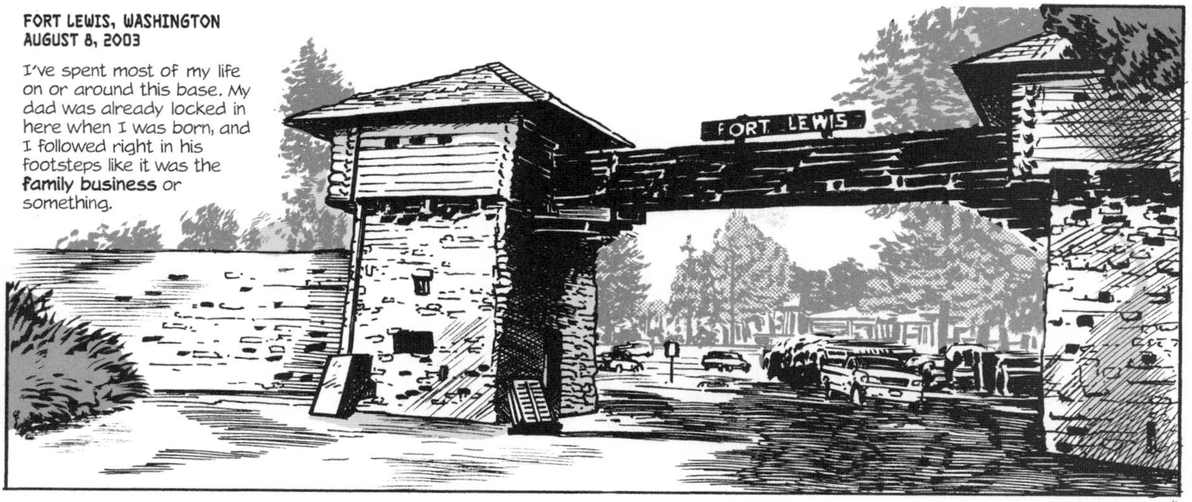
FORT LEWIS, WASHINGTON
AUGUST 8, 2003
I've spent most of my life on or around this base. My dad was already locked in here when I was born, and I followed right in his footsteps like it was the **family business** or something.
FORT LEWIS

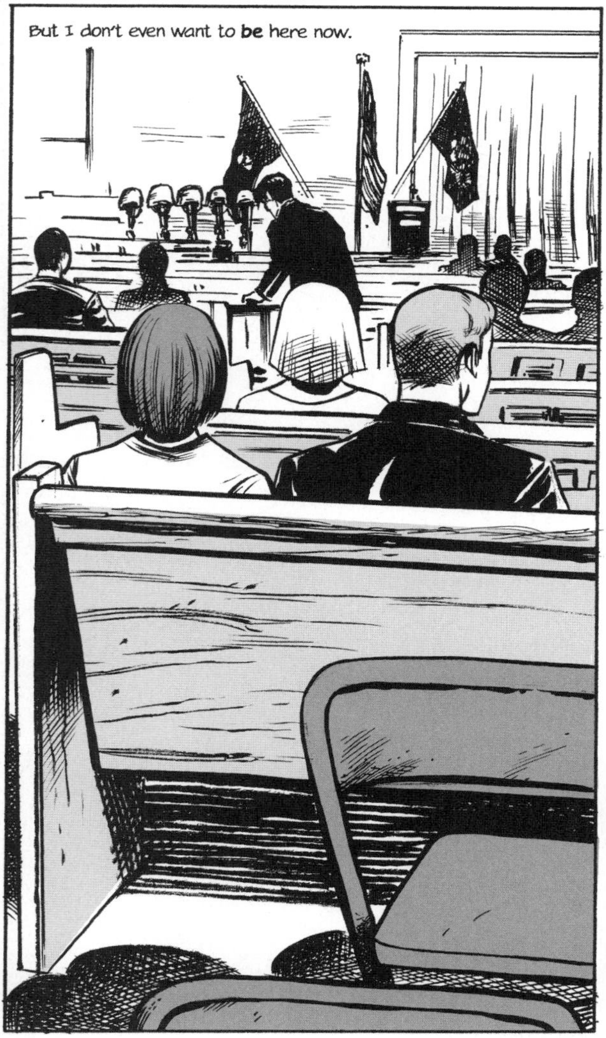
But I don't even want to **be** here now.

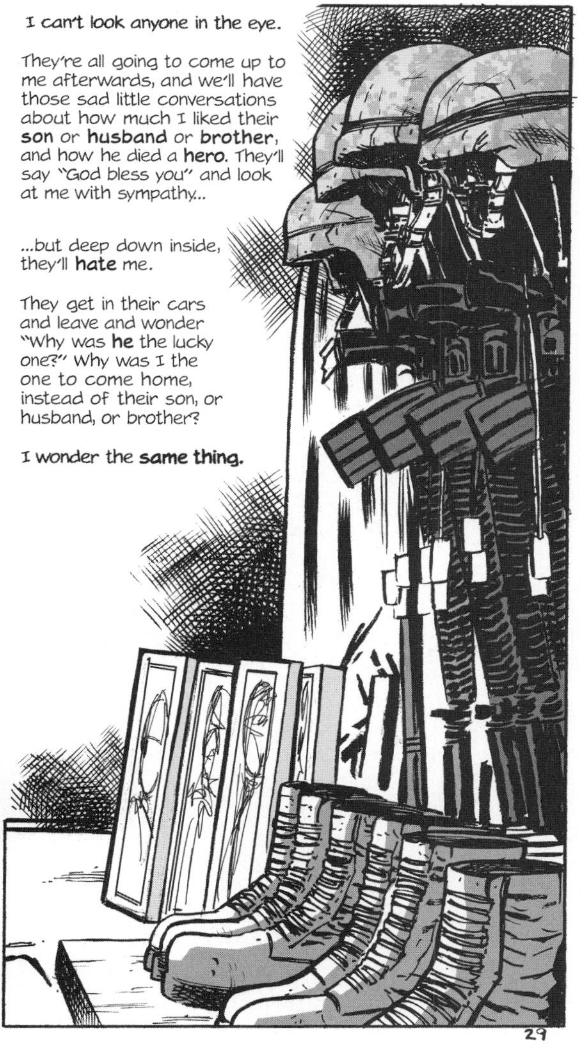
I can't look anyone in the eye.
They're all going to come up to me afterwards, and we'll have those sad little conversations about how much I liked their **son** or **husband** or **brother**, and how he died a **hero**. They'll say "God bless you" and look at me with sympathy...
...but deep down inside, they'll **hate** me.
They get in their cars and leave and wonder "Why was **he** the lucky one?" Why was I the one to come home, instead of their son, or husband, or brother?
I wonder the **same thing.**

It is a very rare thing for a man to choose the **TIME** and **PLACE** of his passing.

Perhaps it would be **BETTER** if we could. It might be easier for our loved ones to **PREPARE** for such a thing, and for us to say every **WORD** we ever meant to **SAY** while we still have the **CHANCE**.

The **TRUTH** is that we are **NOT EQUIPPED** for such a responsibility. Even if we **COULD** control our exit from this world, there would always be one last bit of **UNFINISHED BUSINESS**; one last twinge of **REGRET** for that phone call you didn't make.

Perhaps we **CANNOT** control our **DEATH**...

...but we **CAN** control how we **LIVE OUR LIVES.**

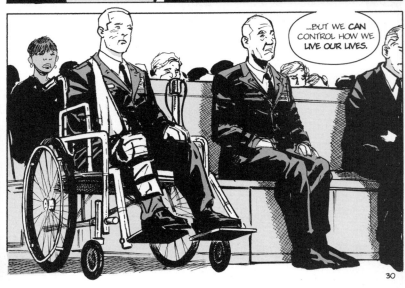

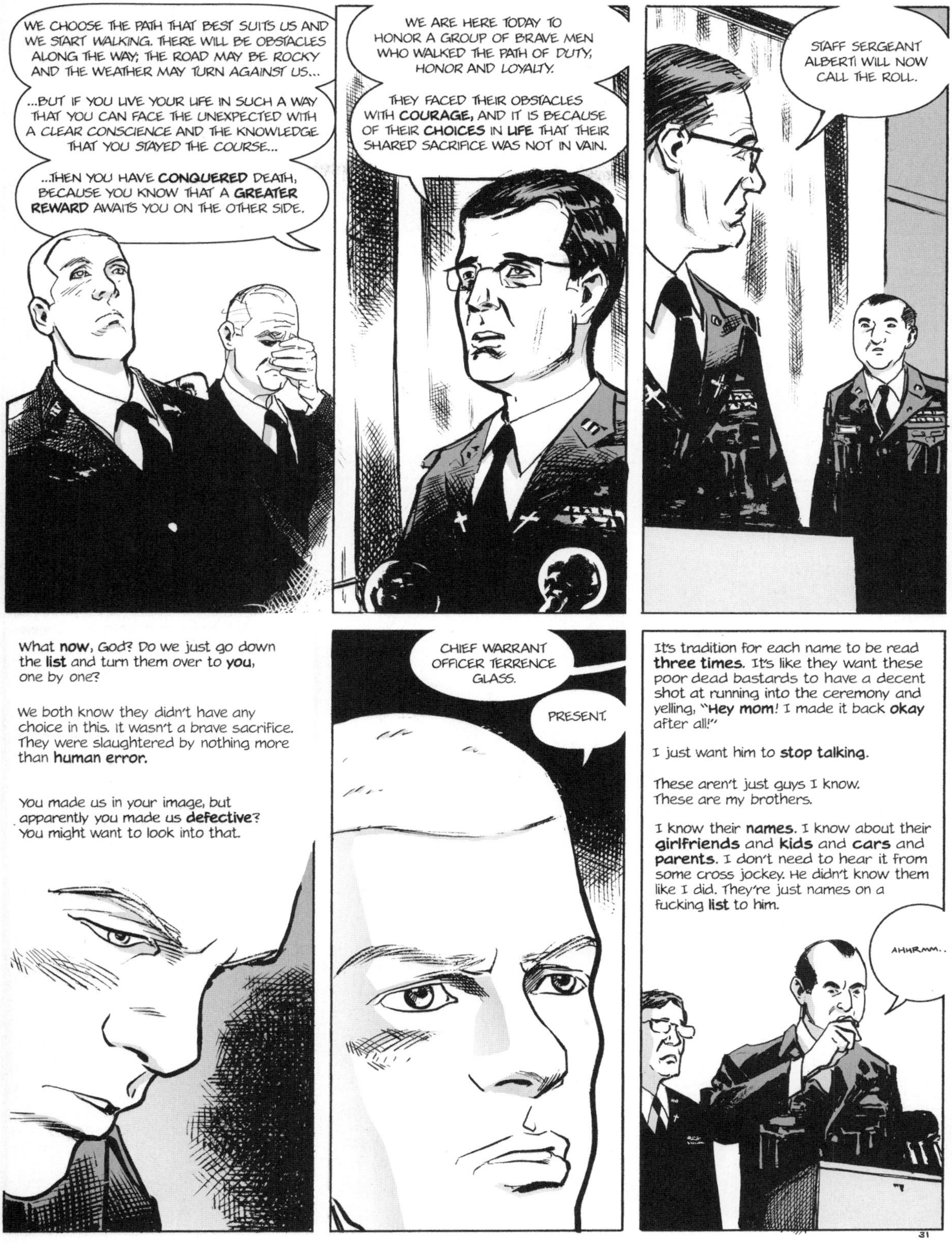
WE CHOOSE THE PATH THAT BEST SUITS US AND WE START WALKING. THERE WILL BE OBSTACLES ALONG THE WAY; THE ROAD MAY BE ROCKY AND THE WEATHER MAY TURN AGAINST US...
...BUT IF YOU LIVE YOUR LIFE IN SUCH A WAY THAT YOU CAN FACE THE UNEXPECTED WITH A CLEAR CONSCIENCE AND THE KNOWLEDGE THAT YOU STAYED THE COURSE...
...THEN YOU HAVE **CONQUERED** DEATH, BECAUSE YOU KNOW THAT A **GREATER REWARD** AWAITS YOU ON THE OTHER SIDE.
WE ARE HERE TODAY TO HONOR A GROUP OF BRAVE MEN WHO WALKED THE PATH OF DUTY, HONOR AND LOYALTY.
THEY FACED THEIR OBSTACLES WITH **COURAGE,** AND IT IS BECAUSE OF THEIR **CHOICES** IN **LIFE** THAT THEIR SHARED SACRIFICE WAS NOT IN VAIN.
STAFF SERGEANT ALBERTI WILL NOW CALL THE ROLL.
What **now**, God? Do we just go down the **list** and turn them over to **you**, one by one?
We both know they didn't have any choice in this. It wasn't a brave sacrifice. They were slaughtered by nothing more than **human error.**
You made us in your image, but apparently you made us **defective**? You might want to look into that.
CHIEF WARRANT OFFICER TERRENCE GLASS.
PRESENT.
It's tradition for each name to be read **three times**. It's like they want these poor dead bastards to have a decent shot at running into the ceremony and yelling, "**Hey mom**! I made it back **okay** after all!"
I just want him to **stop talking**.
These aren't just guys I know. These are my brothers.
I know their **names**. I know about their **girlfriends** and **kids** and **cars** and **parents**. I don't need to hear it from some cross jockey. He didn't know them like I did. They're just names on a fucking **list** to him.
AHHRMM..

Captain Austin Doyle. Wife, two kids. | **Master Sergeant Shemar Casey.** Divorced, one son. | **Sergeant First Class Ernest Pasco.** Single. | **Sergeant First Class Eugene Plymale.** Engaged with a daughter. | **Staff Sergeant Edgar Sanz.** Married, no kids.

Jesus, it's getting hard to breathe. I need to get **out**.

Staff Sergeant Christopher Lutz. Single. | **Sergeant First Class Peter Amherst.** Divorced. | **Staff Sergeant Owen Reemer.** Single. | **Sergeant First Class James Day.** Single. | **Staff Sergeant Stephen Ritter.** Pregnant girlfriend. | **Staff Sergeant David Brooker.** Single, no kids. Awful card player.

Last recitation of the last name, and everything in the room is just **frozen**.

There's nobody left to surprise now. Nobody **can** be in denial.

Sometimes, you can't really accept it until you hear someone else **say** it: "This person is **dead**, and I've just told a whole room full of people, so it must be true."

Rest in peace, guys. I hope they've got a good **bar** where you're going, 'cause you're gonna need a nice stiff drink when you hear **this** shit.

Killed by friendly fire. **Passed over** for posthumous honors. **Fucked up** and **forgotten**.

You deserve **better**.

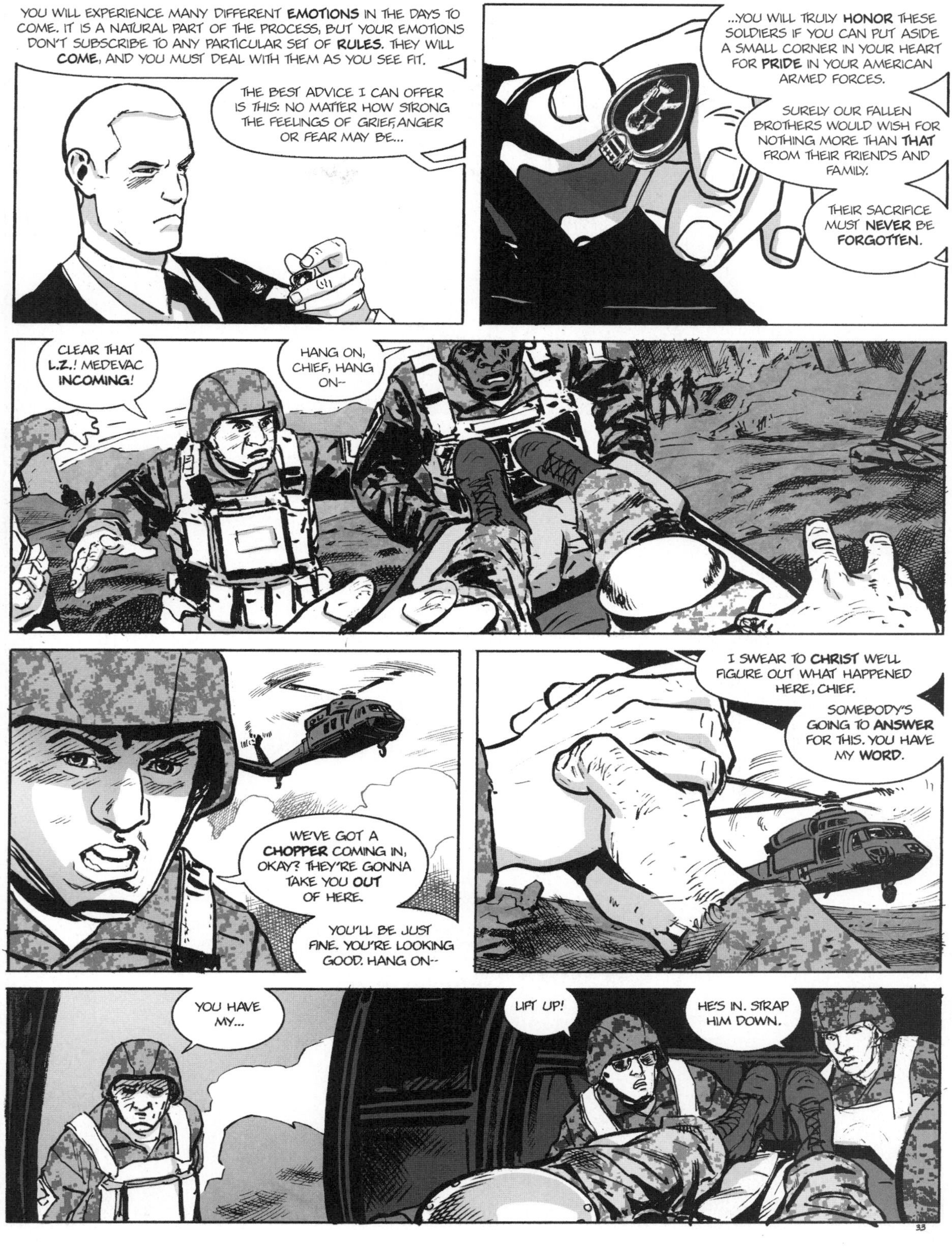
YOU WILL EXPERIENCE MANY DIFFERENT **EMOTIONS** IN THE DAYS TO COME. IT IS A NATURAL PART OF THE PROCESS, BUT YOUR EMOTIONS DON'T SUBSCRIBE TO ANY PARTICULAR SET OF **RULES**. THEY WILL **COME**, AND YOU MUST DEAL WITH THEM AS YOU SEE FIT.
THE BEST ADVICE I CAN OFFER IS THIS: NO MATTER HOW STRONG THE FEELINGS OF GRIEF, ANGER OR FEAR MAY BE...
...YOU WILL TRULY **HONOR** THESE SOLDIERS IF YOU CAN PUT ASIDE A SMALL CORNER IN YOUR HEART FOR **PRIDE** IN YOUR AMERICAN ARMED FORCES.
SURELY OUR FALLEN BROTHERS WOULD WISH FOR NOTHING MORE THAN **THAT** FROM THEIR FRIENDS AND FAMILY.
THEIR SACRIFICE MUST **NEVER** BE **FORGOTTEN**.
CLEAR THAT **L.Z.**! MEDEVAC **INCOMING**!
HANG ON, CHIEF, HANG ON--
WE'VE GOT A **CHOPPER** COMING IN, OKAY? THEY'RE GONNA TAKE YOU **OUT** OF HERE.
YOU'LL BE JUST FINE. YOU'RE LOOKING GOOD. HANG ON--
I SWEAR TO **CHRIST** WE'LL FIGURE OUT WHAT HAPPENED HERE, CHIEF.
SOMEBODY'S GOING TO **ANSWER** FOR THIS. YOU HAVE MY **WORD**.
YOU HAVE MY...
LIFT UP!
HE'S IN. STRAP HIM DOWN.

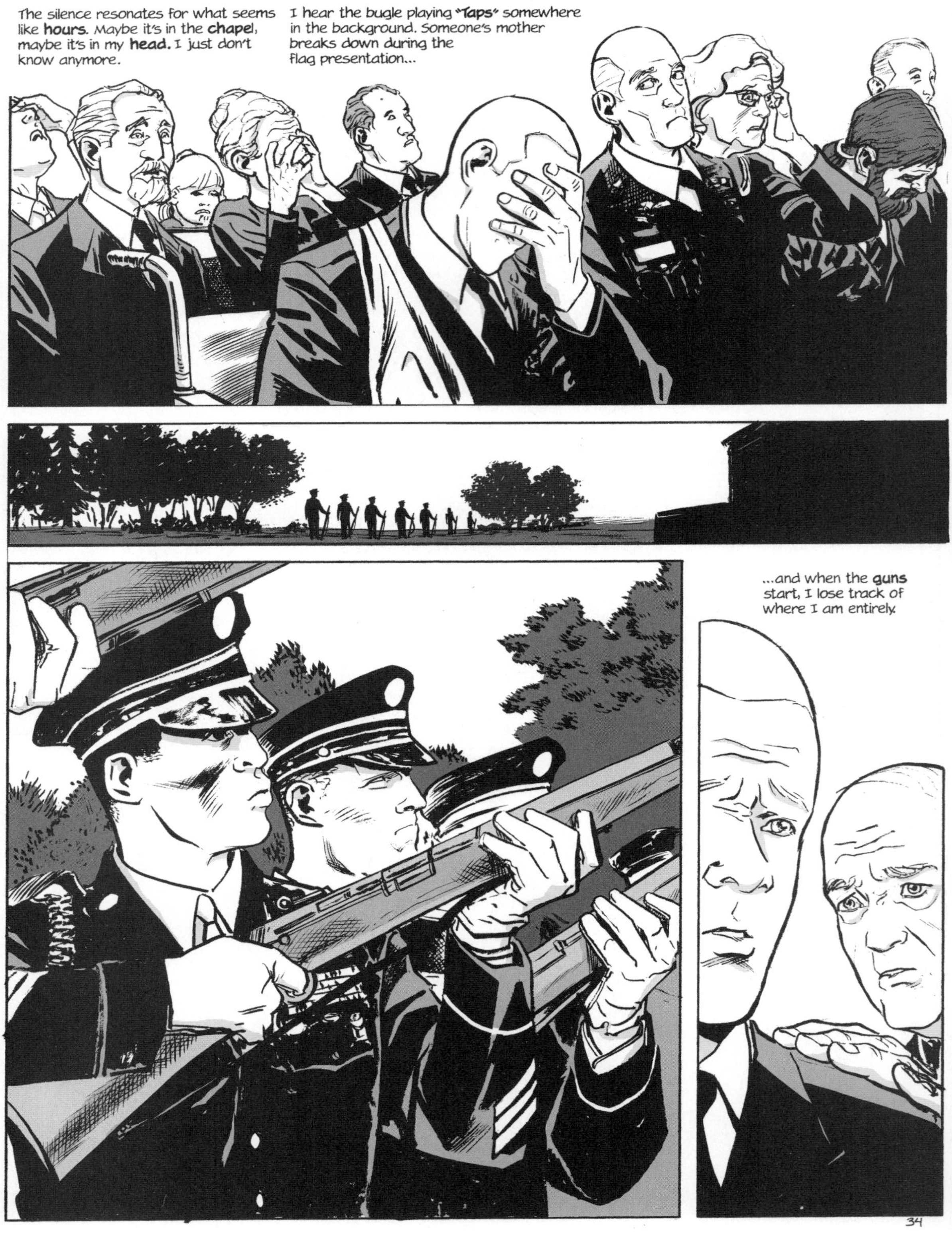
The silence resonates for what seems like **hours**. Maybe it's in the **chapel**, maybe it's in my **head**. I just don't know anymore.
I hear the bugle playing **"Taps"** somewhere in the background. Someone's mother breaks down during the flag presentation...
...and when the **guns** start, I lose track of where I am entirely.

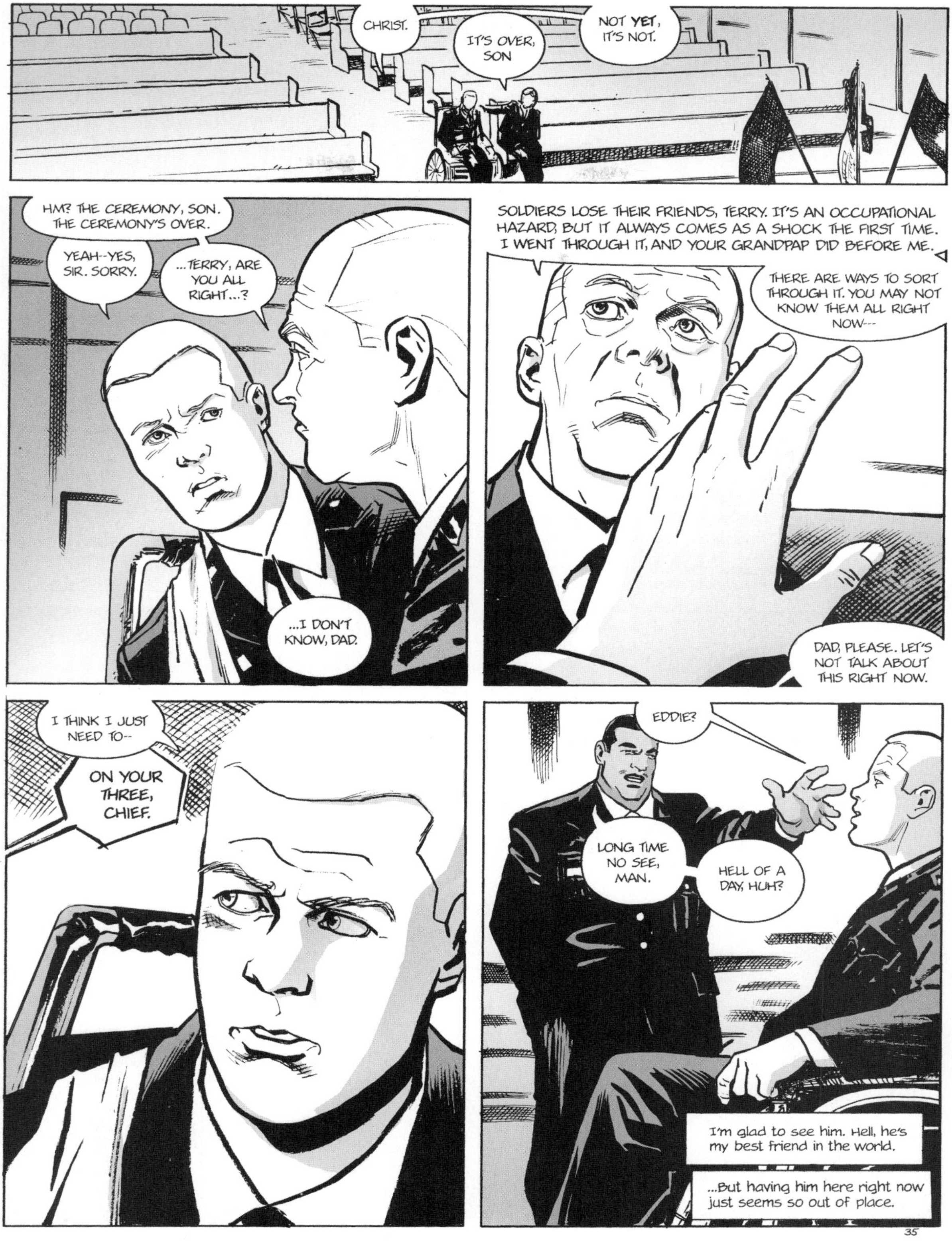
CHRIST.
IT'S OVER, SON
NOT YET, IT'S NOT.
HM? THE CEREMONY, SON. THE CEREMONY'S OVER.
YEAH--YES, SIR. SORRY.
...TERRY, ARE YOU ALL RIGHT...?
...I DON'T KNOW, DAD.
SOLDIERS LOSE THEIR FRIENDS, TERRY. IT'S AN OCCUPATIONAL HAZARD, BUT IT ALWAYS COMES AS A SHOCK THE FIRST TIME. I WENT THROUGH IT, AND YOUR GRANDPAP DID BEFORE ME.
THERE ARE WAYS TO SORT THROUGH IT. YOU MAY NOT KNOW THEM ALL RIGHT NOW---
DAD, PLEASE. LET'S NOT TALK ABOUT THIS RIGHT NOW.
I THINK I JUST NEED TO--
ON YOUR THREE, CHIEF.
EDDIE?
LONG TIME NO SEE, MAN.
HELL OF A DAY, HUH?
I'm glad to see him. Hell, he's my best friend in the world.
...But having him here right now just seems so out of place.

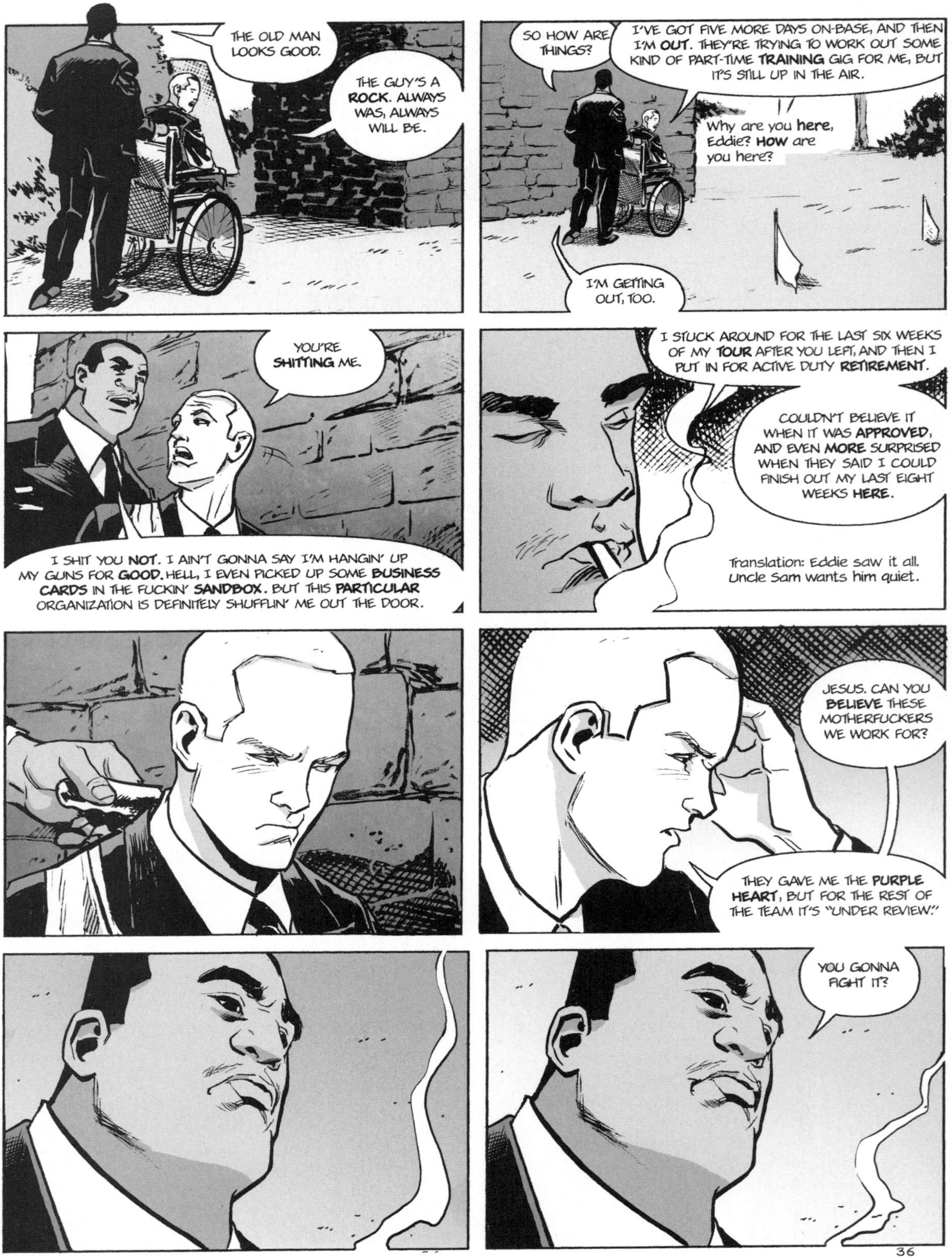
THE OLD MAN LOOKS GOOD.
THE GUY'S A **ROCK**. ALWAYS WAS, ALWAYS WILL BE.
SO HOW ARE THINGS?
I'VE GOT FIVE MORE DAYS ON-BASE, AND THEN I'M **OUT**. THEY'RE TRYING TO WORK OUT SOME KIND OF PART-TIME **TRAINING** GIG FOR ME, BUT IT'S STILL UP IN THE AIR.
Why are you **here**, Eddie? **How** are you here?
I'M GETTING OUT, TOO.
YOU'RE **SHITTING** ME.
I SHIT YOU **NOT**. I AIN'T GONNA SAY I'M HANGIN' UP MY GUNS FOR **GOOD**. HELL, I EVEN PICKED UP SOME **BUSINESS CARDS** IN THE FUCKIN' **SANDBOX**. BUT THIS **PARTICULAR** ORGANIZATION IS DEFINITELY SHUFFLIN' ME OUT THE DOOR.
I STUCK AROUND FOR THE LAST SIX WEEKS OF MY **TOUR** AFTER YOU LEFT, AND THEN I PUT IN FOR ACTIVE DUTY **RETIREMENT**.
COULDN'T BELIEVE IT WHEN IT WAS **APPROVED**, AND EVEN **MORE** SURPRISED WHEN THEY SAID I COULD FINISH OUT MY LAST EIGHT WEEKS **HERE**.
Translation: Eddie saw it all. Uncle Sam wants him quiet.
JESUS. CAN YOU **BELIEVE** THESE MOTHERFUCKERS WE WORK FOR?
THEY GAVE ME THE **PURPLE HEART**, BUT FOR THE REST OF THE TEAM IT'S "UNDER REVIEW."
YOU GONNA FIGHT IT?

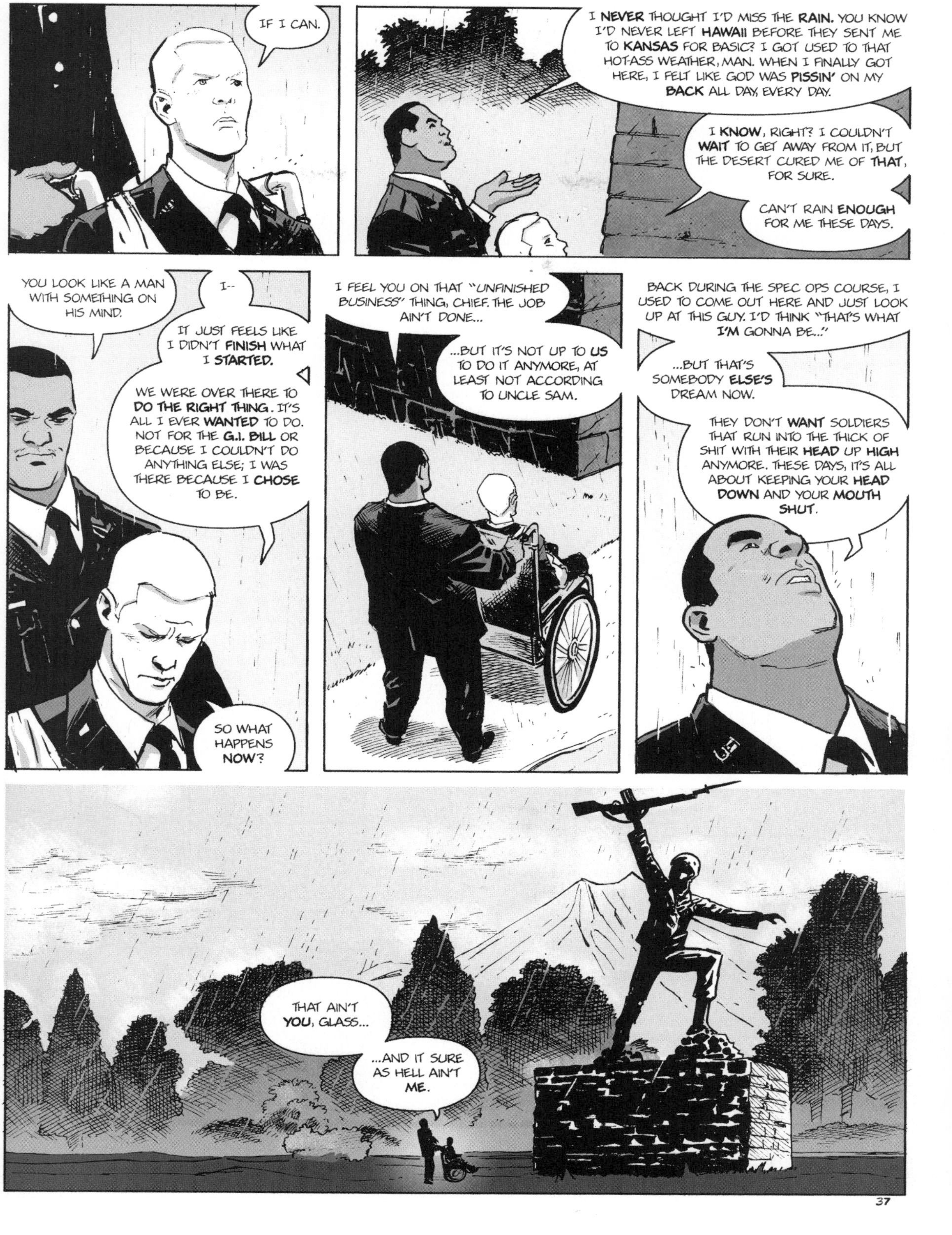
IF I CAN.
I NEVER THOUGHT I'D MISS THE RAIN. YOU KNOW I'D NEVER LEFT HAWAII BEFORE THEY SENT ME TO KANSAS FOR BASIC? I GOT USED TO THAT HOT-ASS WEATHER, MAN. WHEN I FINALLY GOT HERE, I FELT LIKE GOD WAS PISSIN' ON MY BACK ALL DAY, EVERY DAY.
I KNOW, RIGHT? I COULDN'T WAIT TO GET AWAY FROM IT, BUT THE DESERT CURED ME OF THAT, FOR SURE.
CAN'T RAIN ENOUGH FOR ME THESE DAYS.
YOU LOOK LIKE A MAN WITH SOMETHING ON HIS MIND.
I--
IT JUST FEELS LIKE I DIDN'T FINISH WHAT I STARTED.
WE WERE OVER THERE TO DO THE RIGHT THING. IT'S ALL I EVER WANTED TO DO. NOT FOR THE G.I. BILL OR BECAUSE I COULDN'T DO ANYTHING ELSE; I WAS THERE BECAUSE I CHOSE TO BE.
SO WHAT HAPPENS NOW?
I FEEL YOU ON THAT "UNFINISHED BUSINESS" THING, CHIEF. THE JOB AIN'T DONE...
...BUT IT'S NOT UP TO US TO DO IT ANYMORE, AT LEAST NOT ACCORDING TO UNCLE SAM.
BACK DURING THE SPEC OPS COURSE, I USED TO COME OUT HERE AND JUST LOOK UP AT THIS GUY. I'D THINK "THAT'S WHAT I'M GONNA BE..."
...BUT THAT'S SOMEBODY ELSE'S DREAM NOW.
THEY DON'T WANT SOLDIERS THAT RUN INTO THE THICK OF SHIT WITH THEIR HEAD UP HIGH ANYMORE. THESE DAYS, IT'S ALL ABOUT KEEPING YOUR HEAD DOWN AND YOUR MOUTH SHUT.
THAT AIN'T YOU, GLASS...
...AND IT SURE AS HELL AIN'T ME.

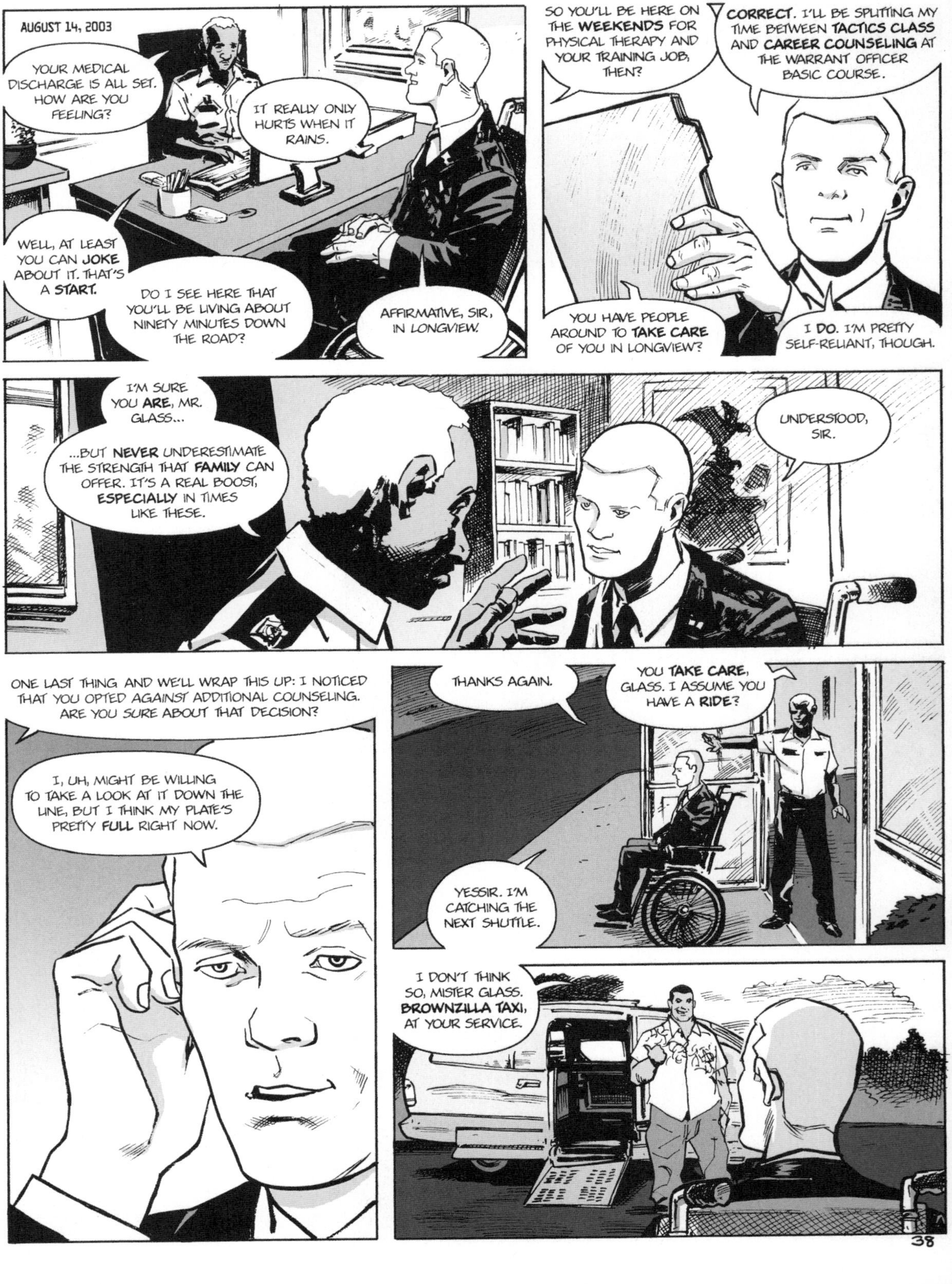
AUGUST 14, 2003
YOUR MEDICAL DISCHARGE IS ALL SET. HOW ARE YOU FEELING?
IT REALLY ONLY HURTS WHEN IT RAINS.
WELL, AT LEAST YOU CAN JOKE ABOUT IT. THAT'S A START.
DO I SEE HERE THAT YOU'LL BE LIVING ABOUT NINETY MINUTES DOWN THE ROAD?
AFFIRMATIVE, SIR, IN LONGVIEW.
SO YOU'LL BE HERE ON THE WEEKENDS FOR PHYSICAL THERAPY AND YOUR TRAINING JOB, THEN?
CORRECT. I'LL BE SPLITTING MY TIME BETWEEN TACTICS CLASS AND CAREER COUNSELING AT THE WARRANT OFFICER BASIC COURSE.
YOU HAVE PEOPLE AROUND TO TAKE CARE OF YOU IN LONGVIEW?
I DO. I'M PRETTY SELF-RELIANT, THOUGH.
I'M SURE YOU ARE, MR. GLASS...
...BUT NEVER UNDERESTIMATE THE STRENGTH THAT FAMILY CAN OFFER. IT'S A REAL BOOST, ESPECIALLY IN TIMES LIKE THESE.
UNDERSTOOD, SIR.
ONE LAST THING AND WE'LL WRAP THIS UP: I NOTICED THAT YOU OPTED AGAINST ADDITIONAL COUNSELING. ARE YOU SURE ABOUT THAT DECISION?
I, UH, MIGHT BE WILLING TO TAKE A LOOK AT IT DOWN THE LINE, BUT I THINK MY PLATE'S PRETTY FULL RIGHT NOW.
THANKS AGAIN.
YOU TAKE CARE, GLASS. I ASSUME YOU HAVE A RIDE?
YESSIR. I'M CATCHING THE NEXT SHUTTLE.
I DON'T THINK SO, MISTER GLASS. BROWNZILLA TAXI, AT YOUR SERVICE.

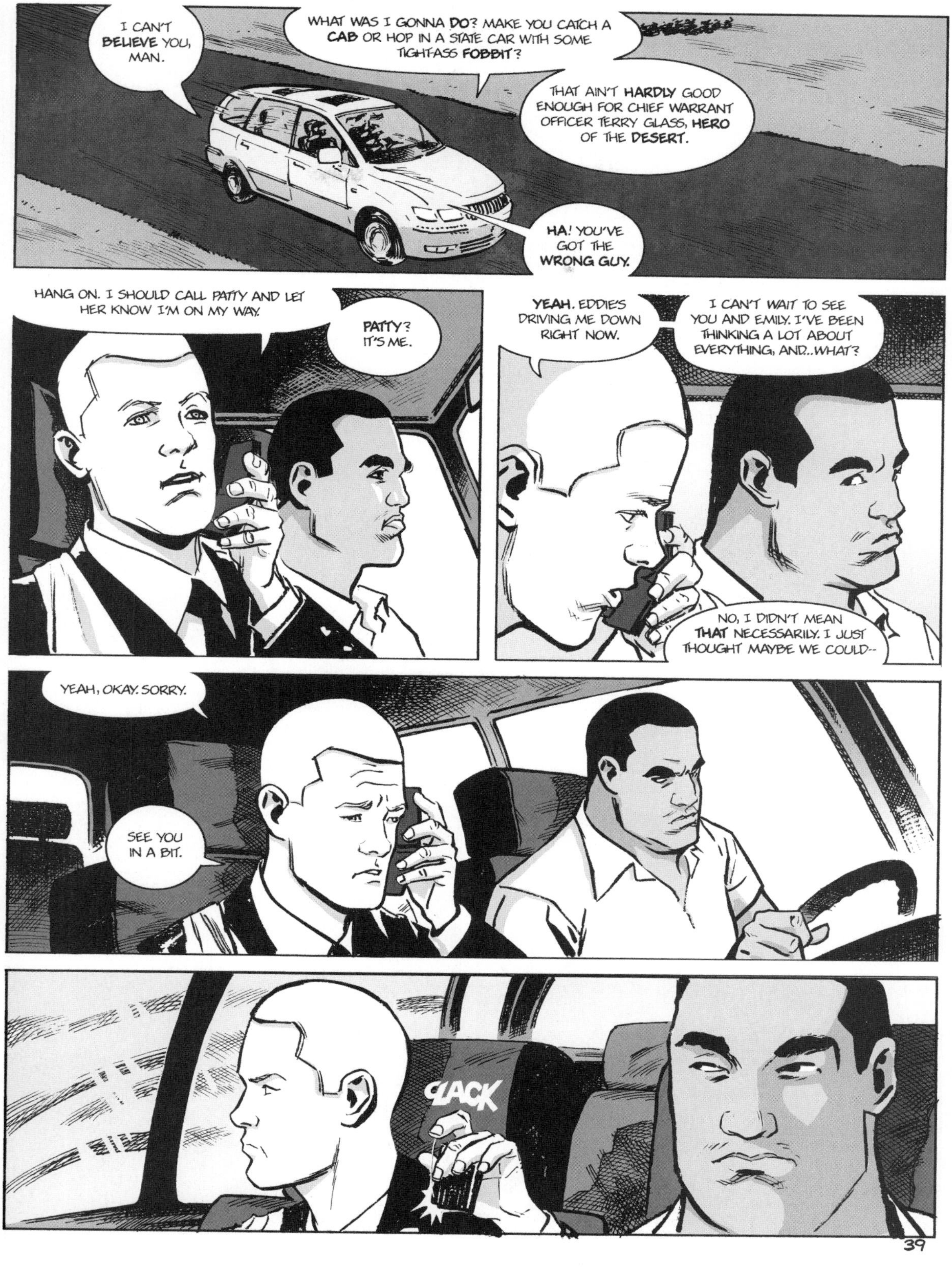
I CAN'T BELIEVE YOU, MAN.
WHAT WAS I GONNA DO? MAKE YOU CATCH A CAB OR HOP IN A STATE CAR WITH SOME TIGHTASS FOBBIT?
THAT AIN'T HARDLY GOOD ENOUGH FOR CHIEF WARRANT OFFICER TERRY GLASS, HERO OF THE DESERT.
HA! YOU'VE GOT THE WRONG GUY.
HANG ON. I SHOULD CALL PATTY AND LET HER KNOW I'M ON MY WAY.
PATTY? IT'S ME.
YEAH. EDDIE'S DRIVING ME DOWN RIGHT NOW.
I CAN'T WAIT TO SEE YOU AND EMILY. I'VE BEEN THINKING A LOT ABOUT EVERYTHING, AND...WHAT?
NO, I DIDN'T MEAN THAT NECESSARILY. I JUST THOUGHT MAYBE WE COULD--
YEAH, OKAY. SORRY.
SEE YOU IN A BIT.
CLACK

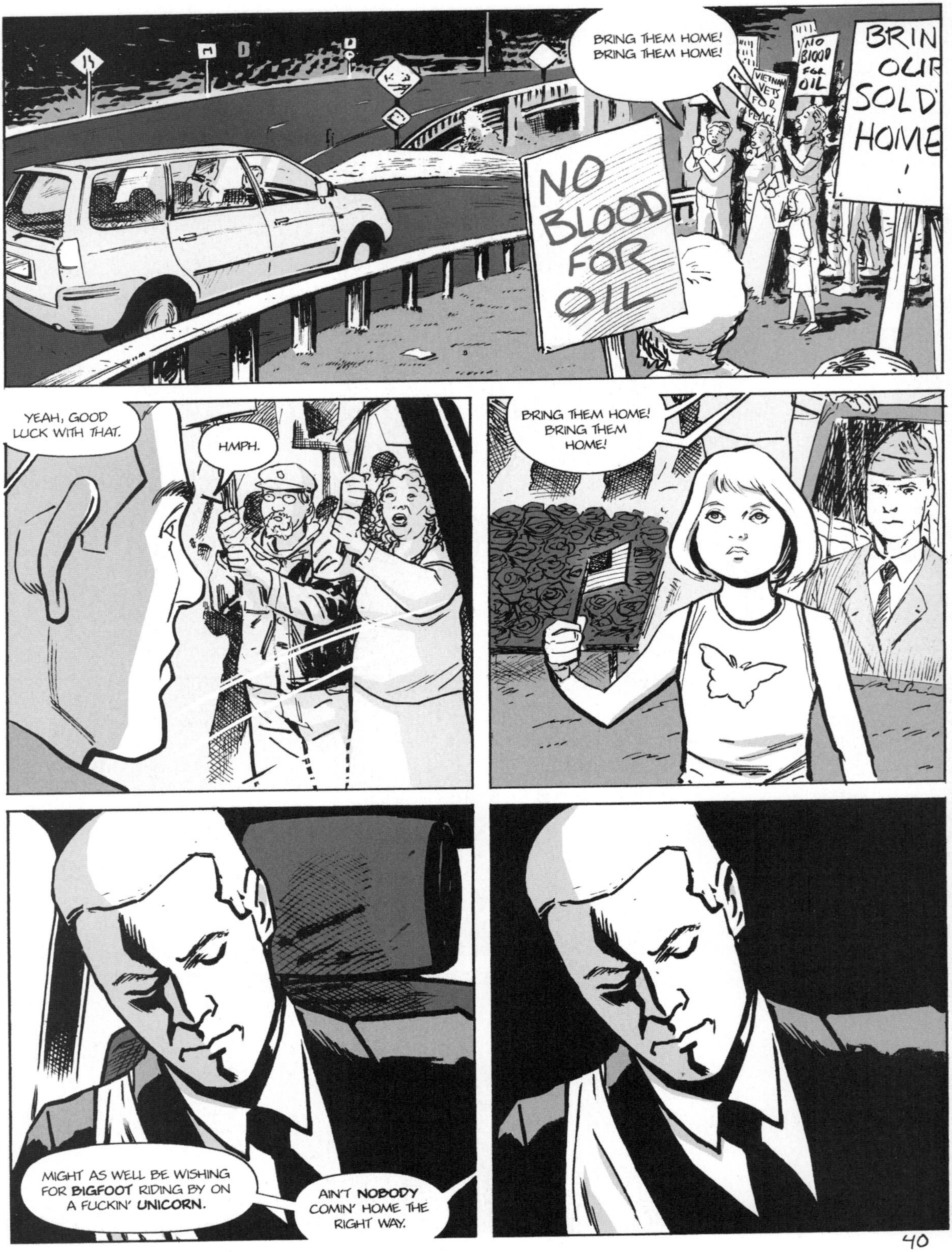
BRING THEM HOME!
BRING THEM HOME!
VIETNAM VETS FOR PEACE
NO BLOOD FOR OIL
BRING OUR SOLD' HOME!
NO BLOOD FOR OIL
YEAH, GOOD LUCK WITH THAT.
HMPH.
BRING THEM HOME! BRING THEM HOME!
MIGHT AS WELL BE WISHING FOR **BIGFOOT** RIDING BY ON A FUCKIN' **UNICORN**.
AIN'T **NOBODY** COMIN' HOME THE RIGHT WAY.

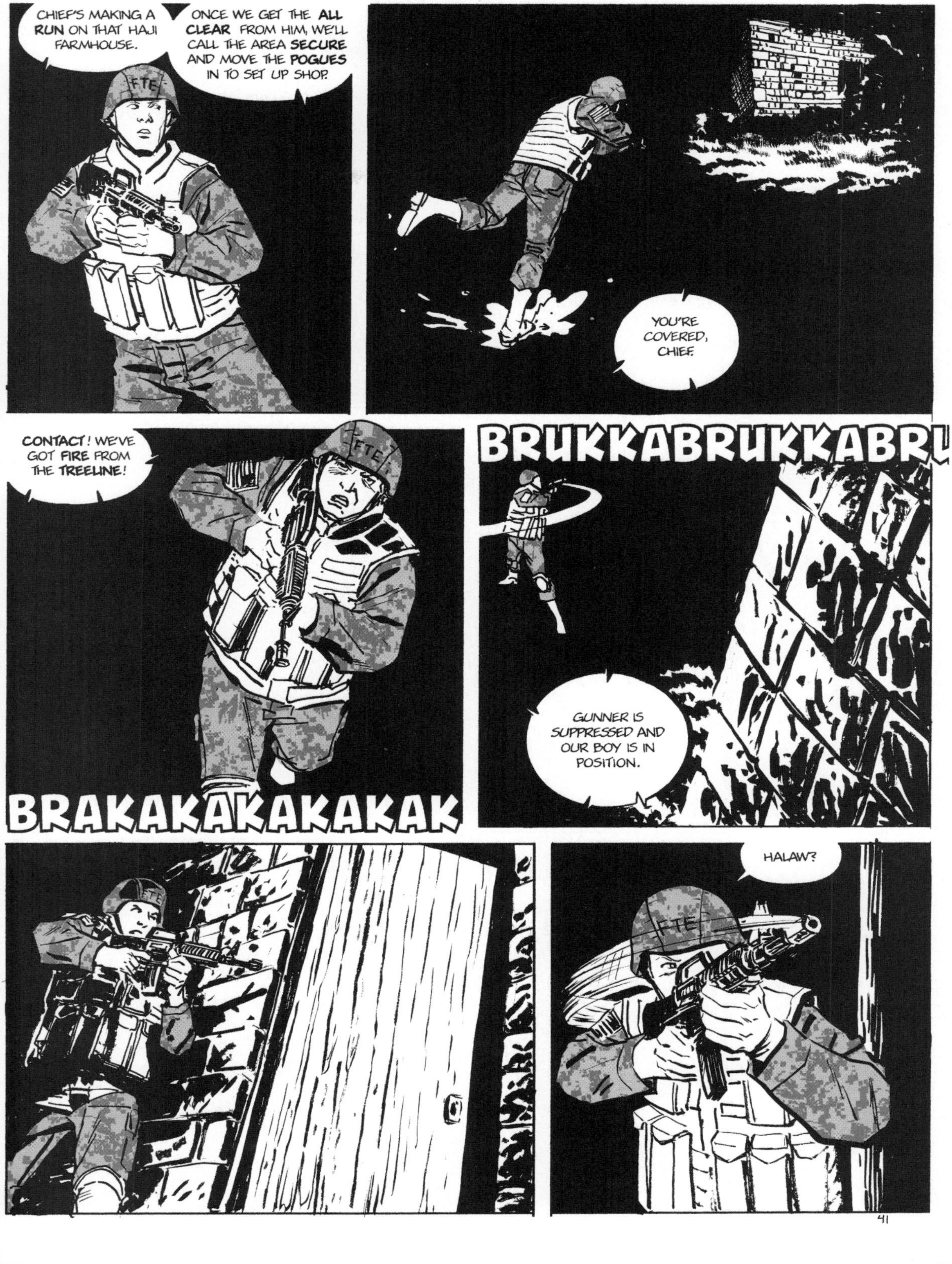
CHIEF'S MAKING A RUN ON THAT HAJI FARMHOUSE.
ONCE WE GET THE ALL CLEAR FROM HIM, WE'LL CALL THE AREA SECURE AND MOVE THE POGUES IN TO SET UP SHOP.
YOU'RE COVERED, CHIEF.
CONTACT! WE'VE GOT FIRE FROM THE TREELINE!
BRAKAKAKAKAKAKAK
BRUKKABRUKKABRU
GUNNER IS SUPPRESSED AND OUR BOY IS IN POSITION.
HALAW?

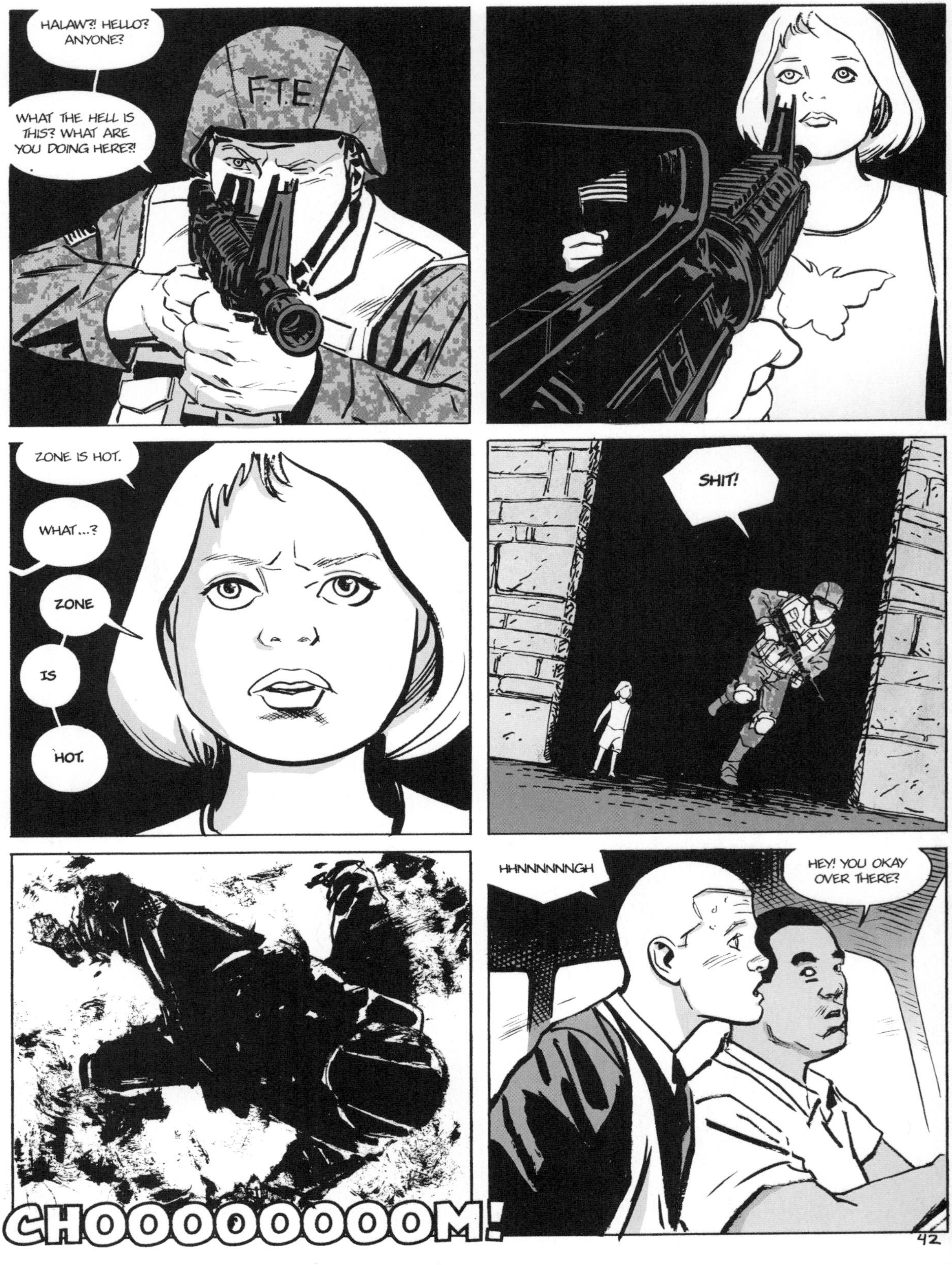
HALAW?! HELLO? ANYONE?
F.T.E.
WHAT THE HELL IS THIS? WHAT ARE YOU DOING HERE?!
ZONE IS HOT.
WHAT...?
ZONE
IS
HOT.
SHIT!
CHOOOOOOOOOM!
HHNNNNNNGH
HEY! YOU OKAY OVER THERE?

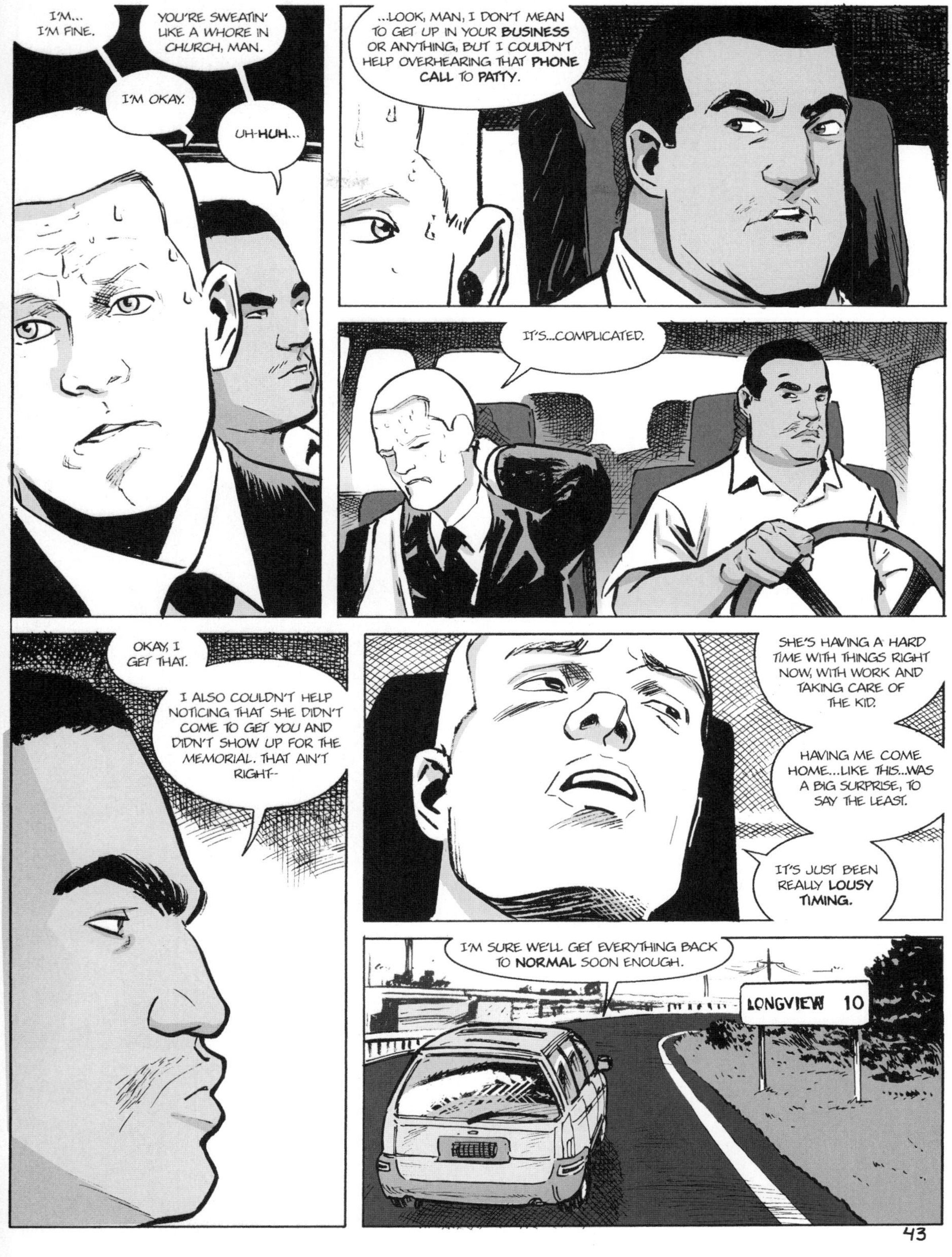
I'M... I'M FINE.
YOU'RE SWEATIN' LIKE A WHORE IN CHURCH, MAN.
I'M OKAY.
UH-HUH...
...LOOK, MAN, I DON'T MEAN TO GET UP IN YOUR BUSINESS OR ANYTHING, BUT I COULDN'T HELP OVERHEARING THAT PHONE CALL TO PATTY.
IT'S...COMPLICATED.
OKAY, I GET THAT.
I ALSO COULDN'T HELP NOTICING THAT SHE DIDN'T COME TO GET YOU AND DIDN'T SHOW UP FOR THE MEMORIAL. THAT AIN'T RIGHT--
SHE'S HAVING A HARD TIME WITH THINGS RIGHT NOW, WITH WORK AND TAKING CARE OF THE KID.
HAVING ME COME HOME...LIKE THIS...WAS A BIG SURPRISE, TO SAY THE LEAST.
IT'S JUST BEEN REALLY LOUSY TIMING.
I'M SURE WE'LL GET EVERYTHING BACK TO NORMAL SOON ENOUGH.
LONGVIEW 10

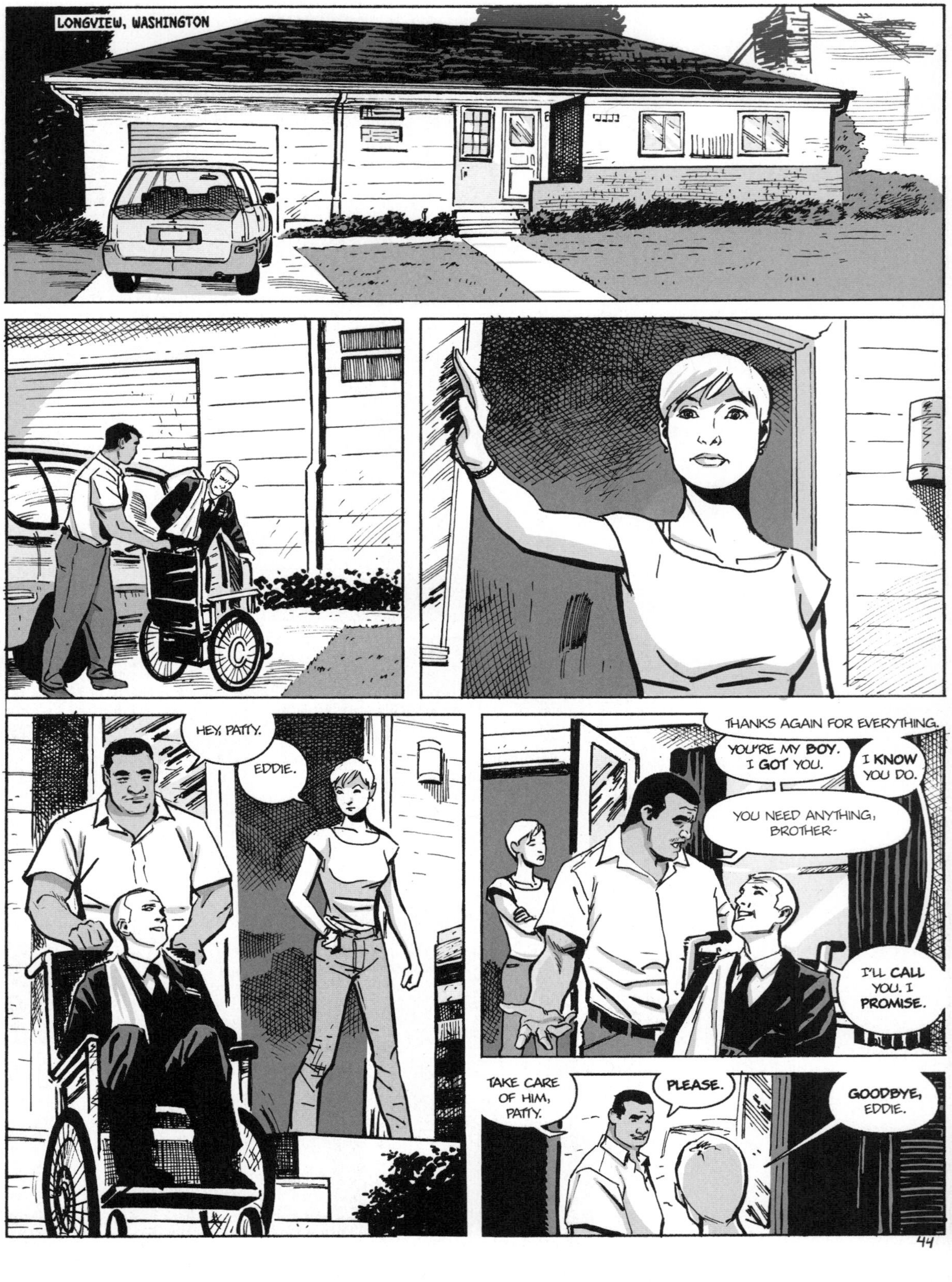
LONGVIEW, WASHINGTON
HEY, PATTY.
EDDIE.
THANKS AGAIN FOR EVERYTHING.
YOU'RE MY BOY. I GOT YOU.
I KNOW YOU DO.
YOU NEED ANYTHING, BROTHER-
I'LL CALL YOU. I PROMISE.
TAKE CARE OF HIM, PATTY.
PLEASE.
GOODBYE, EDDIE.

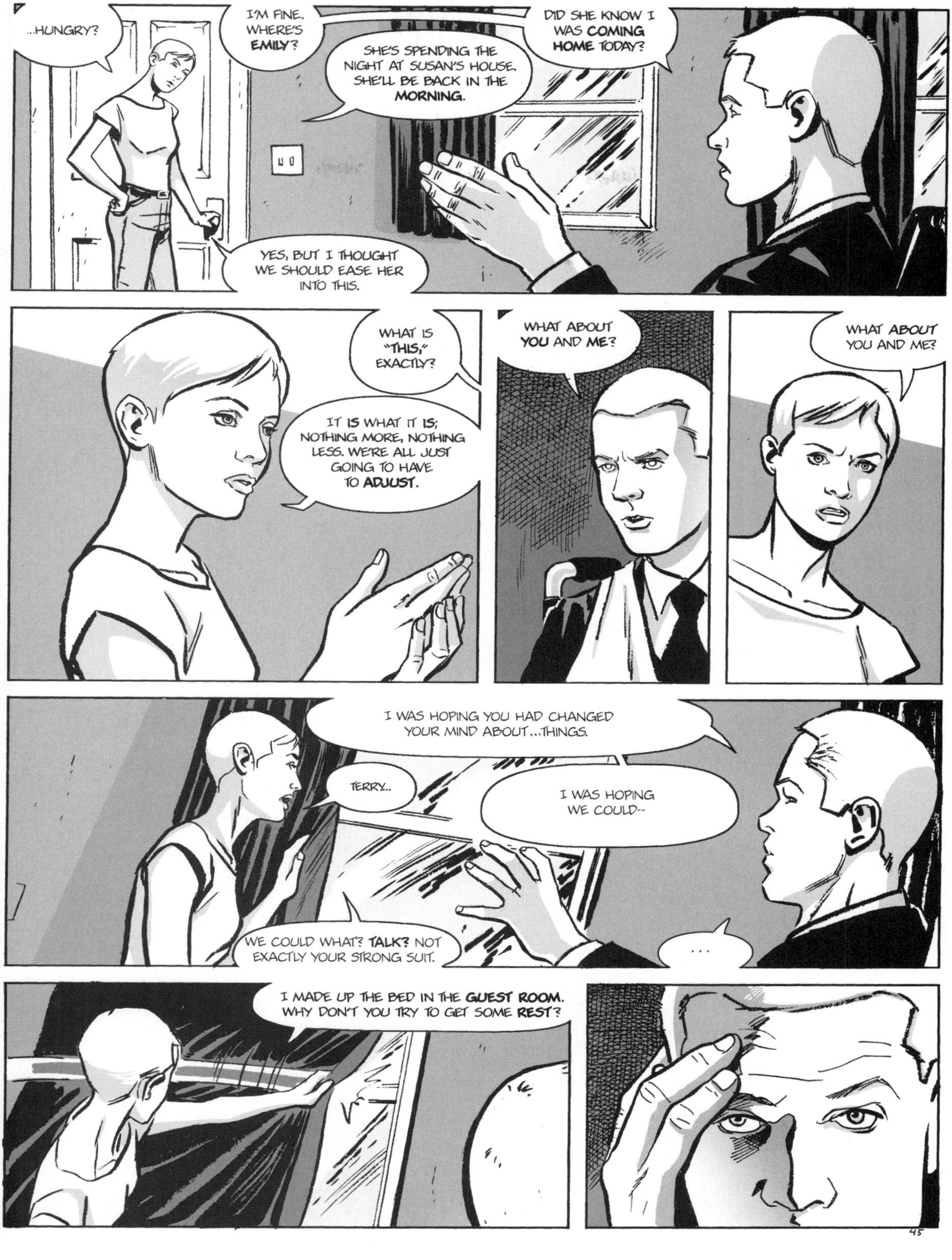
...HUNGRY?
I'M FINE. WHERE'S EMILY?
SHE'S SPENDING THE NIGHT AT SUSAN'S HOUSE. SHE'LL BE BACK IN THE MORNING.
DID SHE KNOW I WAS COMING HOME TODAY?
YES, BUT I THOUGHT WE SHOULD EASE HER INTO THIS.
WHAT IS "THIS," EXACTLY?
IT IS WHAT IT IS; NOTHING MORE, NOTHING LESS. WE'RE ALL JUST GOING TO HAVE TO ADJUST.
WHAT ABOUT YOU AND ME?
WHAT ABOUT YOU AND ME?
I WAS HOPING YOU HAD CHANGED YOUR MIND ABOUT...THINGS.
TERRY...
I WAS HOPING WE COULD--
WE COULD WHAT? TALK? NOT EXACTLY YOUR STRONG SUIT.
. . .
I MADE UP THE BED IN THE GUEST ROOM. WHY DON'T YOU TRY TO GET SOME REST?

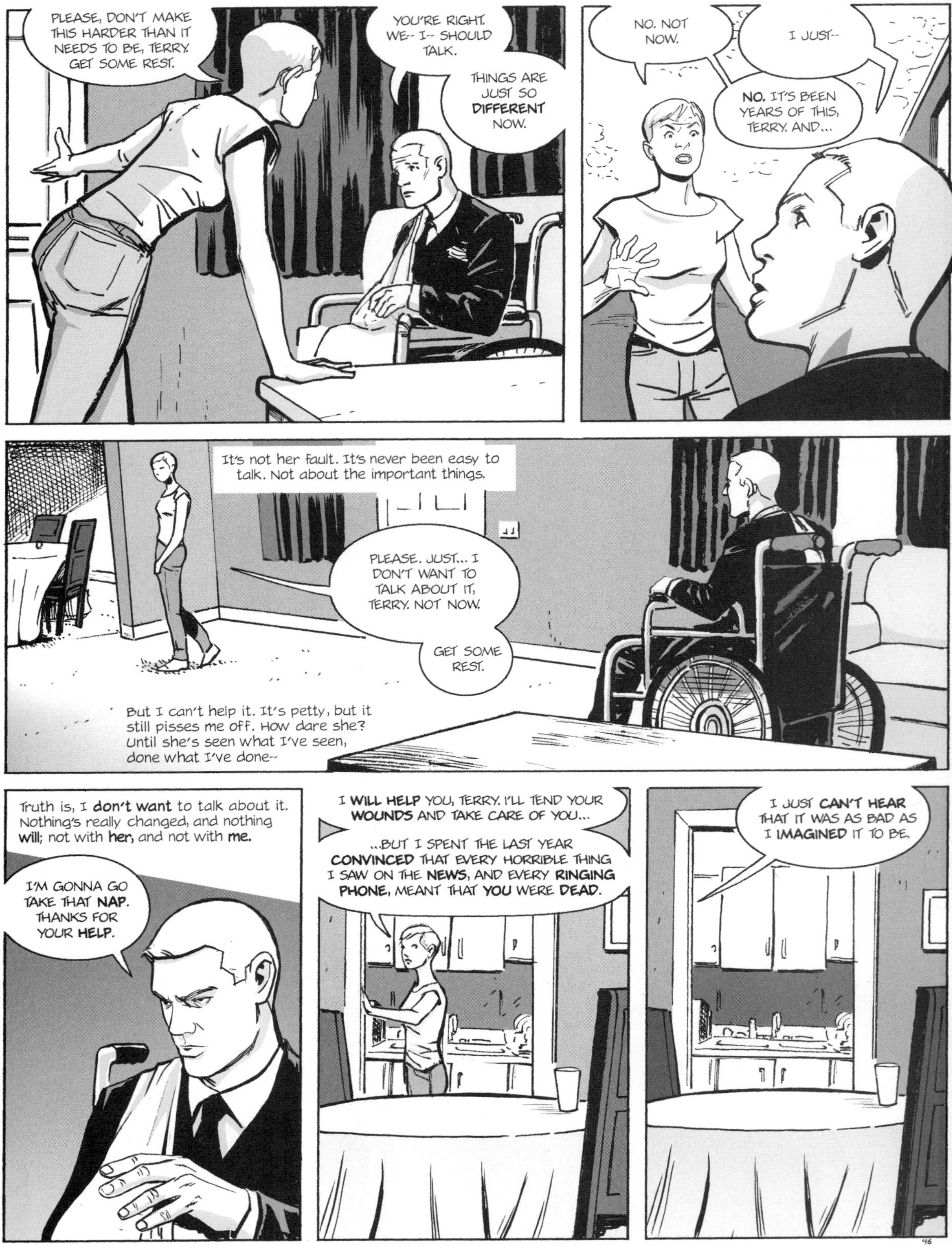

PLEASE, DON'T MAKE THIS HARDER THAN IT NEEDS TO BE, TERRY. GET SOME REST.
YOU'RE RIGHT. WE-- I-- SHOULD TALK.
THINGS ARE JUST SO **DIFFERENT** NOW.
NO. NOT NOW.
I JUST--
NO. IT'S BEEN YEARS OF THIS, TERRY. AND...
It's not her fault. It's never been easy to talk. Not about the important things.
PLEASE. JUST... I DON'T WANT TO TALK ABOUT IT, TERRY. NOT NOW.
GET SOME REST.
But I can't help it. It's petty, but it still pisses me off. How dare she? Until she's seen what I've seen, done what I've done--
Truth is, I **don't want** to talk about it. Nothing's really changed, and nothing **will**; not with **her**, and not with **me.**
I'M GONNA GO TAKE THAT **NAP**. THANKS FOR YOUR **HELP**.
I **WILL HELP** YOU, TERRY. I'LL TEND YOUR **WOUNDS** AND TAKE CARE OF YOU...
...BUT I SPENT THE LAST YEAR **CONVINCED** THAT EVERY HORRIBLE THING I SAW ON THE **NEWS**, AND EVERY **RINGING PHONE**, MEANT THAT **YOU** WERE **DEAD**.
I JUST **CAN'T HEAR** THAT IT WAS AS BAD AS I **IMAGINED** IT TO BE.

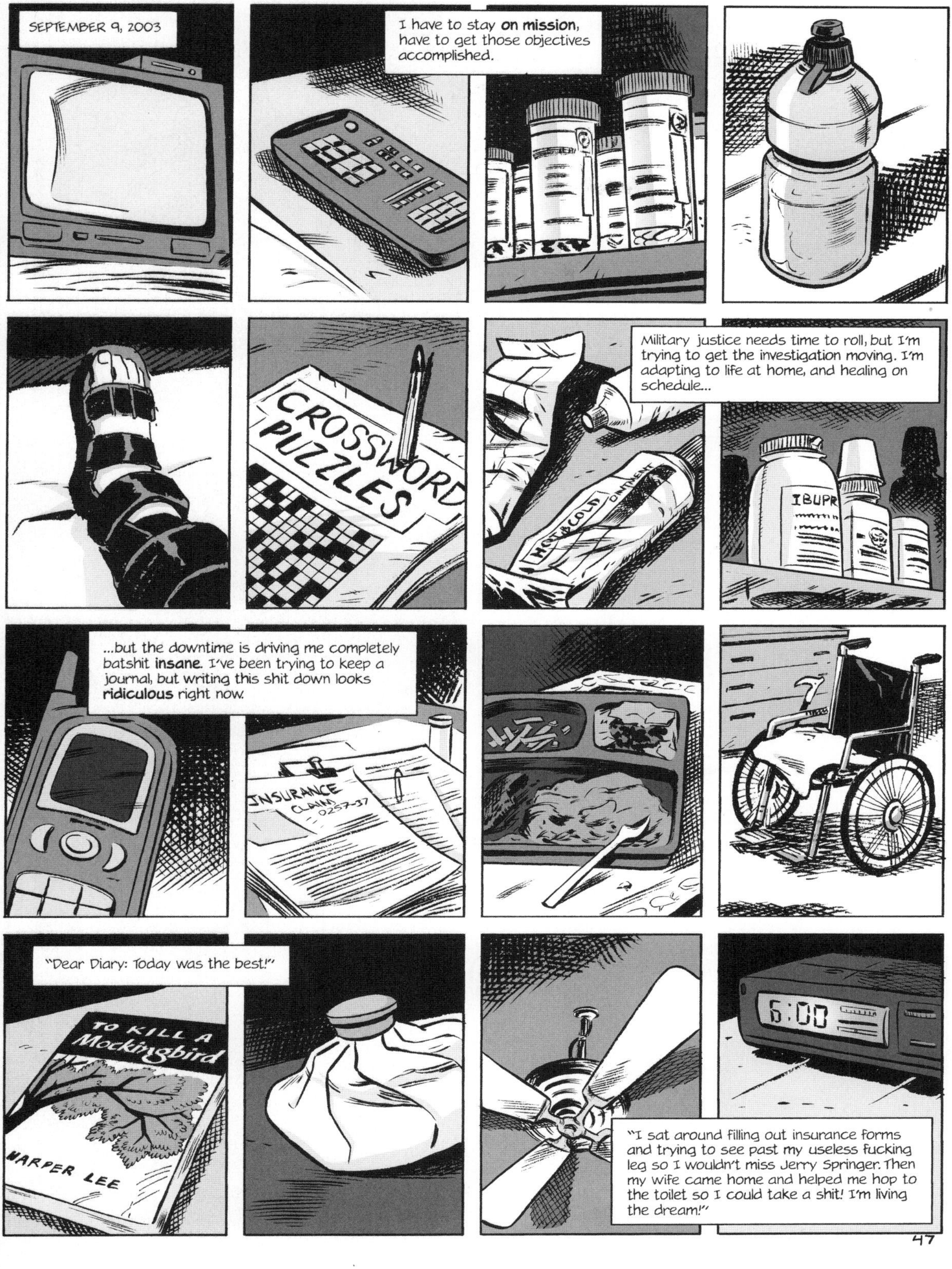
SEPTEMBER 9, 2003
I have to stay **on mission**, have to get those objectives accomplished.
CROSSWORD PUZZLES
Military justice needs time to roll, but I'm trying to get the investigation moving. I'm adapting to life at home, and healing on schedule...
HOT & COLD OINTMENT
IBUPR
...but the downtime is driving me completely batshit **insane**. I've been trying to keep a journal, but writing this shit down looks **ridiculous** right now.
INSURANCE CLAIM 0257-37
"Dear Diary: Today was the best!"
TO KILL A Mockingbird
HARPER LEE
6:00
"I sat around filling out insurance forms and trying to see past my useless fucking leg so I wouldn't miss Jerry Springer. Then my wife came home and helped me hop to the toilet so I could take a shit! I'm living the dream!"

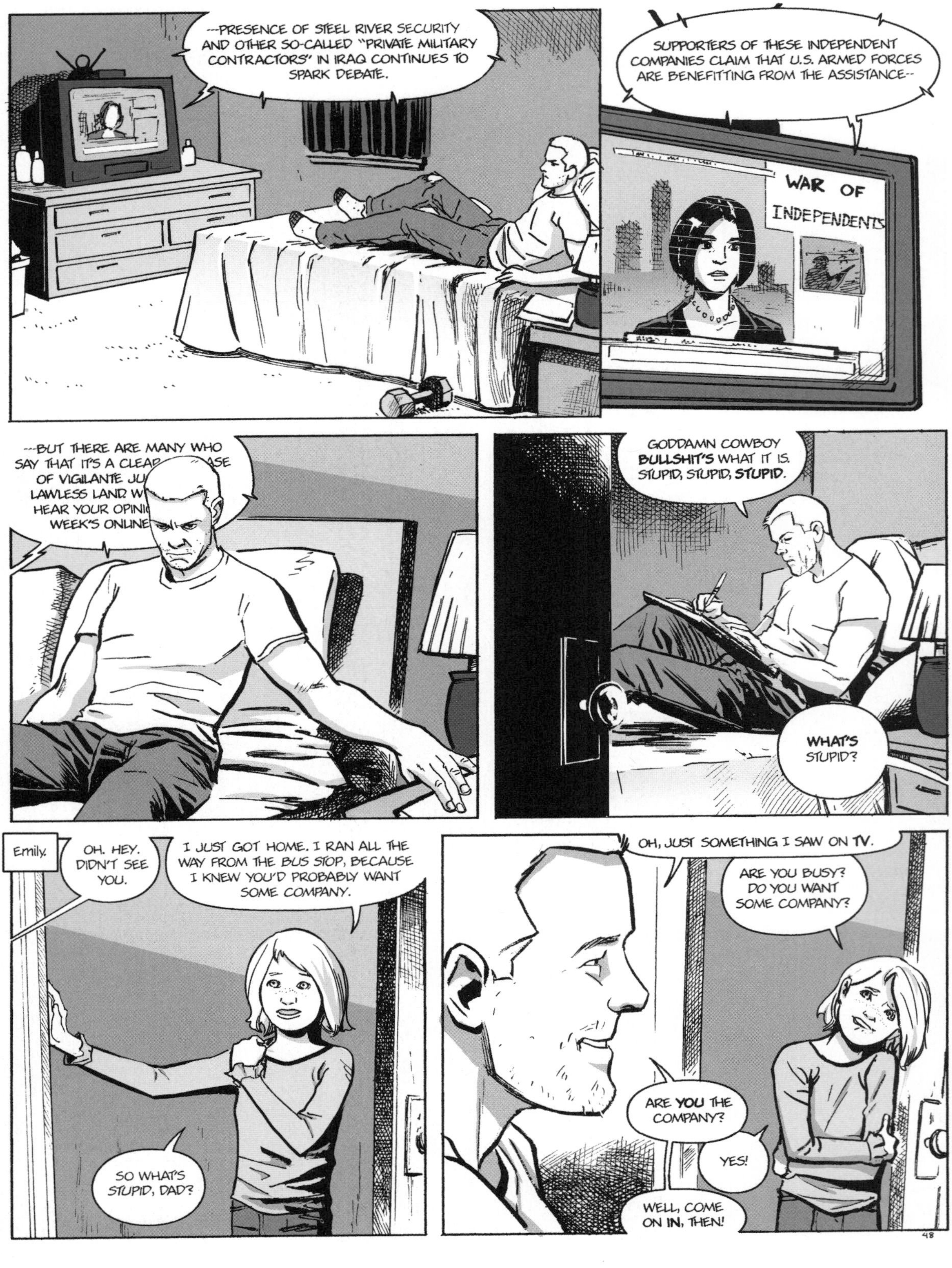

--PRESENCE OF STEEL RIVER SECURITY AND OTHER SO-CALLED "PRIVATE MILITARY CONTRACTORS" IN IRAQ CONTINUES TO SPARK DEBATE.
SUPPORTERS OF THESE INDEPENDENT COMPANIES CLAIM THAT U.S. ARMED FORCES ARE BENEFITTING FROM THE ASSISTANCE--
WAR OF INDEPENDENTS
--BUT THERE ARE MANY WHO SAY THAT IT'S A CLEAR CASE OF VIGILANTE JU LAWLESS LAND. W HEAR YOUR OPINI WEEK'S ONLINE
GODDAMN COWBOY BULLSHIT'S WHAT IT IS. STUPID, STUPID, STUPID.
WHAT'S STUPID?
Emily.
OH. HEY. DIDN'T SEE YOU.
I JUST GOT HOME. I RAN ALL THE WAY FROM THE BUS STOP, BECAUSE I KNEW YOU'D PROBABLY WANT SOME COMPANY.
SO WHAT'S STUPID, DAD?
OH, JUST SOMETHING I SAW ON TV.
ARE YOU BUSY? DO YOU WANT SOME COMPANY?
ARE YOU THE COMPANY?
YES!
WELL, COME ON IN, THEN!

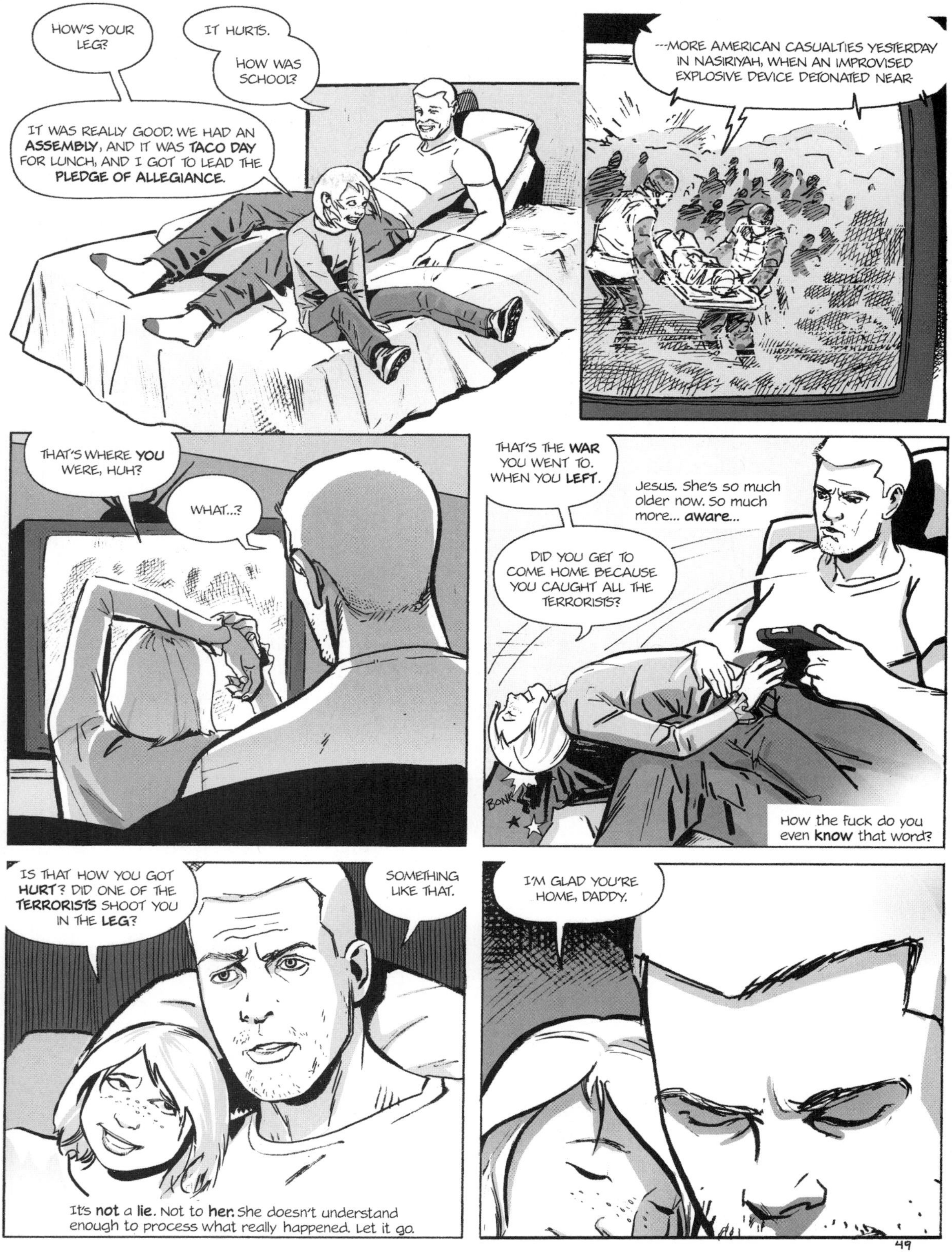
HOW'S YOUR LEG?
IT HURTS.
HOW WAS SCHOOL?
IT WAS REALLY GOOD. WE HAD AN ASSEMBLY, AND IT WAS TACO DAY FOR LUNCH, AND I GOT TO LEAD THE PLEDGE OF ALLEGIANCE.
--MORE AMERICAN CASUALTIES YESTERDAY IN NASIRIYAH, WHEN AN IMPROVISED EXPLOSIVE DEVICE DETONATED NEAR-
THAT'S WHERE YOU WERE, HUH?
WHAT...?
THAT'S THE WAR YOU WENT TO. WHEN YOU LEFT.
Jesus. She's so much older now. So much more... aware...
DID YOU GET TO COME HOME BECAUSE YOU CAUGHT ALL THE TERRORISTS?
BONK
How the fuck do you even know that word?
IS THAT HOW YOU GOT HURT? DID ONE OF THE TERRORISTS SHOOT YOU IN THE LEG?
SOMETHING LIKE THAT.
It's not a lie. Not to her. She doesn't understand enough to process what really happened. Let it go.
I'M GLAD YOU'RE HOME, DADDY.

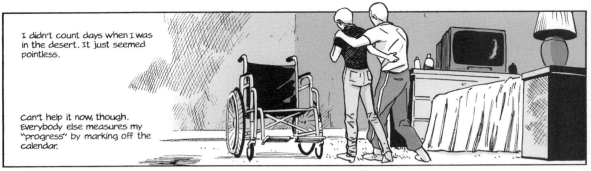

I didn't count days when I was in the desert. It just seemed pointless.

Can't help it now, though. Everybody else measures my "progress" by marking off the calendar.

I guess I don't look at the actual dates. I don't really have to; my life has such a routine lately that I can figure out what day it is just by looking around me.

Monday, Wednesday, Friday: Back on base, teaching Terry Glass' patented "How Not To Die 101" class.

If I'm being helped out of a handicapped van, it must be around eighteen-thirty. If I'm being helped in, it's oh-seven-hundred.

Tuesday and Thursday: Physical therapy.

Weekends: Back at the house, being a goddamn liability. It's been two months since I got back to the real world, and I still can't even get myself to the shower.

I'm tired of being needy. I bet Patty and Emily are pretty well tired of it, too.

They all say, "Don't push it, Terry." They say it'll happen when it's supposed to happen.

I'm already "pushing it," though. I'm pushing my luck with these people around me, pushing my problems on everybody else.

I can't stand up in front of a bunch of hard-ass shooters and pretend that I have anything to teach them. Not when I'm fucking weak, anyway.

I'm supposed to be an example. I have to show them all what it's like to get knocked down and then get back up like it ain't no thing.

When your body's broken, people get used to seeing you that way; they underestimate you until you start looking normal. So I have to fix my body, have to look normal again.

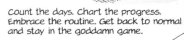

Count the days. Chart the progress. Embrace the routine. Get back to normal and stay in the goddamn game.

And whatever you do...

...Don't ever let them find out you're full of shit.

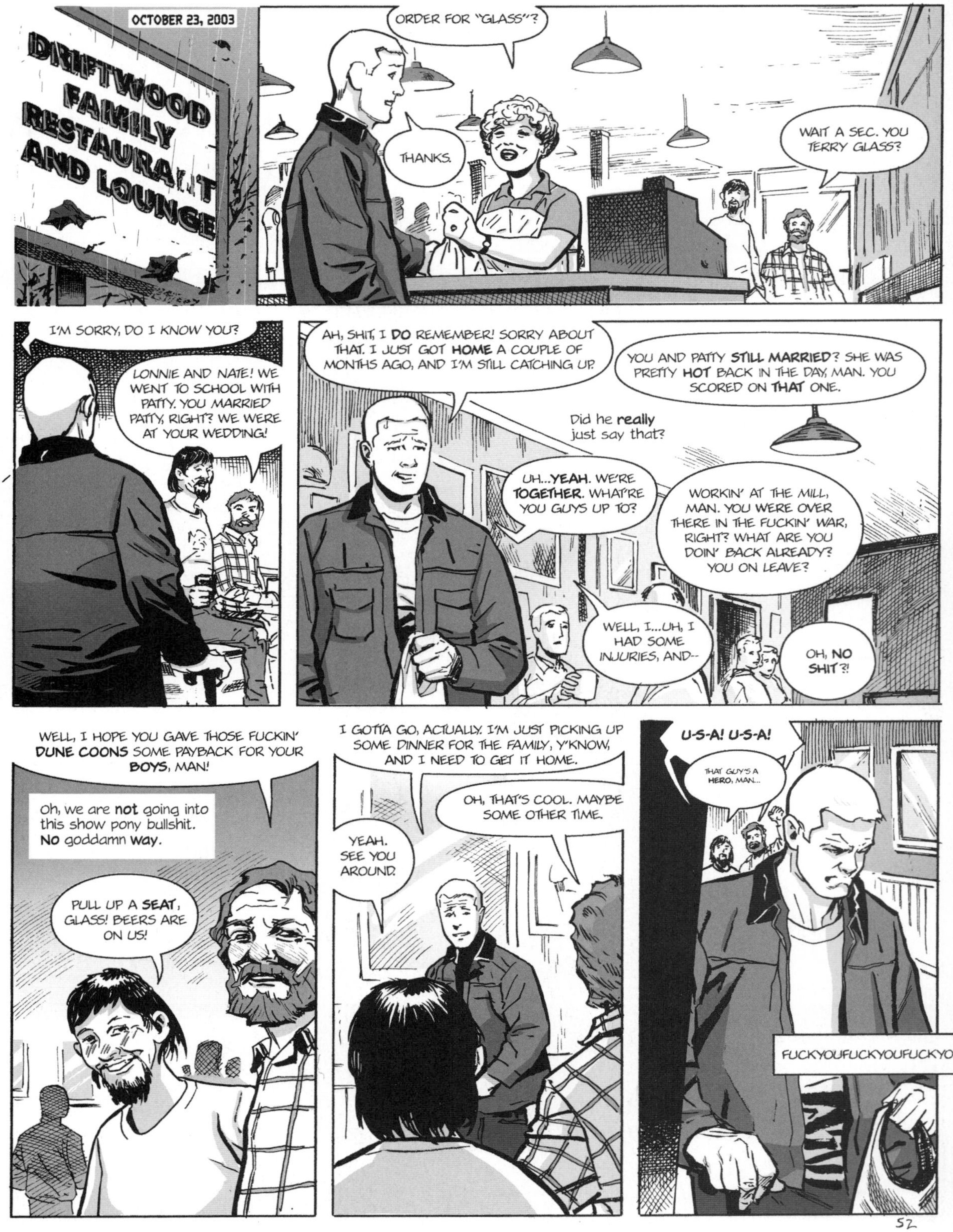
OCTOBER 23, 2003
DRIFTWOOD FAMILY RESTAURANT AND LOUNGE
ORDER FOR "GLASS"?
THANKS.
WAIT A SEC. YOU TERRY GLASS?
I'M SORRY, DO I KNOW YOU?
LONNIE AND NATE! WE WENT TO SCHOOL WITH PATTY. YOU MARRIED PATTY, RIGHT? WE WERE AT YOUR WEDDING!
AH, SHIT, I DO REMEMBER! SORRY ABOUT THAT. I JUST GOT HOME A COUPLE OF MONTHS AGO, AND I'M STILL CATCHING UP.
YOU AND PATTY STILL MARRIED? SHE WAS PRETTY HOT BACK IN THE DAY, MAN. YOU SCORED ON THAT ONE.
Did he really just say that?
UH...YEAH. WE'RE TOGETHER. WHAT'RE YOU GUYS UP TO?
WORKIN' AT THE MILL, MAN. YOU WERE OVER THERE IN THE FUCKIN' WAR, RIGHT? WHAT ARE YOU DOIN' BACK ALREADY? YOU ON LEAVE?
WELL, I...UH, I HAD SOME INJURIES, AND--
OH, NO SHIT?!
WELL, I HOPE YOU GAVE THOSE FUCKIN' DUNE COONS SOME PAYBACK FOR YOUR BOYS, MAN!
Oh, we are not going into this show pony bullshit. NO goddamn way.
PULL UP A SEAT, GLASS! BEERS ARE ON US!
I GOTTA GO, ACTUALLY. I'M JUST PICKING UP SOME DINNER FOR THE FAMILY, Y'KNOW, AND I NEED TO GET IT HOME.
OH, THAT'S COOL. MAYBE SOME OTHER TIME.
YEAH. SEE YOU AROUND.
U-S-A! U-S-A!
THAT GUY'S A HERO, MAN...
FUCKYOUFUCKYOUFUCKYOU

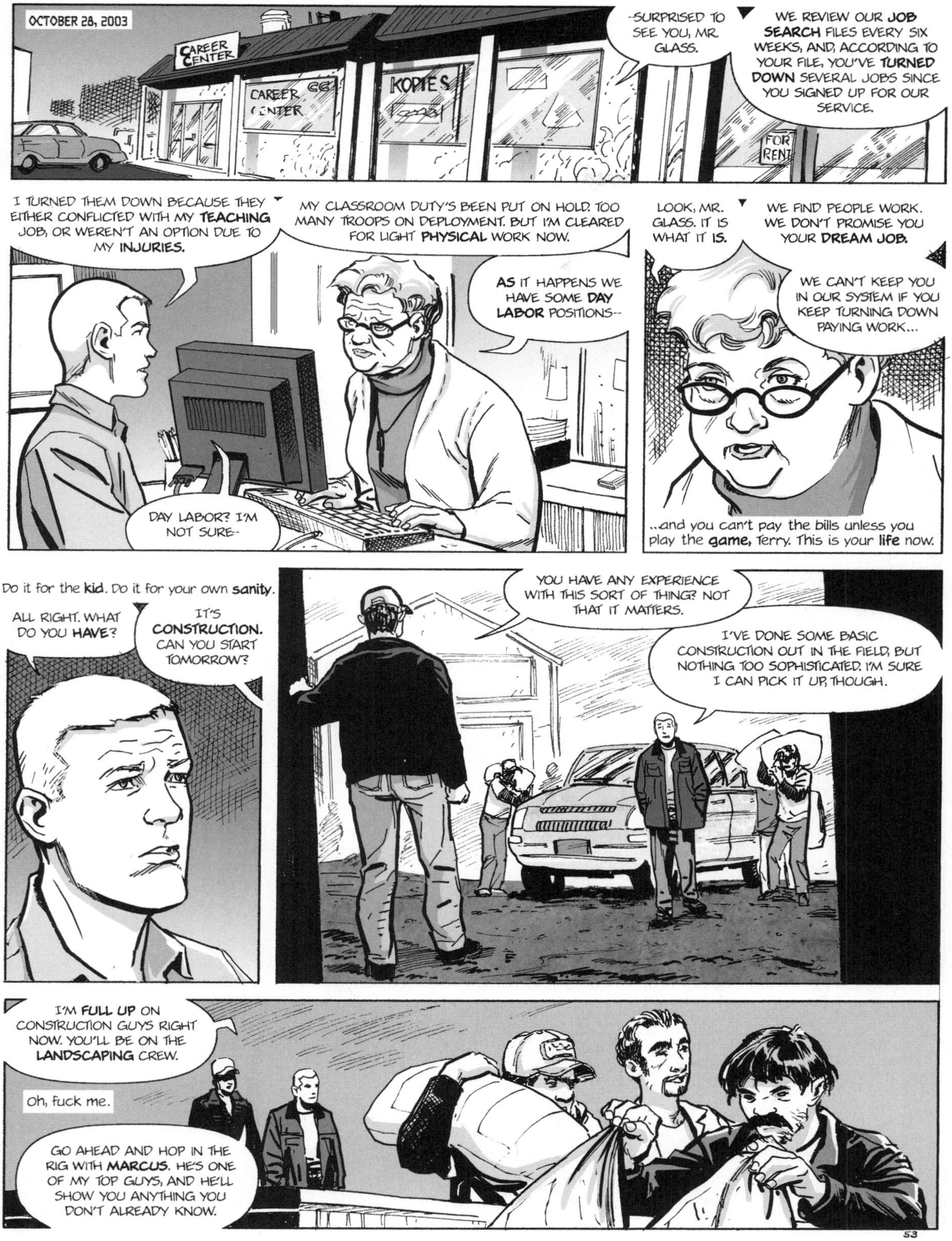

OCTOBER 28, 2003
CAREER CENTER
CAREER CENTER
KOPIES
FOR RENT
-SURPRISED TO SEE YOU, MR. GLASS.
WE REVIEW OUR JOB SEARCH FILES EVERY SIX WEEKS, AND, ACCORDING TO YOUR FILE, YOU'VE TURNED DOWN SEVERAL JOBS SINCE YOU SIGNED UP FOR OUR SERVICE.
I TURNED THEM DOWN BECAUSE THEY EITHER CONFLICTED WITH MY TEACHING JOB, OR WEREN'T AN OPTION DUE TO MY INJURIES.
MY CLASSROOM DUTY'S BEEN PUT ON HOLD. TOO MANY TROOPS ON DEPLOYMENT. BUT I'M CLEARED FOR LIGHT PHYSICAL WORK NOW.
AS IT HAPPENS WE HAVE SOME DAY LABOR POSITIONS--
DAY LABOR? I'M NOT SURE-
LOOK, MR. GLASS. IT IS WHAT IT IS.
WE FIND PEOPLE WORK. WE DON'T PROMISE YOU YOUR DREAM JOB.
WE CAN'T KEEP YOU IN OUR SYSTEM IF YOU KEEP TURNING DOWN PAYING WORK...
..and you can't pay the bills unless you play the game, Terry. This is your life now.
Do it for the kid. Do it for your own sanity.
ALL RIGHT. WHAT DO YOU HAVE?
IT'S CONSTRUCTION. CAN YOU START TOMORROW?
YOU HAVE ANY EXPERIENCE WITH THIS SORT OF THING? NOT THAT IT MATTERS.
I'VE DONE SOME BASIC CONSTRUCTION OUT IN THE FIELD, BUT NOTHING TOO SOPHISTICATED. I'M SURE I CAN PICK IT UP, THOUGH.
I'M FULL UP ON CONSTRUCTION GUYS RIGHT NOW. YOU'LL BE ON THE LANDSCAPING CREW.
Oh, fuck me.
GO AHEAD AND HOP IN THE RIG WITH MARCUS. HE'S ONE OF MY TOP GUYS, AND HE'LL SHOW YOU ANYTHING YOU DON'T ALREADY KNOW.

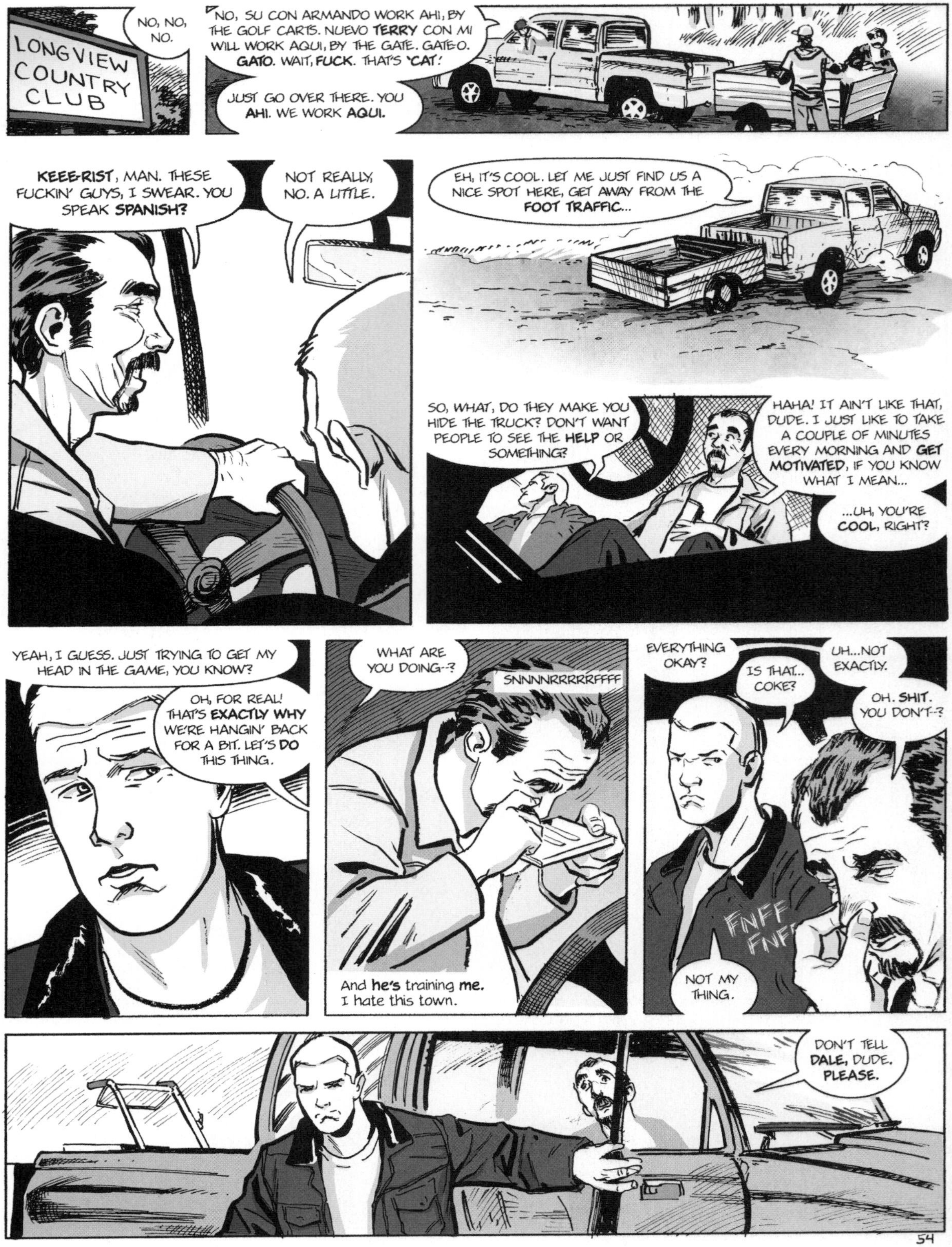
LONGVIEW COUNTRY CLUB
NO, NO, NO.
NO, SU CON ARMANDO WORK AHI, BY THE GOLF CARTS. NUEVO TERRY CON MI WILL WORK AQUI, BY THE GATE. GATE-O. GATO. WAIT, FUCK. THAT'S 'CAT.'
JUST GO OVER THERE. YOU AHI. WE WORK AQUI.
KEEE-RIST, MAN. THESE FUCKIN' GUYS, I SWEAR. YOU SPEAK SPANISH?
NOT REALLY, NO. A LITTLE.
EH, IT'S COOL. LET ME JUST FIND US A NICE SPOT HERE, GET AWAY FROM THE FOOT TRAFFIC...
SO, WHAT, DO THEY MAKE YOU HIDE THE TRUCK? DON'T WANT PEOPLE TO SEE THE HELP OR SOMETHING?
HAHA! IT AIN'T LIKE THAT, DUDE. I JUST LIKE TO TAKE A COUPLE OF MINUTES EVERY MORNING AND GET MOTIVATED, IF YOU KNOW WHAT I MEAN...
...UH, YOU'RE COOL, RIGHT?
YEAH, I GUESS. JUST TRYING TO GET MY HEAD IN THE GAME, YOU KNOW?
OH, FOR REAL! THAT'S EXACTLY WHY WE'RE HANGIN' BACK FOR A BIT. LET'S DO THIS THING.
WHAT ARE YOU DOING--?
SNNNNRRRRRFFFF
And he's training me. I hate this town.
EVERYTHING OKAY?
UH...NOT EXACTLY.
IS THAT... COKE?
OH. SHIT. YOU DON'T--?
FNFF FNFF
NOT MY THING.
DON'T TELL DALE, DUDE. PLEASE.

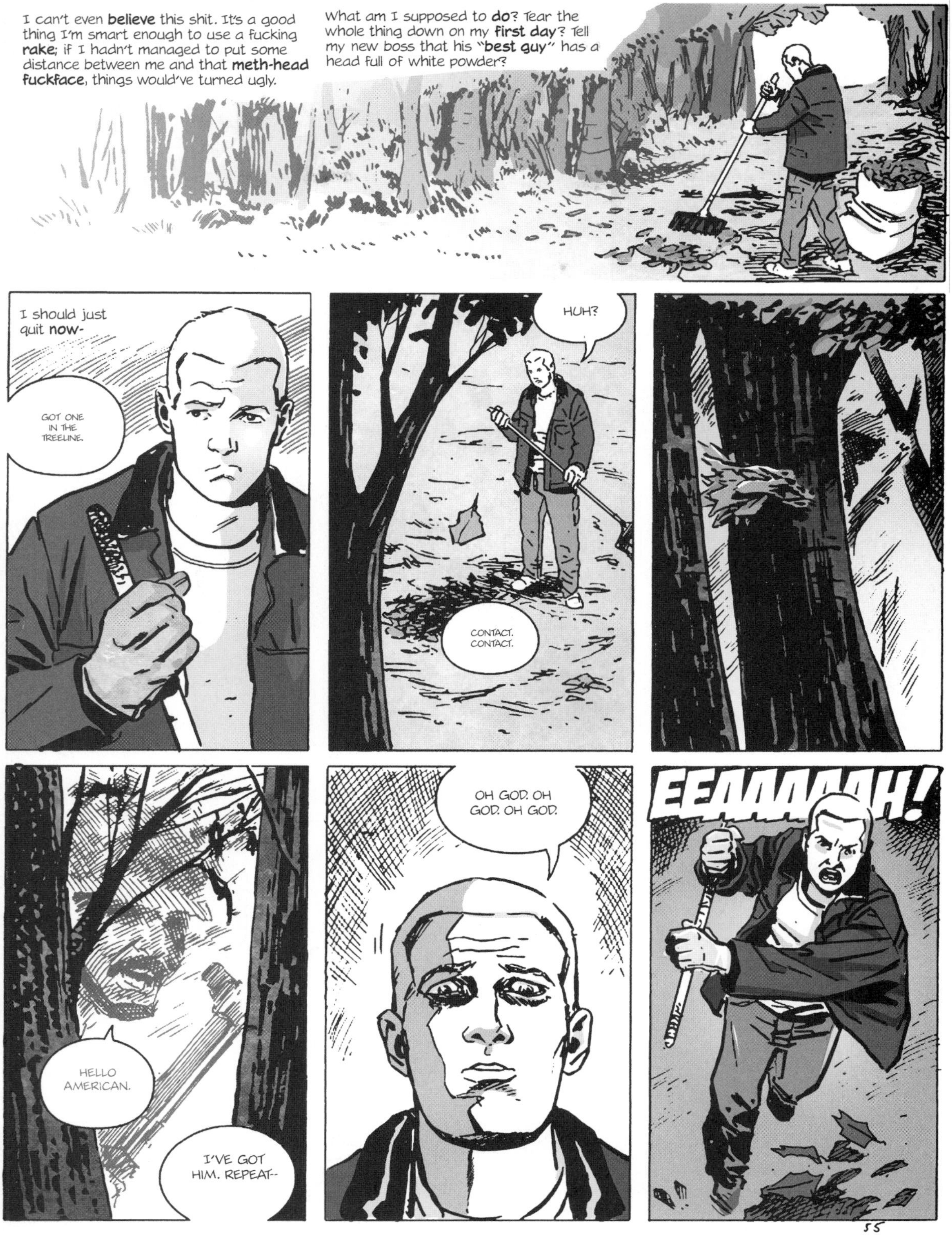

I can't even **believe** this shit. It's a good thing I'm smart enough to use a fucking **rake**; if I hadn't managed to put some distance between me and that **meth-head fuckface**, things would've turned ugly.
What am I supposed to **do**? Tear the whole thing down on my **first day**? Tell my new boss that his **"best guy"** has a head full of white powder?
I should just quit **now**-
GOT ONE IN THE TREELINE.
HUH?
CONTACT. CONTACT.
HELLO AMERICAN.
I'VE GOT HIM. REPEAT--
OH GOD. OH GOD. OH GOD.
EEAAAAAH!

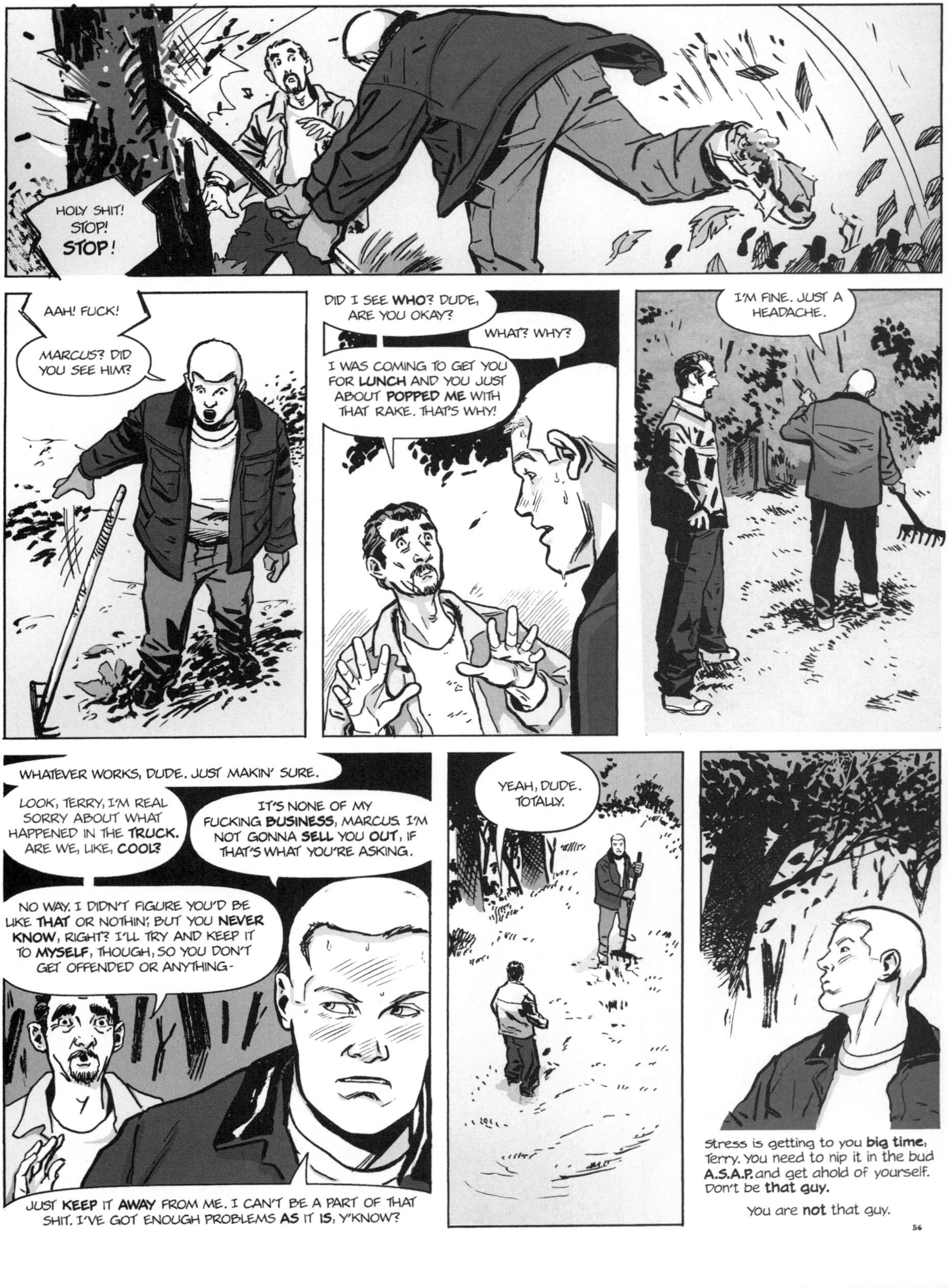

HOLY SHIT! STOP! STOP!
AAH! FUCK!
MARCUS? DID YOU SEE HIM?
DID I SEE WHO? DUDE, ARE YOU OKAY?
WHAT? WHY?
I WAS COMING TO GET YOU FOR LUNCH AND YOU JUST ABOUT POPPED ME WITH THAT RAKE. THAT'S WHY!
I'M FINE. JUST A HEADACHE.
WHATEVER WORKS, DUDE. JUST MAKIN' SURE.
LOOK, TERRY, I'M REAL SORRY ABOUT WHAT HAPPENED IN THE TRUCK. ARE WE, LIKE, COOL?
IT'S NONE OF MY FUCKING BUSINESS, MARCUS. I'M NOT GONNA SELL YOU OUT, IF THAT'S WHAT YOU'RE ASKING.
NO WAY. I DIDN'T FIGURE YOU'D BE LIKE THAT OR NOTHIN; BUT YOU NEVER KNOW, RIGHT? I'LL TRY AND KEEP IT TO MYSELF, THOUGH, SO YOU DON'T GET OFFENDED OR ANYTHING-
JUST KEEP IT AWAY FROM ME. I CAN'T BE A PART OF THAT SHIT. I'VE GOT ENOUGH PROBLEMS AS IT IS, Y'KNOW?
YEAH, DUDE. TOTALLY.
Stress is getting to you big time, Terry. You need to nip it in the bud A.S.A.P. and get ahold of yourself. Don't be that guy.
You are not that guy.

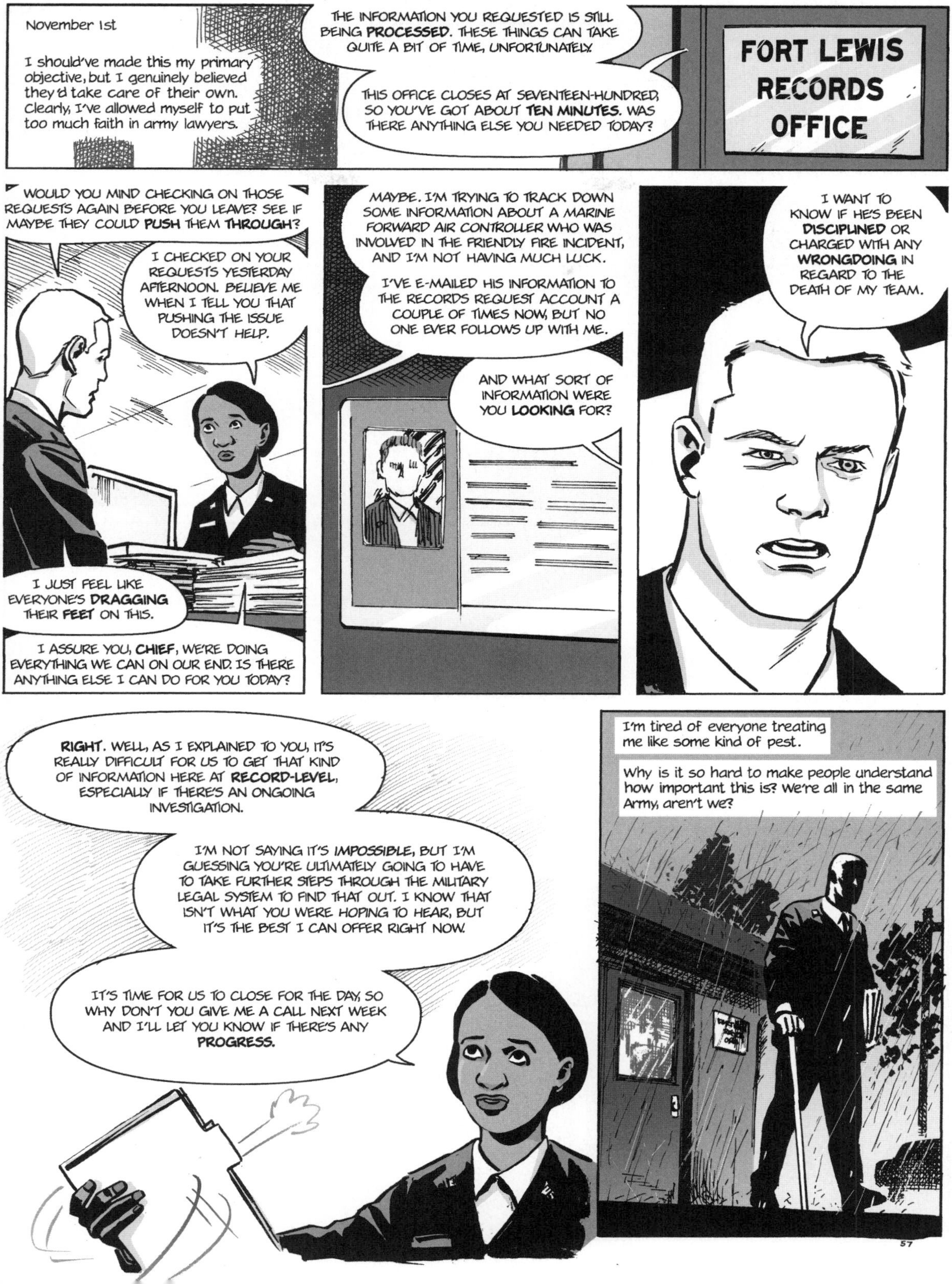
November 1st
I should've made this my primary objective, but I genuinely believed they'd take care of their own. Clearly, I've allowed myself to put too much faith in army lawyers.
THE INFORMATION YOU REQUESTED IS STILL BEING PROCESSED. THESE THINGS CAN TAKE QUITE A BIT OF TIME, UNFORTUNATELY.
THIS OFFICE CLOSES AT SEVENTEEN-HUNDRED, SO YOU'VE GOT ABOUT TEN MINUTES. WAS THERE ANYTHING ELSE YOU NEEDED TODAY?
FORT LEWIS RECORDS OFFICE
WOULD YOU MIND CHECKING ON THOSE REQUESTS AGAIN BEFORE YOU LEAVE? SEE IF MAYBE THEY COULD PUSH THEM THROUGH?
I CHECKED ON YOUR REQUESTS YESTERDAY AFTERNOON. BELIEVE ME WHEN I TELL YOU THAT PUSHING THE ISSUE DOESN'T HELP.
I JUST FEEL LIKE EVERYONE'S DRAGGING THEIR FEET ON THIS.
I ASSURE YOU, CHIEF, WE'RE DOING EVERYTHING WE CAN ON OUR END. IS THERE ANYTHING ELSE I CAN DO FOR YOU TODAY?
MAYBE. I'M TRYING TO TRACK DOWN SOME INFORMATION ABOUT A MARINE FORWARD AIR CONTROLLER WHO WAS INVOLVED IN THE FRIENDLY FIRE INCIDENT, AND I'M NOT HAVING MUCH LUCK.
I'VE E-MAILED HIS INFORMATION TO THE RECORDS REQUEST ACCOUNT A COUPLE OF TIMES NOW, BUT NO ONE EVER FOLLOWS UP WITH ME.
AND WHAT SORT OF INFORMATION WERE YOU LOOKING FOR?
I WANT TO KNOW IF HE'S BEEN DISCIPLINED OR CHARGED WITH ANY WRONGDOING IN REGARD TO THE DEATH OF MY TEAM.
RIGHT. WELL, AS I EXPLAINED TO YOU, IT'S REALLY DIFFICULT FOR US TO GET THAT KIND OF INFORMATION HERE AT RECORD-LEVEL, ESPECIALLY IF THERE'S AN ONGOING INVESTIGATION.
I'M NOT SAYING IT'S IMPOSSIBLE, BUT I'M GUESSING YOU'RE ULTIMATELY GOING TO HAVE TO TAKE FURTHER STEPS THROUGH THE MILITARY LEGAL SYSTEM TO FIND THAT OUT. I KNOW THAT ISN'T WHAT YOU WERE HOPING TO HEAR, BUT IT'S THE BEST I CAN OFFER RIGHT NOW.
IT'S TIME FOR US TO CLOSE FOR THE DAY, SO WHY DON'T YOU GIVE ME A CALL NEXT WEEK AND I'LL LET YOU KNOW IF THERE'S ANY PROGRESS.
I'm tired of everyone treating me like some kind of pest.
Why is it so hard to make people understand how important this is? We're all in the same Army, aren't we?

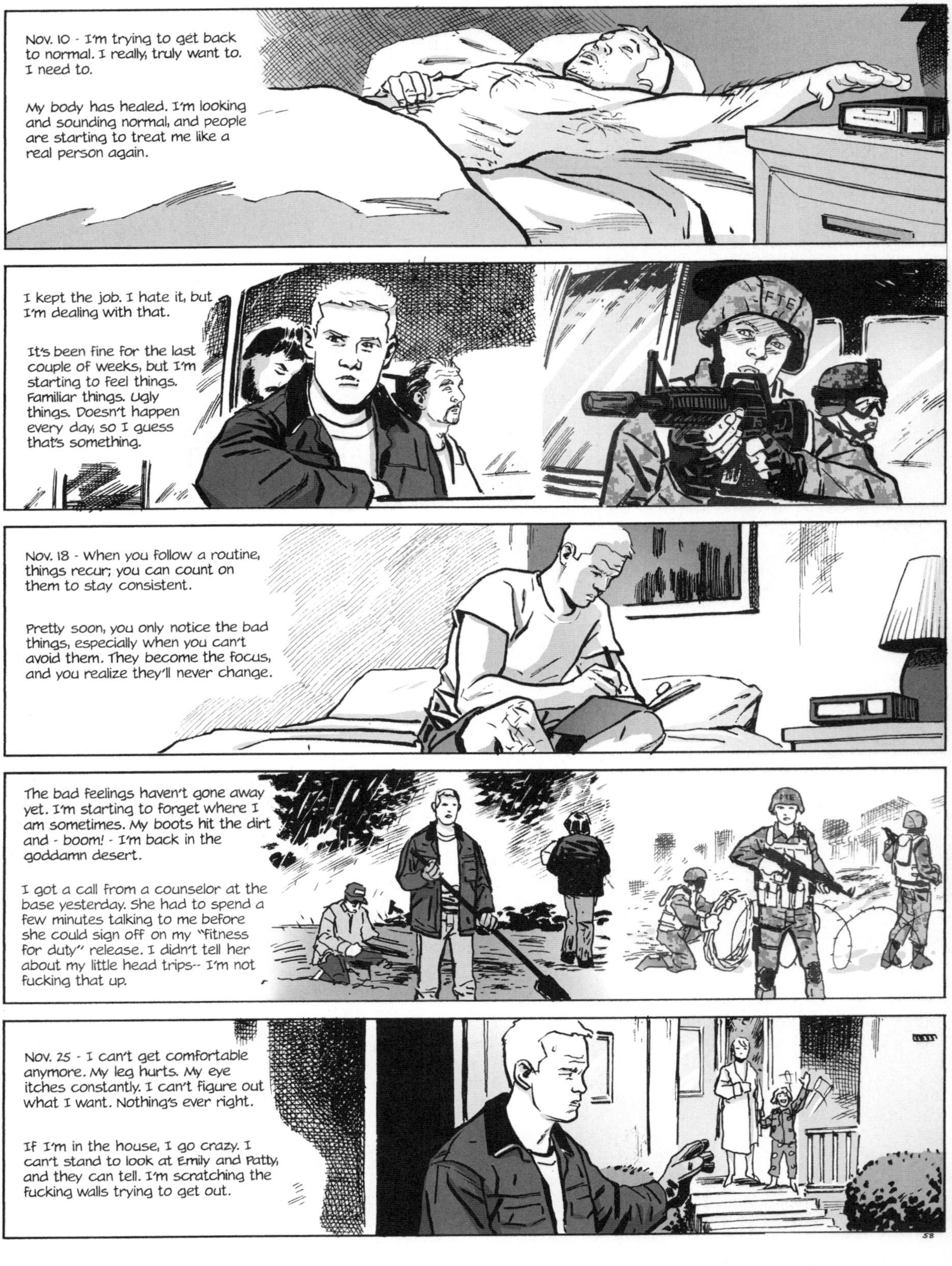
Nov. 10 - I'm trying to get back to normal. I really, truly want to. I need to.
My body has healed. I'm looking and sounding normal, and people are starting to treat me like a real person again.
I kept the job. I hate it, but I'm dealing with that.
It's been fine for the last couple of weeks, but I'm starting to feel things. Familiar things. Ugly things. Doesn't happen every day, so I guess that's something.
FTE
Nov. 18 - When you follow a routine, things recur; you can count on them to stay consistent.
Pretty soon, you only notice the bad things, especially when you can't avoid them. They become the focus, and you realize they'll never change.
The bad feelings haven't gone away yet. I'm starting to forget where I am sometimes. My boots hit the dirt and - boom! - I'm back in the goddamn desert.
I got a call from a counselor at the base yesterday. She had to spend a few minutes talking to me before she could sign off on my "fitness for duty" release. I didn't tell her about my little head trips-- I'm not fucking that up.
FTE
Nov. 25 - I can't get comfortable anymore. My leg hurts. My eye itches constantly. I can't figure out what I want. Nothing's ever right.
If I'm in the house, I go crazy. I can't stand to look at Emily and Patty, and they can tell. I'm scratching the fucking walls trying to get out.

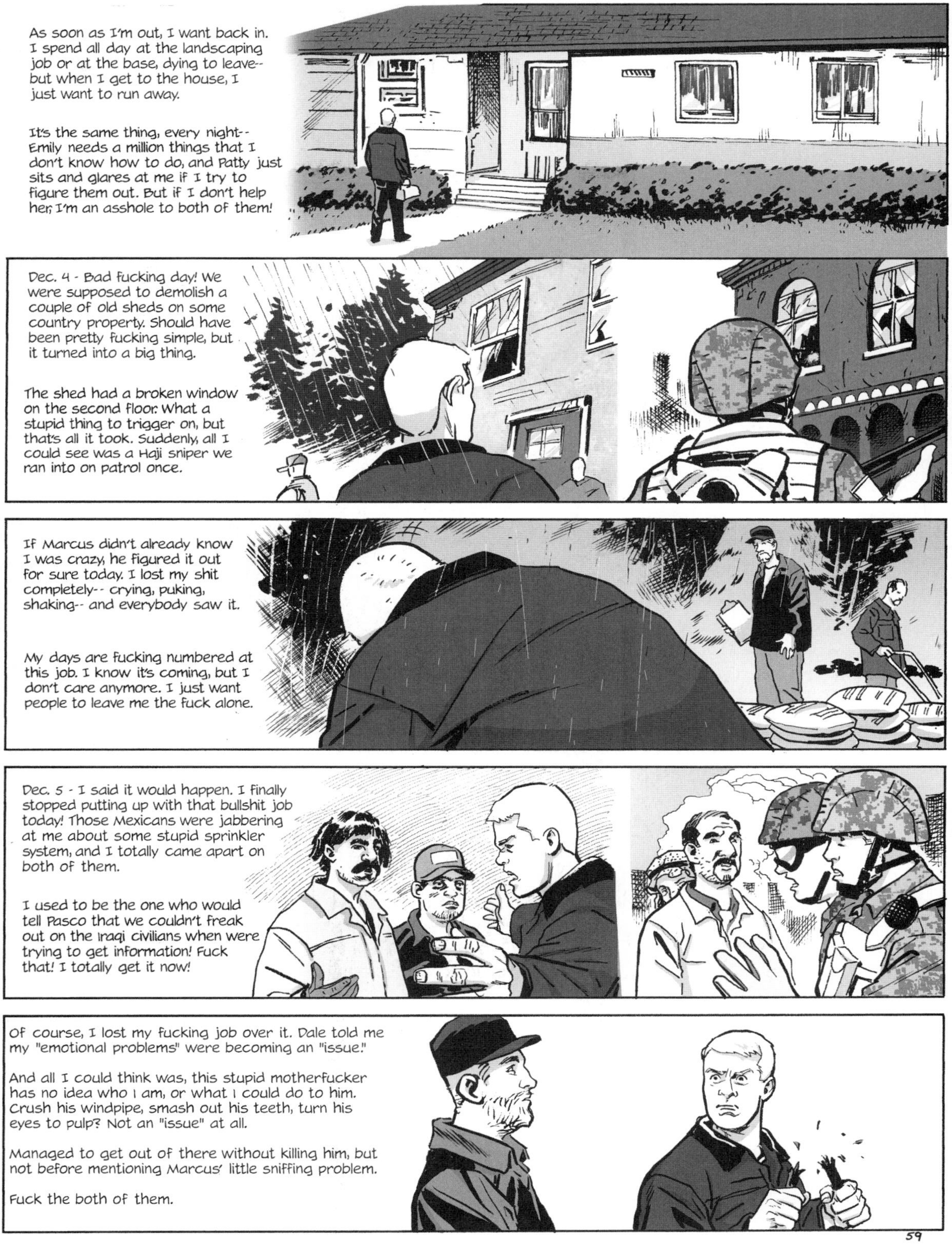

As soon as I'm out, I want back in. I spend all day at the landscaping job or at the base, dying to leave-- but when I get to the house, I just want to run away.
It's the same thing, every night-- Emily needs a million things that I don't know how to do, and Patty just sits and glares at me if I try to figure them out. But if I don't help her, I'm an asshole to both of them!
Dec. 4 - Bad fucking day! We were supposed to demolish a couple of old sheds on some country property. Should have been pretty fucking simple, but it turned into a big thing.
The shed had a broken window on the second floor. What a stupid thing to trigger on, but that's all it took. Suddenly, all I could see was a Haji sniper we ran into on patrol once.
If Marcus didn't already know I was crazy, he figured it out for sure today. I lost my shit completely-- crying, puking, shaking-- and everybody saw it.
My days are fucking numbered at this job. I know it's coming, but I don't care anymore. I just want people to leave me the fuck alone.
Dec. 5 - I said it would happen. I finally stopped putting up with that bullshit job today! Those Mexicans were jabbering at me about some stupid sprinkler system, and I totally came apart on both of them.
I used to be the one who would tell Pasco that we couldn't freak out on the Iraqi civilians when were trying to get information! Fuck that! I totally get it now!
Of course, I lost my fucking job over it. Dale told me my "emotional problems" were becoming an "issue."
And all I could think was, this stupid motherfucker has no idea who I am, or what I could do to him. Crush his windpipe, smash out his teeth, turn his eyes to pulp? Not an "issue" at all.
Managed to get out of there without killing him, but not before mentioning Marcus' little sniffing problem.
Fuck the both of them.

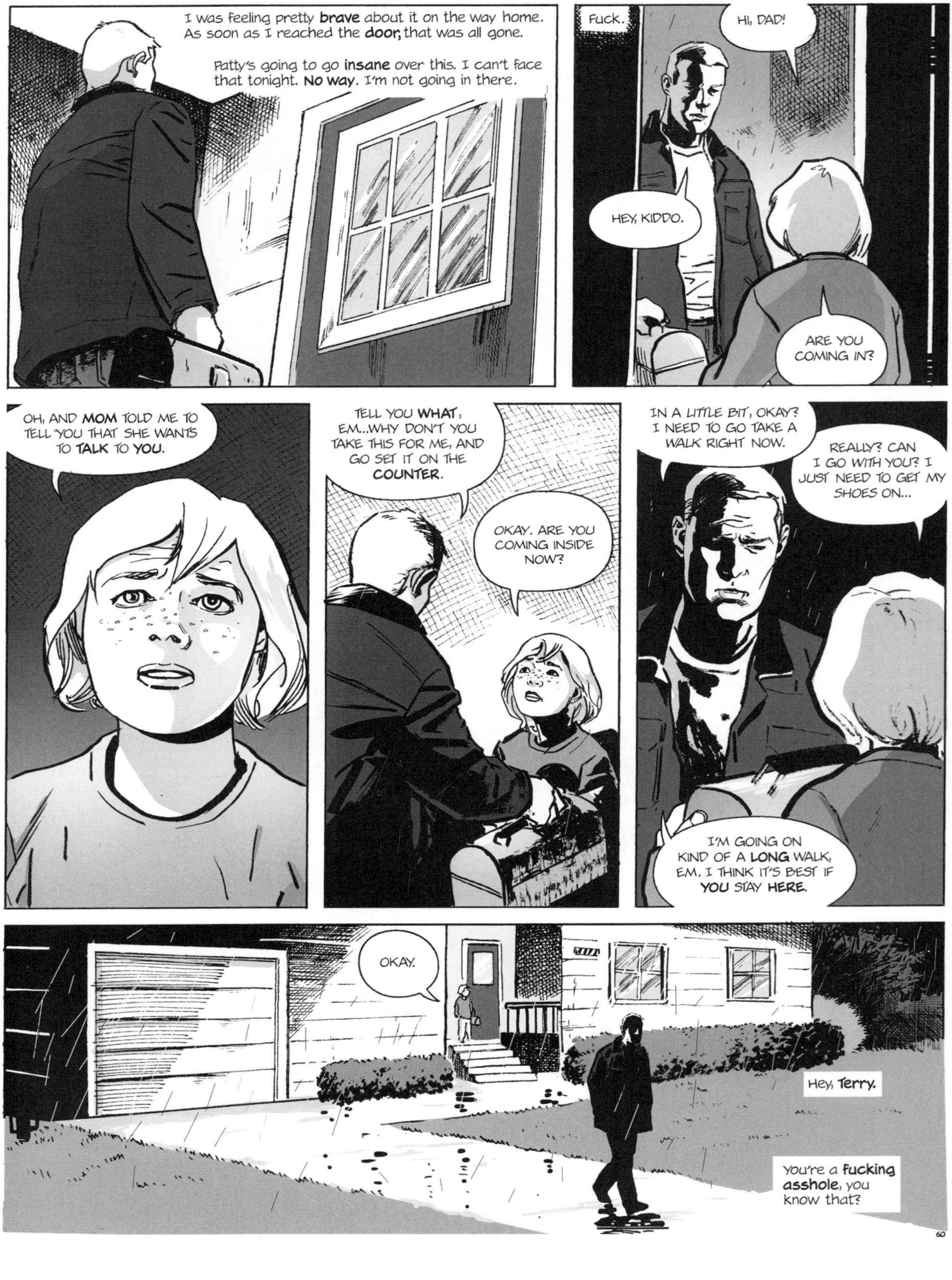
I was feeling pretty brave about it on the way home. As soon as I reached the door, that was all gone.
Patty's going to go insane over this. I can't face that tonight. No way. I'm not going in there.
Fuck.
HI, DAD!
HEY, KIDDO.
ARE YOU COMING IN?
OH, AND MOM TOLD ME TO TELL YOU THAT SHE WANTS TO TALK TO YOU.
TELL YOU WHAT, EM...WHY DON'T YOU TAKE THIS FOR ME, AND GO SET IT ON THE COUNTER.
OKAY. ARE YOU COMING INSIDE NOW?
IN A LITTLE BIT, OKAY? I NEED TO GO TAKE A WALK RIGHT NOW.
REALLY? CAN I GO WITH YOU? I JUST NEED TO GET MY SHOES ON...
I'M GOING ON KIND OF A LONG WALK, EM. I THINK IT'S BEST IF YOU STAY HERE.
OKAY.
Hey, Terry.
You're a fucking asshole, you know that?

YOU READY FOR ANOTHER ONE?

BZZZ BZZZ

YEAH. THANKS.

GREAT.

PATTY HOME

BZZZ BZZZ

WHAT?

GEE, I DON'T KNOW, MAYBE I DIDN'T ANSWER BECAUSE I DON'T **FEEL** LIKE **TALKING**. BUT HEY, YOU'VE CALLED **SEVENTEEN TIMES** NOW AND I FINALLY PICKED UP, SO I GUESS **YOU WIN!**

I DON'T HAVE TO **TELL** YOU WHERE I AM. AND WHY DO YOU **GIVE A SHIT**, ANYWAY?

LOOK, I'LL BE HOME IN A **LITTLE BIT.** YOU CAN YELL AT ME **THEN.**

WHAT? WHAT'S SO HARD TO UNDERSTAND? **HERE,** SEE IF YOU CAN UNDERSTAND **THIS:**

LEAVE. ME. THE. FUCK. ALONE! IT'S WHAT YOU'RE **GOOD** AT, ISN'T IT?!

JESUS FUCKING CHRIST!

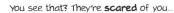

You see that? They're **scared** of you...

...because they all **know** you're fucking **crazy.**

You need to go home and **clean up** your **mess,** boy. You fucked up for **real** this time, and everybody **knows** it.

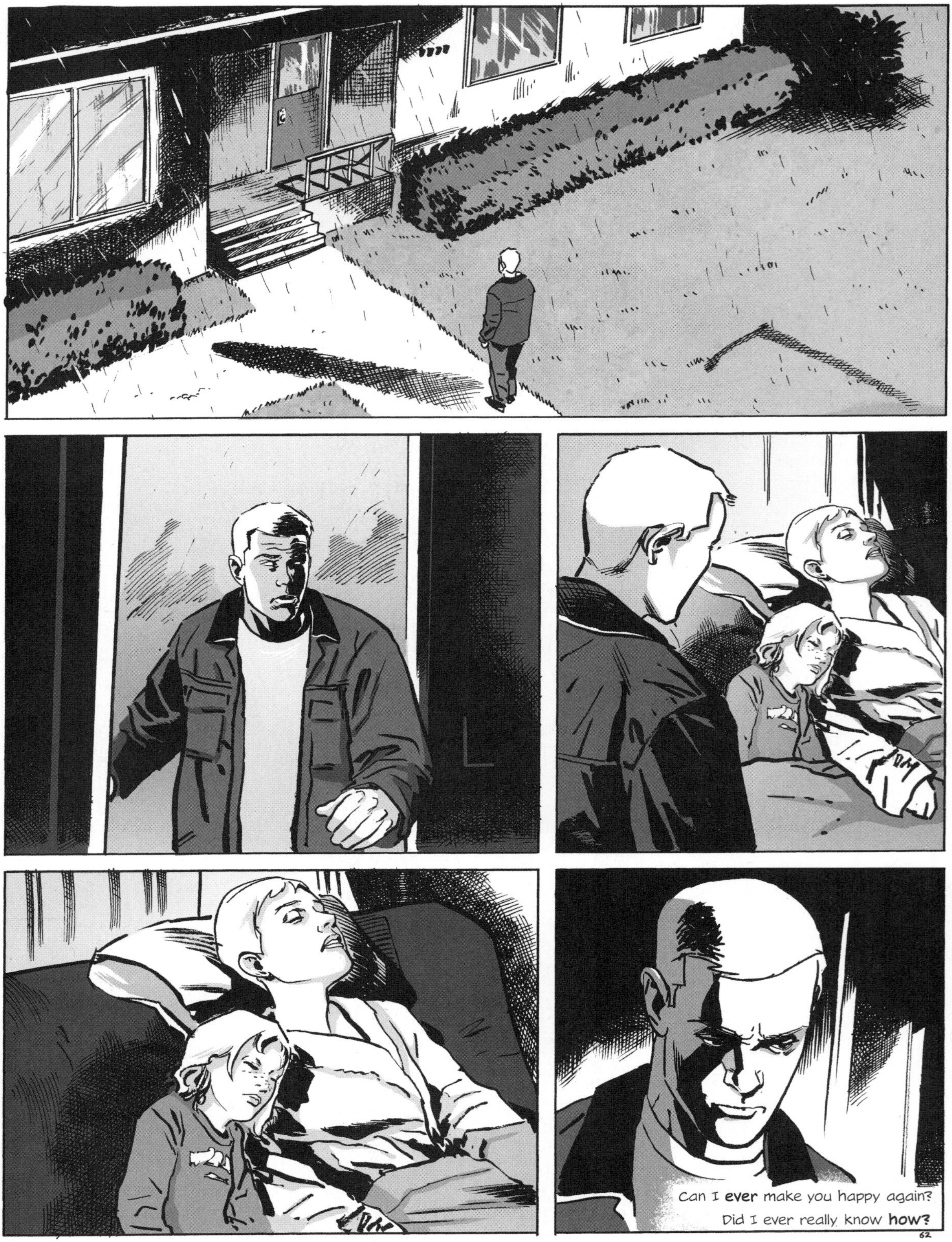
Can I **ever** make you happy again?
Did I ever really know **how?**

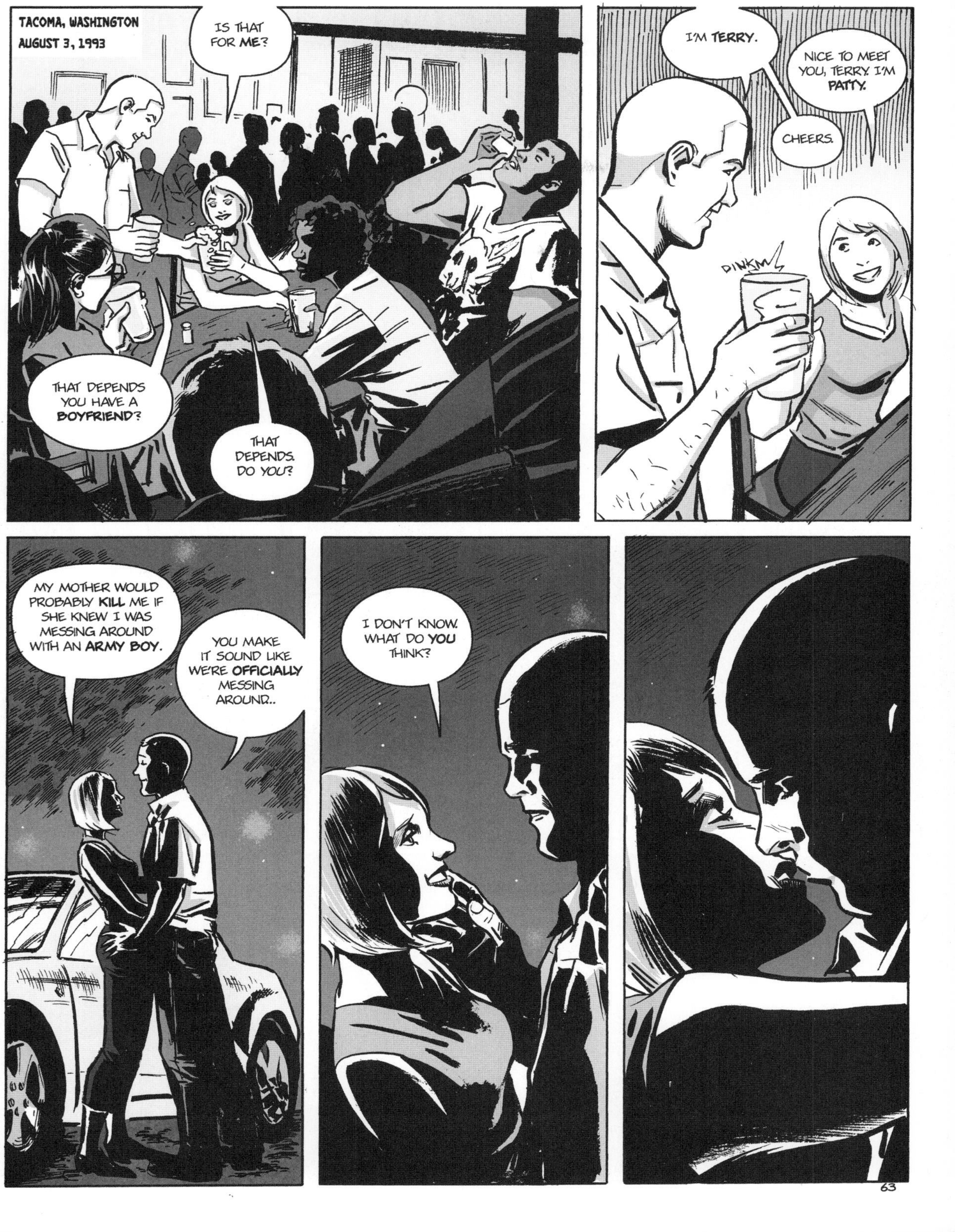
TACOMA, WASHINGTON
AUGUST 3, 1993
IS THAT FOR ME?
THAT DEPENDS YOU HAVE A BOYFRIEND?
THAT DEPENDS. DO YOU?
I'M TERRY.
NICE TO MEET YOU, TERRY. I'M PATTY.
CHEERS.
DINK
MY MOTHER WOULD PROBABLY KILL ME IF SHE KNEW I WAS MESSING AROUND WITH AN ARMY BOY.
YOU MAKE IT SOUND LIKE WE'RE OFFICIALLY MESSING AROUND..
I DON'T KNOW. WHAT DO YOU THINK?

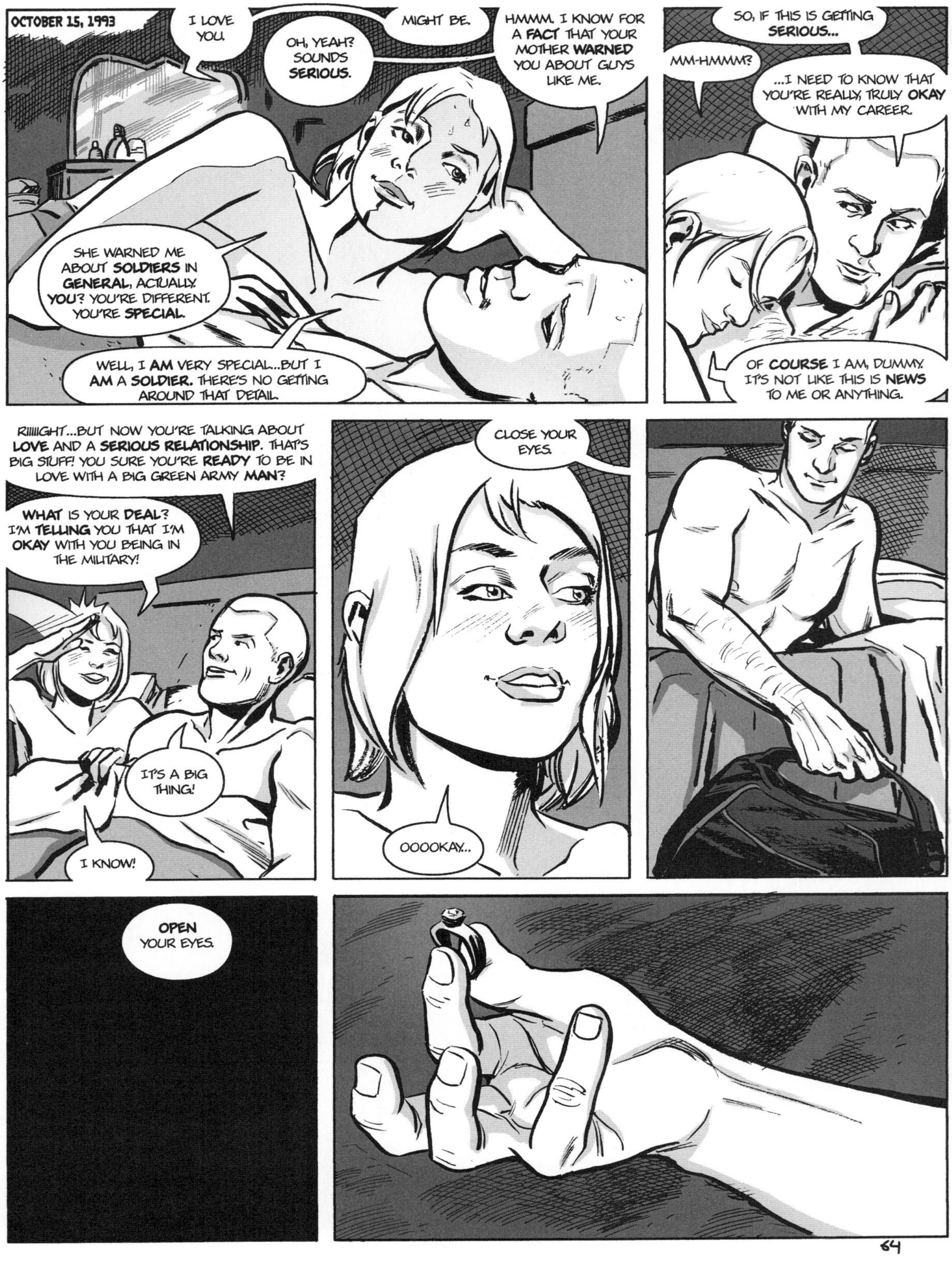

OCTOBER 15, 1993
I LOVE YOU.
OH, YEAH? SOUNDS SERIOUS.
MIGHT BE.
HMMM. I KNOW FOR A FACT THAT YOUR MOTHER WARNED YOU ABOUT GUYS LIKE ME.
SHE WARNED ME ABOUT SOLDIERS IN GENERAL, ACTUALLY. YOU? YOU'RE DIFFERENT. YOU'RE SPECIAL.
WELL, I AM VERY SPECIAL...BUT I AM A SOLDIER. THERE'S NO GETTING AROUND THAT DETAIL.
SO, IF THIS IS GETTING SERIOUS...
MM-HMMM?
...I NEED TO KNOW THAT YOU'RE REALLY, TRULY OKAY WITH MY CAREER.
OF COURSE I AM, DUMMY. IT'S NOT LIKE THIS IS NEWS TO ME OR ANYTHING.
RIIIIGHT...BUT NOW YOU'RE TALKING ABOUT LOVE AND A SERIOUS RELATIONSHIP. THAT'S BIG STUFF! YOU SURE YOU'RE READY TO BE IN LOVE WITH A BIG GREEN ARMY MAN?
WHAT IS YOUR DEAL? I'M TELLING YOU THAT I'M OKAY WITH YOU BEING IN THE MILITARY!
IT'S A BIG THING!
I KNOW!
CLOSE YOUR EYES.
OOOOKAY...
OPEN YOUR EYES.

OH...OH...

PATTY, I -- SORRY, MY HAND IS SHAKING - I WAS WONDERING IF...

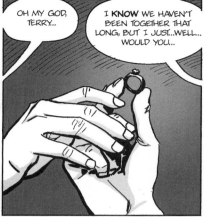

OH MY GOD, TERRY...

I **KNOW** WE HAVEN'T BEEN TOGETHER THAT LONG, BUT I JUST...WELL... WOULD YOU...

YES! YES! **YES!**

HERE. I HOPE IT FITS.

IT'S **PERFECT.**

I LOVE YOU, PATTY.

AW, MAN. I'M BEING CALLED BACK TO THE **BASE** EARLY.

I'M SO **SORRY.** THIS IS BAD TIMING...

IT'S OKAY, TERRY. REALLY. **GO.**

WE HAVE THE **REST** OF OUR **LIVES** TOGETHER, RIGHT?

I got called back to base in the middle of my big proposal. It was a sign, but we didn't see it. We didn't see the others, either, but now it's so obvious.

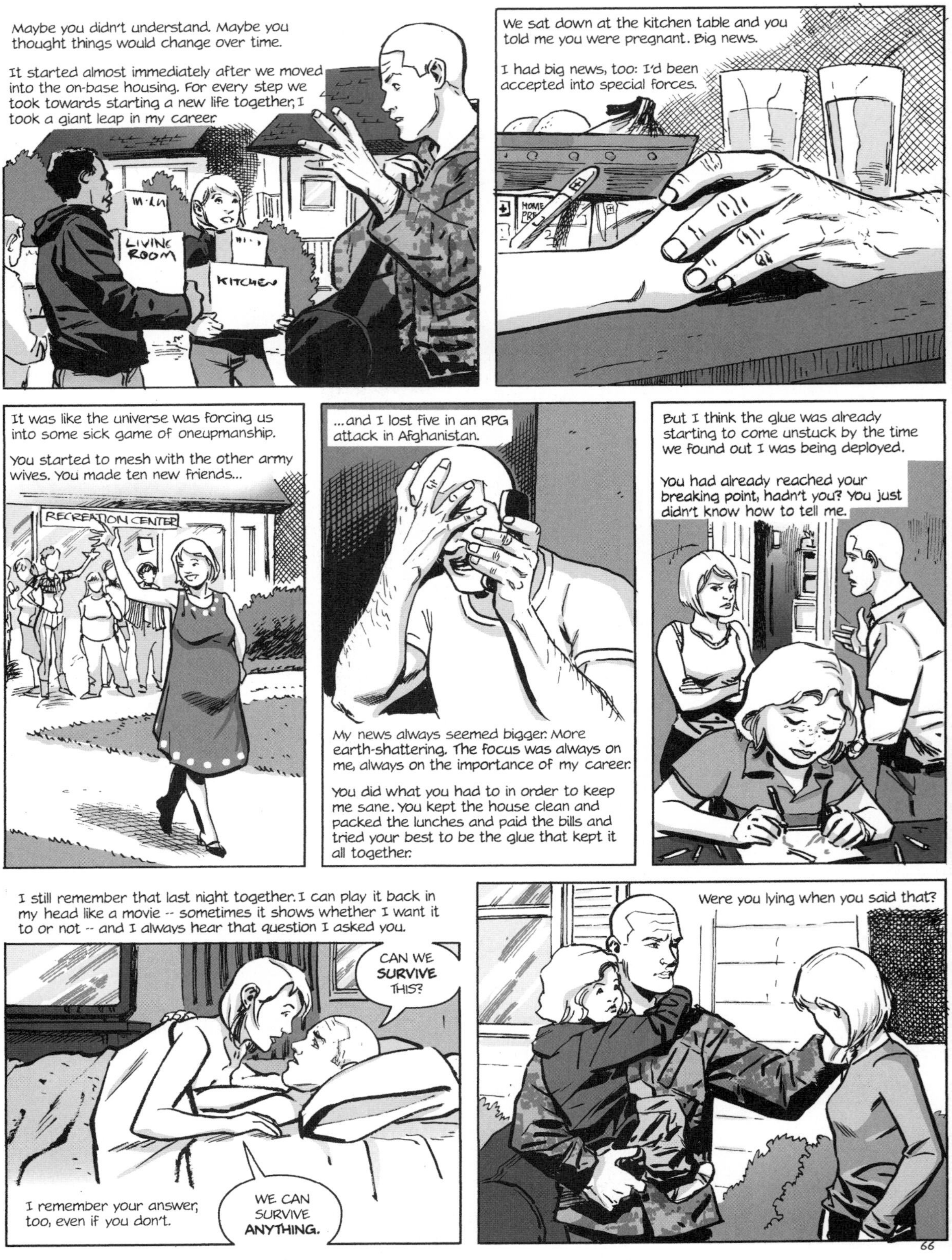

Maybe you didn't understand. Maybe you thought things would change over time.
It started almost immediately after we moved into the on-base housing. For every step we took towards starting a new life together, I took a giant leap in my career.
LIVING ROOM
KITCHEN
We sat down at the kitchen table and you told me you were pregnant. Big news.
I had big news, too: I'd been accepted into special forces.
It was like the universe was forcing us into some sick game of oneupmanship.
You started to mesh with the other army wives. You made ten new friends...
RECREATION CENTER
...and I lost five in an RPG attack in Afghanistan.
My news always seemed bigger. More earth-shattering. The focus was always on me, always on the importance of my career.
You did what you had to in order to keep me sane. You kept the house clean and packed the lunches and paid the bills and tried your best to be the glue that kept it all together.
But I think the glue was already starting to come unstuck by the time we found out I was being deployed.
You had already reached your breaking point, hadn't you? You just didn't know how to tell me.
I still remember that last night together. I can play it back in my head like a movie -- sometimes it shows whether I want it to or not -- and I always hear that question I asked you.
CAN WE **SURVIVE** THIS?
I remember your answer, too, even if you don't.
WE CAN SURVIVE **ANYTHING.**
Were you lying when you said that?

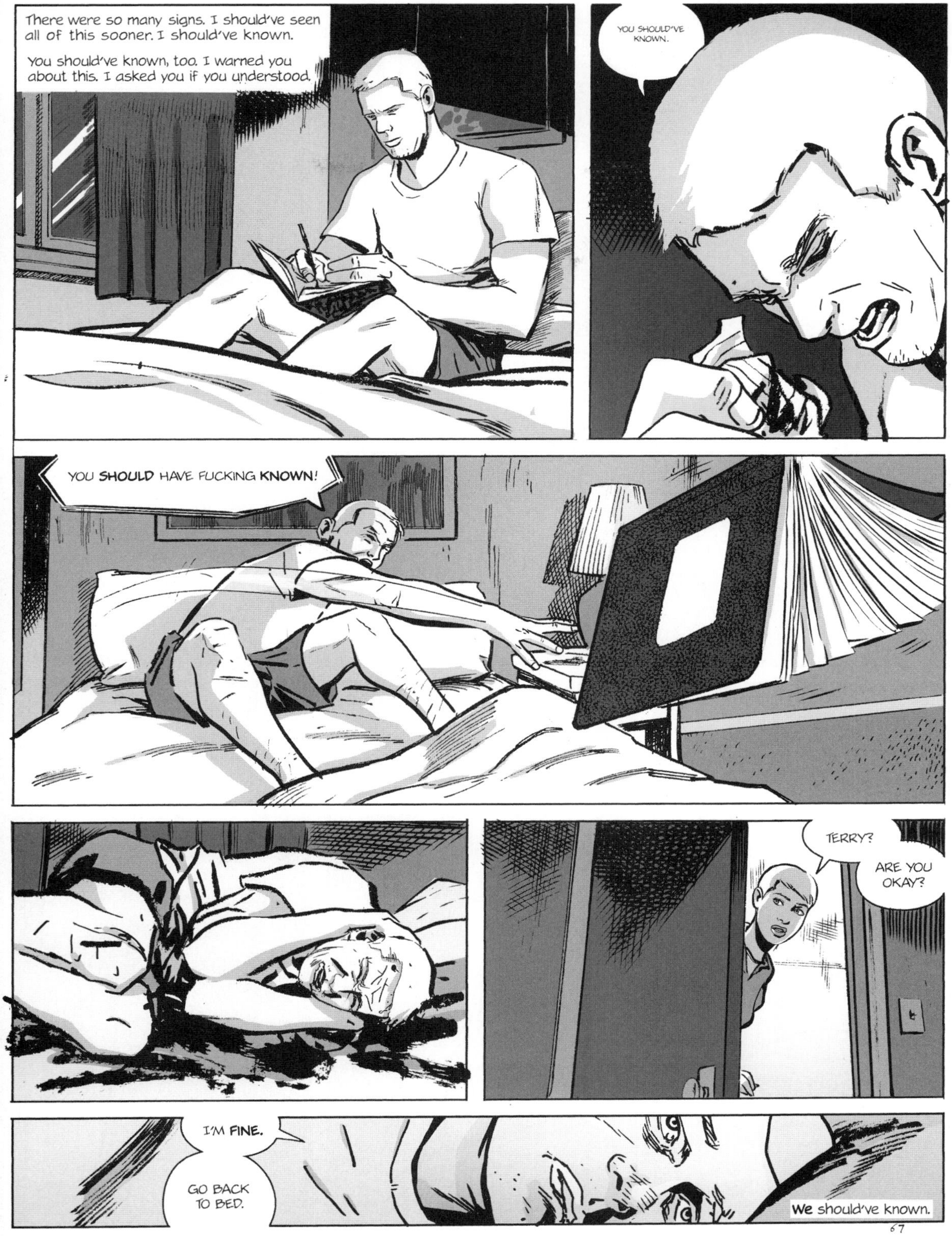

There were so many signs. I should've seen all of this sooner. I should've known.
You should've known, too. I warned you about this. I asked you if you understood.
YOU SHOULD'VE KNOWN.
YOU **SHOULD** HAVE FUCKING **KNOWN**!
TERRY?
ARE YOU OKAY?
I'M **FINE**.
GO BACK TO BED.
We should've known.

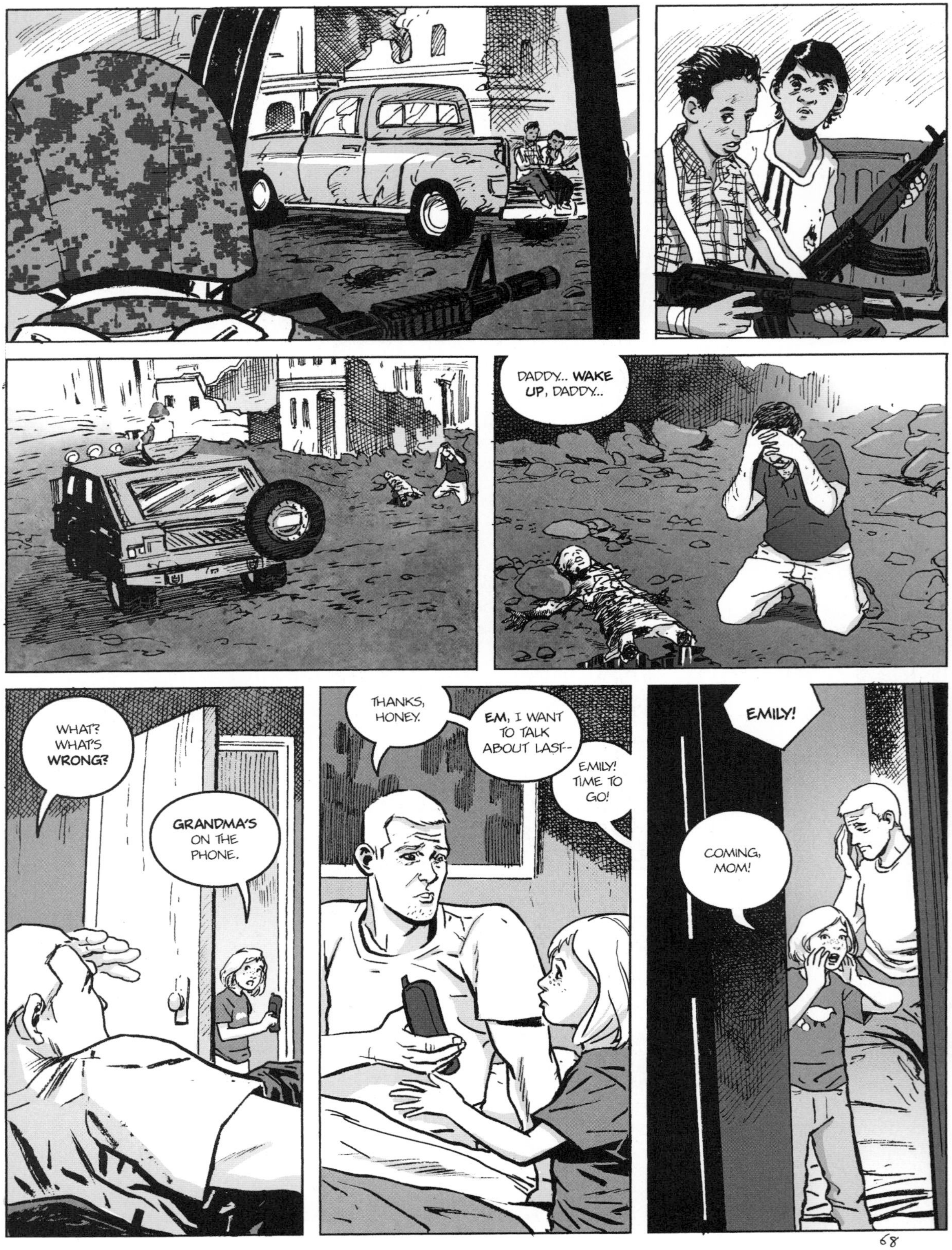
DADDY... WAKE UP, DADDY...
WHAT? WHAT'S WRONG?
GRANDMA'S ON THE PHONE.
THANKS, HONEY.
EM, I WANT TO TALK ABOUT LAST-
EMILY! TIME TO GO!
EMILY!
COMING, MOM!

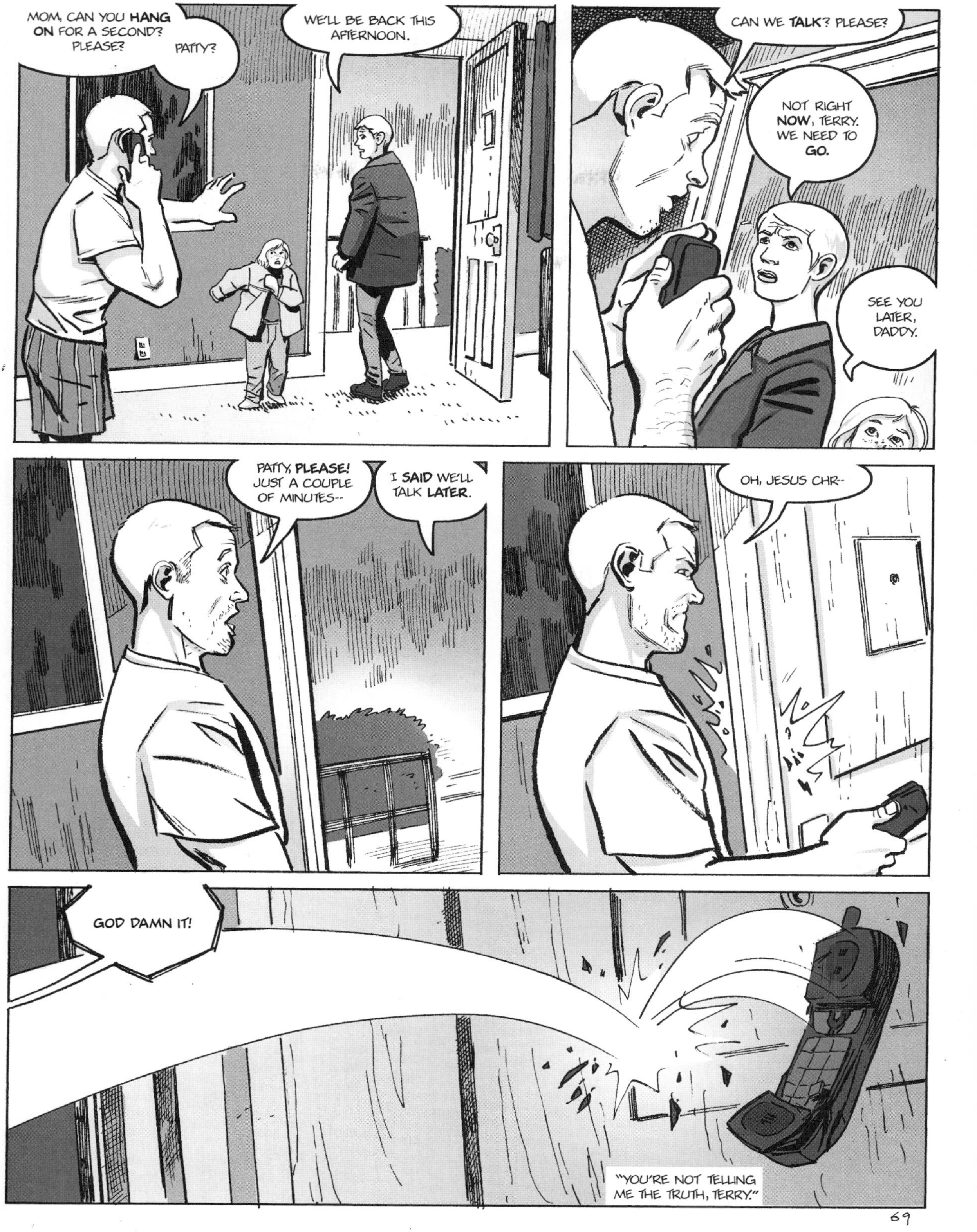
MOM, CAN YOU HANG ON FOR A SECOND? PLEASE?
PATTY?
WE'LL BE BACK THIS AFTERNOON.
CAN WE TALK? PLEASE?
NOT RIGHT NOW, TERRY. WE NEED TO GO.
SEE YOU LATER, DADDY.
PATTY, PLEASE! JUST A COUPLE OF MINUTES--
I SAID WE'LL TALK LATER.
OH, JESUS CHR-
GOD DAMN IT!
"YOU'RE NOT TELLING ME THE TRUTH, TERRY."

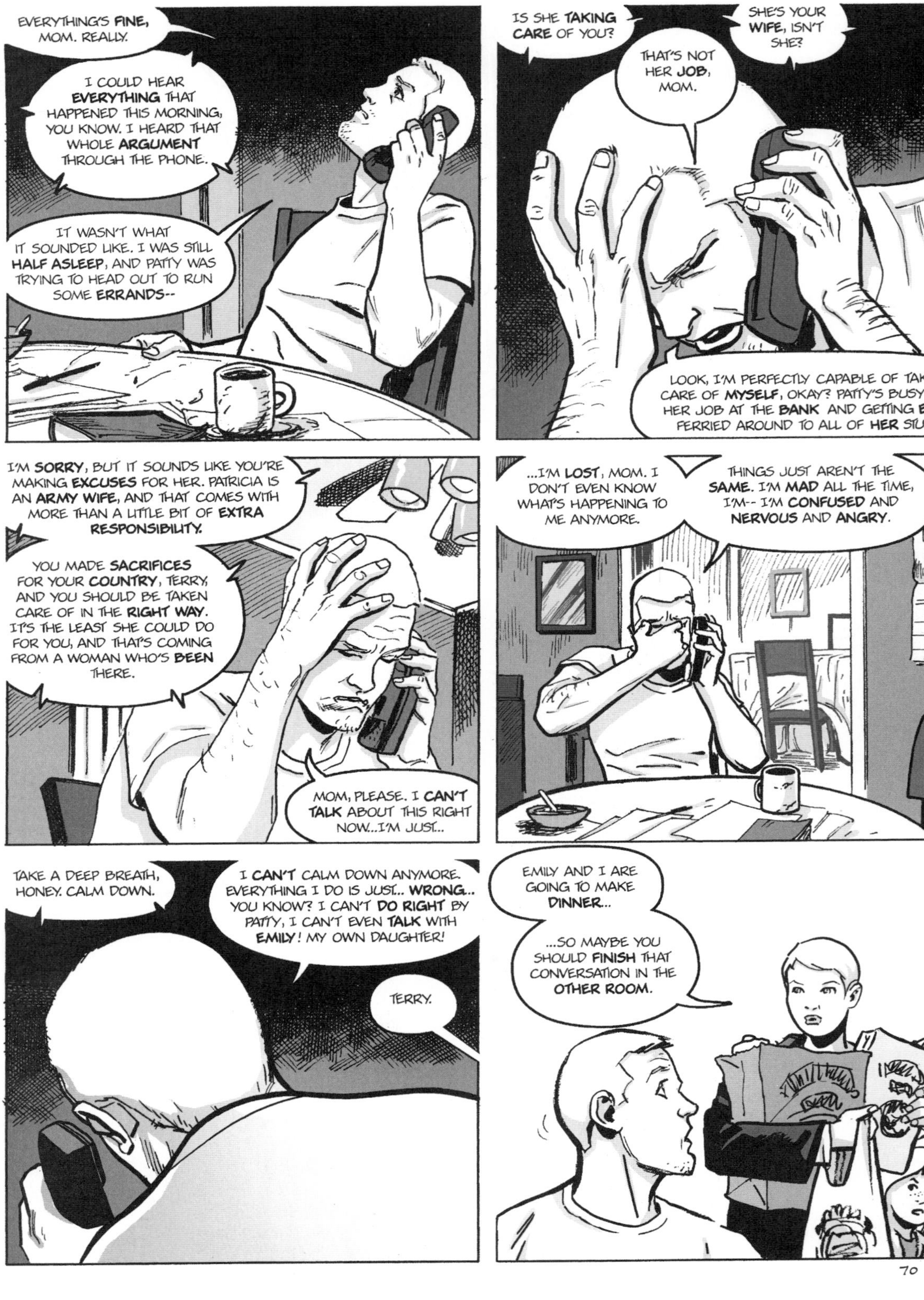
EVERYTHING'S FINE, MOM. REALLY.
I COULD HEAR EVERYTHING THAT HAPPENED THIS MORNING, YOU KNOW. I HEARD THAT WHOLE ARGUMENT THROUGH THE PHONE.
IT WASN'T WHAT IT SOUNDED LIKE. I WAS STILL HALF ASLEEP, AND PATTY WAS TRYING TO HEAD OUT TO RUN SOME ERRANDS--
IS SHE TAKING CARE OF YOU?
THAT'S NOT HER JOB, MOM.
SHE'S YOUR WIFE, ISN'T SHE?
LOOK, I'M PERFECTLY CAPABLE OF TAKING CARE OF MYSELF, OKAY? PATTY'S BUSY WITH HER JOB AT THE BANK AND GETTING EMILY FERRIED AROUND TO ALL OF HER STUFF..
I'M SORRY, BUT IT SOUNDS LIKE YOU'RE MAKING EXCUSES FOR HER. PATRICIA IS AN ARMY WIFE, AND THAT COMES WITH MORE THAN A LITTLE BIT OF EXTRA RESPONSIBILITY.
YOU MADE SACRIFICES FOR YOUR COUNTRY, TERRY, AND YOU SHOULD BE TAKEN CARE OF IN THE RIGHT WAY. IT'S THE LEAST SHE COULD DO FOR YOU, AND THAT'S COMING FROM A WOMAN WHO'S BEEN THERE.
MOM, PLEASE. I CAN'T TALK ABOUT THIS RIGHT NOW...I'M JUST...
...I'M LOST, MOM. I DON'T EVEN KNOW WHAT'S HAPPENING TO ME ANYMORE.
THINGS JUST AREN'T THE SAME. I'M MAD ALL THE TIME, I'M-- I'M CONFUSED AND NERVOUS AND ANGRY.
TAKE A DEEP BREATH, HONEY. CALM DOWN.
I CAN'T CALM DOWN ANYMORE. EVERYTHING I DO IS JUST... WRONG... YOU KNOW? I CAN'T DO RIGHT BY PATTY, I CAN'T EVEN TALK WITH EMILY! MY OWN DAUGHTER!
TERRY.
EMILY AND I ARE GOING TO MAKE DINNER...
...SO MAYBE YOU SHOULD FINISH THAT CONVERSATION IN THE OTHER ROOM.

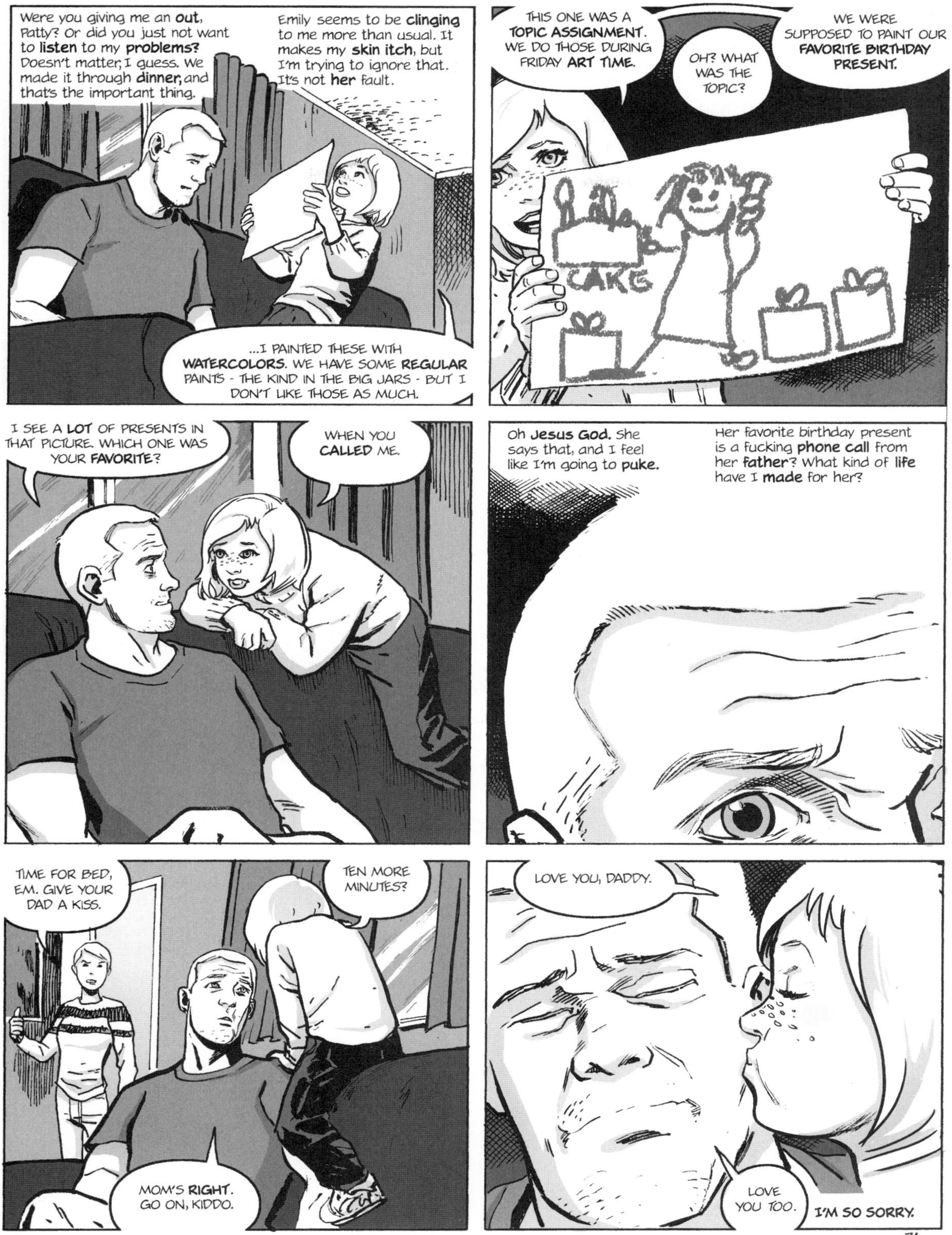

Were you giving me an **out**, Patty? Or did you just not want to **listen** to my **problems?** Doesn't matter, I guess. We made it through **dinner**, and that's the important thing.
Emily seems to be **clinging** to me more than usual. It makes my **skin itch**, but I'm trying to ignore that. It's not **her** fault.
...I PAINTED THESE WITH **WATERCOLORS**. WE HAVE SOME **REGULAR** PAINTS - THE KIND IN THE BIG JARS - BUT I DON'T LIKE THOSE AS MUCH.
THIS ONE WAS A **TOPIC ASSIGNMENT**. WE DO THOSE DURING FRIDAY **ART TIME**.
OH? WHAT WAS THE TOPIC?
WE WERE SUPPOSED TO PAINT OUR **FAVORITE BIRTHDAY PRESENT.**
CAKE
I SEE A **LOT** OF PRESENTS IN THAT PICTURE. WHICH ONE WAS YOUR **FAVORITE**?
WHEN YOU **CALLED** ME.
Oh **Jesus God**. She says that, and I feel like I'm going to **puke**.
Her favorite birthday present is a fucking **phone call** from her **father**? What kind of **life** have I **made** for her?
TIME FOR BED, EM. GIVE YOUR DAD A KISS.
TEN MORE MINUTES?
MOM'S **RIGHT**. GO ON, KIDDO.
LOVE YOU, DADDY.
LOVE YOU TOO.
I'M SO SORRY.

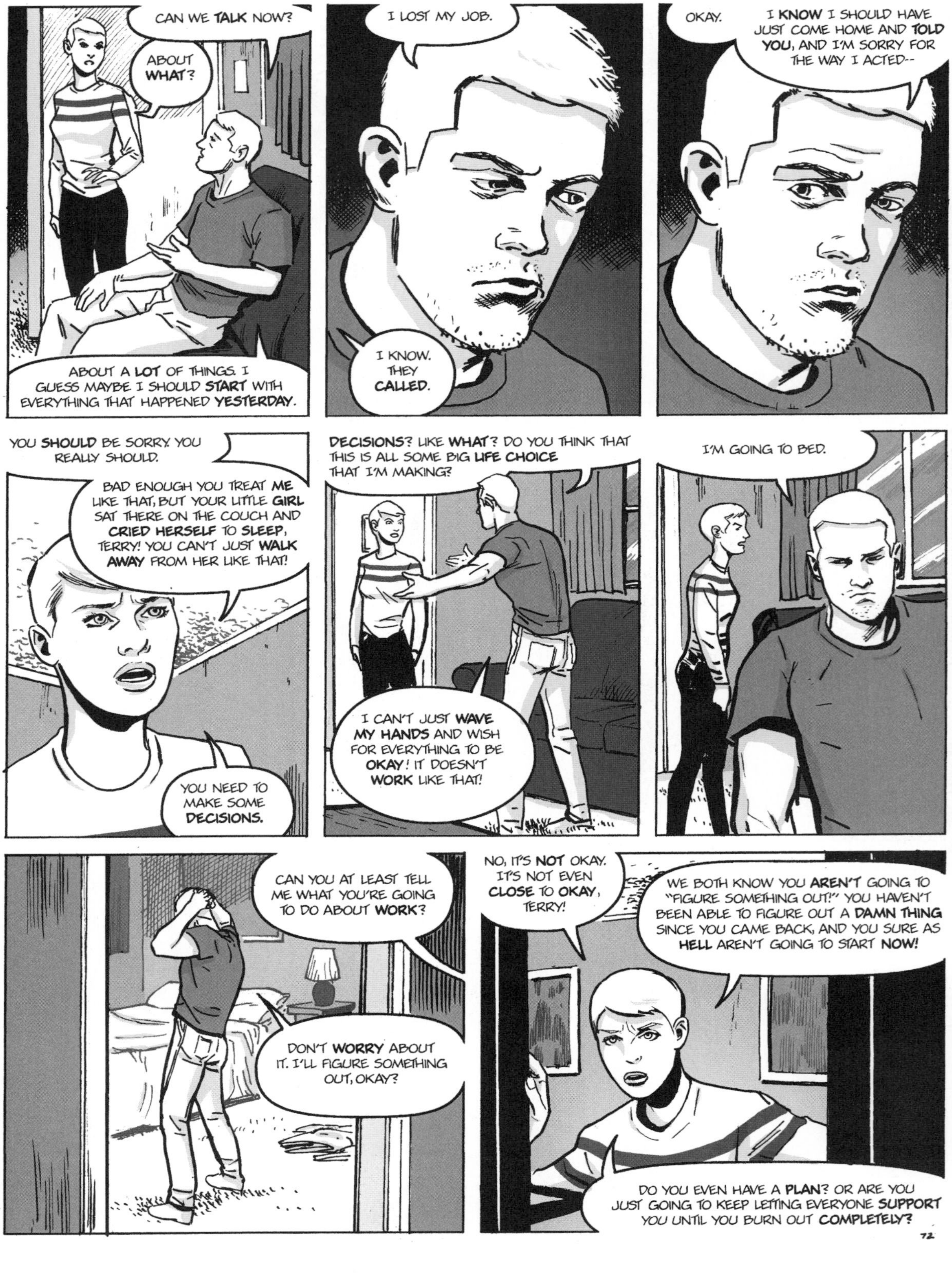
CAN WE TALK NOW?
ABOUT WHAT?
ABOUT A LOT OF THINGS. I GUESS MAYBE I SHOULD START WITH EVERYTHING THAT HAPPENED YESTERDAY.
I LOST MY JOB.
I KNOW. THEY CALLED.
OKAY.
I KNOW I SHOULD HAVE JUST COME HOME AND TOLD YOU, AND I'M SORRY FOR THE WAY I ACTED--
YOU SHOULD BE SORRY. YOU REALLY SHOULD.
BAD ENOUGH YOU TREAT ME LIKE THAT, BUT YOUR LITTLE GIRL SAT THERE ON THE COUCH AND CRIED HERSELF TO SLEEP, TERRY! YOU CAN'T JUST WALK AWAY FROM HER LIKE THAT!
YOU NEED TO MAKE SOME DECISIONS.
DECISIONS? LIKE WHAT? DO YOU THINK THAT THIS IS ALL SOME BIG LIFE CHOICE THAT I'M MAKING?
I CAN'T JUST WAVE MY HANDS AND WISH FOR EVERYTHING TO BE OKAY! IT DOESN'T WORK LIKE THAT!
I'M GOING TO BED.
CAN YOU AT LEAST TELL ME WHAT YOU'RE GOING TO DO ABOUT WORK?
DON'T WORRY ABOUT IT. I'LL FIGURE SOMETHING OUT, OKAY?
NO, IT'S NOT OKAY. IT'S NOT EVEN CLOSE TO OKAY, TERRY!
WE BOTH KNOW YOU AREN'T GOING TO "FIGURE SOMETHING OUT!" YOU HAVEN'T BEEN ABLE TO FIGURE OUT A DAMN THING SINCE YOU CAME BACK, AND YOU SURE AS HELL AREN'T GOING TO START NOW!
DO YOU EVEN HAVE A PLAN? OR ARE YOU JUST GOING TO KEEP LETTING EVERYONE SUPPORT YOU UNTIL YOU BURN OUT COMPLETELY?

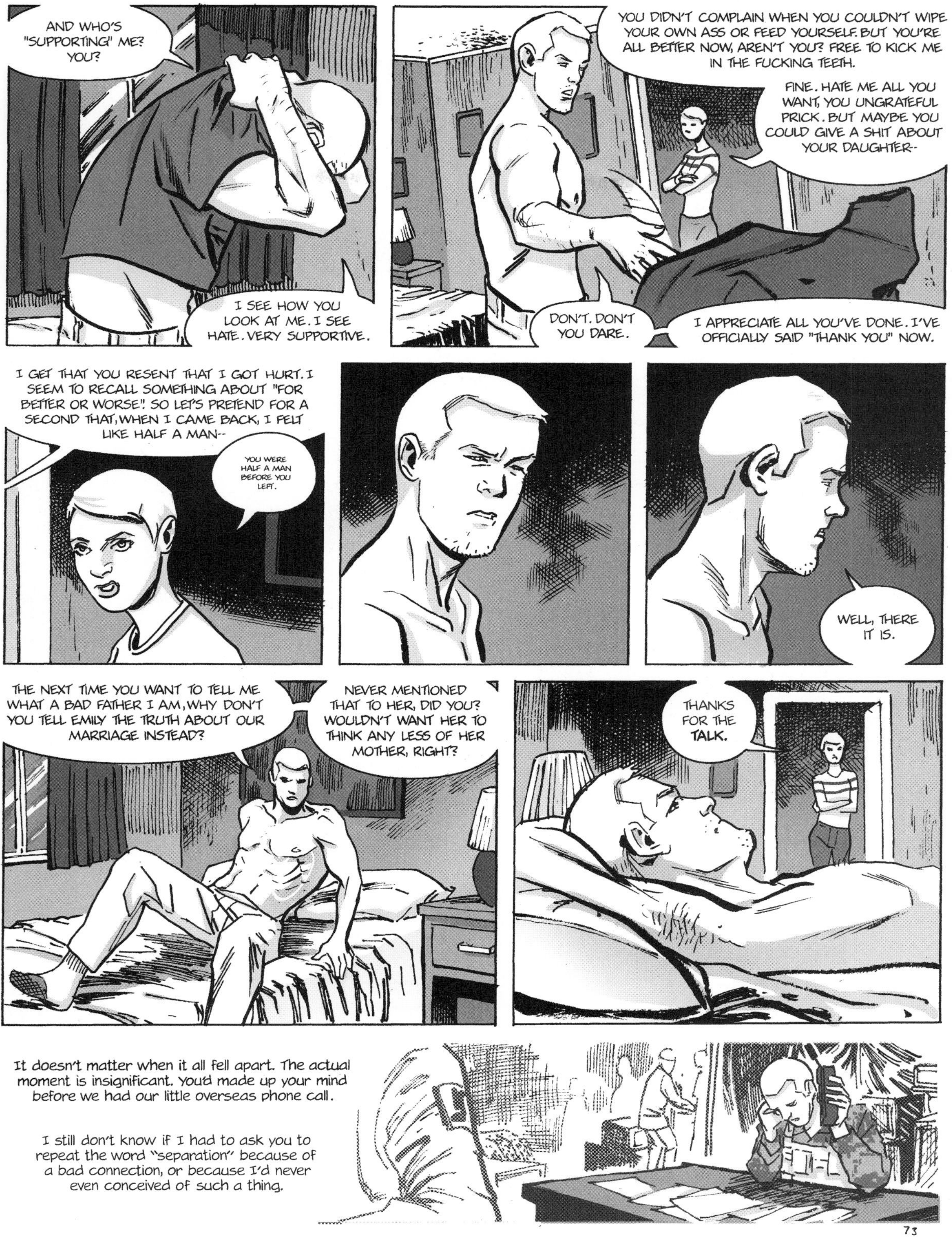
AND WHO'S "SUPPORTING" ME? YOU?
I SEE HOW YOU LOOK AT ME. I SEE HATE. VERY SUPPORTIVE.
YOU DIDN'T COMPLAIN WHEN YOU COULDN'T WIPE YOUR OWN ASS OR FEED YOURSELF. BUT YOU'RE ALL BETTER NOW, AREN'T YOU? FREE TO KICK ME IN THE FUCKING TEETH.
FINE. HATE ME ALL YOU WANT, YOU UNGRATEFUL PRICK. BUT MAYBE YOU COULD GIVE A SHIT ABOUT YOUR DAUGHTER--
I APPRECIATE ALL YOU'VE DONE. I'VE OFFICIALLY SAID "THANK YOU" NOW.
DON'T. DON'T YOU DARE.
I GET THAT YOU RESENT THAT I GOT HURT. I SEEM TO RECALL SOMETHING ABOUT "FOR BETTER OR WORSE". SO LET'S PRETEND FOR A SECOND THAT, WHEN I CAME BACK, I FELT LIKE HALF A MAN--
YOU WERE HALF A MAN BEFORE YOU LEFT.
WELL, THERE IT IS.
THE NEXT TIME YOU WANT TO TELL ME WHAT A BAD FATHER I AM, WHY DON'T YOU TELL EMILY THE TRUTH ABOUT OUR MARRIAGE INSTEAD?
NEVER MENTIONED THAT TO HER, DID YOU? WOULDN'T WANT HER TO THINK ANY LESS OF HER MOTHER, RIGHT?
THANKS FOR THE **TALK.**
It doesn't matter when it all fell apart. The actual moment is insignificant. You'd made up your mind before we had our little overseas phone call.
I still don't know if I had to ask you to repeat the word "separation" because of a bad connection, or because I'd never even conceived of such a thing.

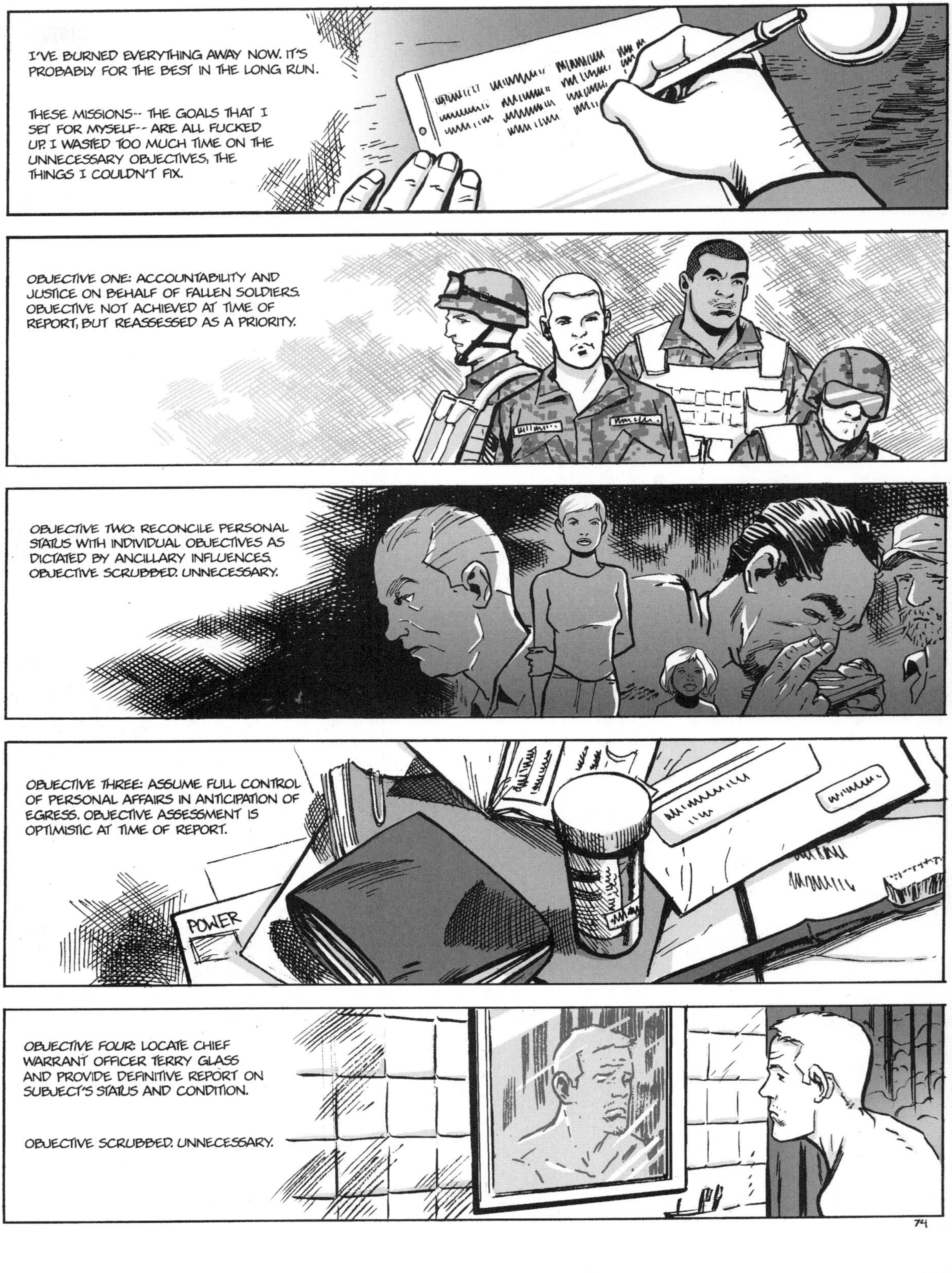
I'VE BURNED EVERYTHING AWAY NOW. IT'S PROBABLY FOR THE BEST IN THE LONG RUN.
THESE MISSIONS-- THE GOALS THAT I SET FOR MYSELF-- ARE ALL FUCKED UP. I WASTED TOO MUCH TIME ON THE UNNECESSARY OBJECTIVES, THE THINGS I COULDN'T FIX.
OBJECTIVE ONE: ACCOUNTABILITY AND JUSTICE ON BEHALF OF FALLEN SOLDIERS. OBJECTIVE NOT ACHIEVED AT TIME OF REPORT, BUT REASSESSED AS A PRIORITY.
OBJECTIVE TWO: RECONCILE PERSONAL STATUS WITH INDIVIDUAL OBJECTIVES AS DICTATED BY ANCILLARY INFLUENCES. OBJECTIVE SCRUBBED. UNNECESSARY.
OBJECTIVE THREE: ASSUME FULL CONTROL OF PERSONAL AFFAIRS IN ANTICIPATION OF EGRESS. OBJECTIVE ASSESSMENT IS OPTIMISTIC AT TIME OF REPORT.
POWER
OBJECTIVE FOUR: LOCATE CHIEF WARRANT OFFICER TERRY GLASS AND PROVIDE DEFINITIVE REPORT ON SUBJECT'S STATUS AND CONDITION.
OBJECTIVE SCRUBBED. UNNECESSARY.

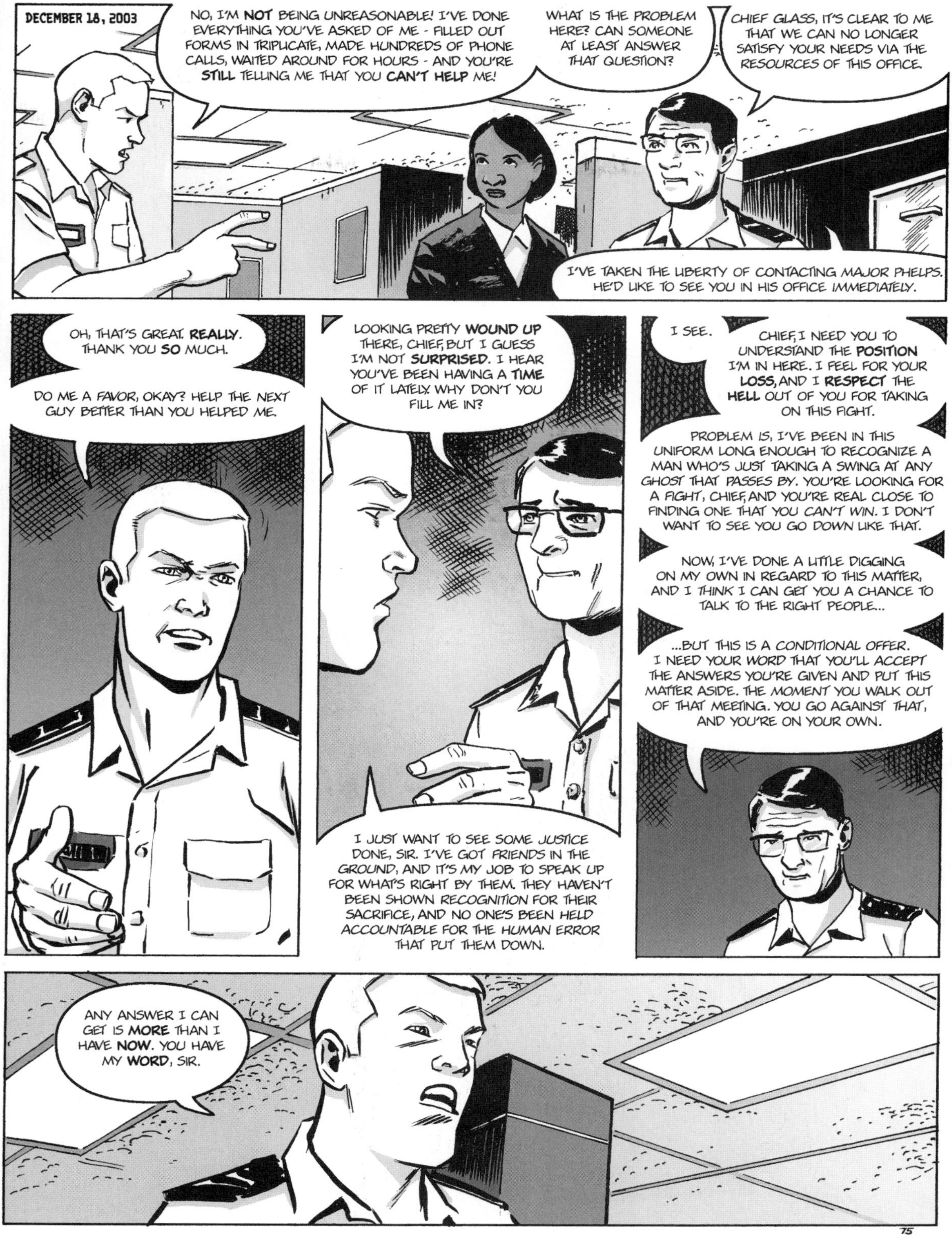
DECEMBER 18, 2003
NO, I'M **NOT** BEING UNREASONABLE! I'VE DONE EVERYTHING YOU'VE ASKED OF ME - FILLED OUT FORMS IN TRIPLICATE, MADE HUNDREDS OF PHONE CALLS, WAITED AROUND FOR HOURS - AND YOU'RE **STILL** TELLING ME THAT YOU **CAN'T HELP** ME!
WHAT IS THE PROBLEM HERE? CAN SOMEONE AT LEAST ANSWER THAT QUESTION?
CHIEF GLASS, IT'S CLEAR TO ME THAT WE CAN NO LONGER SATISFY YOUR NEEDS VIA THE RESOURCES OF THIS OFFICE.
I'VE TAKEN THE LIBERTY OF CONTACTING MAJOR PHELPS. HE'D LIKE TO SEE YOU IN HIS OFFICE IMMEDIATELY.
OH, THAT'S GREAT. **REALLY**. THANK YOU **SO** MUCH.
DO ME A FAVOR, OKAY? HELP THE NEXT GUY BETTER THAN YOU HELPED ME.
LOOKING PRETTY **WOUND UP** THERE, CHIEF, BUT I GUESS I'M NOT **SURPRISED**. I HEAR YOU'VE BEEN HAVING A **TIME** OF IT LATELY. WHY DON'T YOU FILL ME IN?
I JUST WANT TO SEE SOME JUSTICE DONE, SIR. I'VE GOT FRIENDS IN THE GROUND, AND IT'S MY JOB TO SPEAK UP FOR WHAT'S RIGHT BY THEM. THEY HAVEN'T BEEN SHOWN RECOGNITION FOR THEIR SACRIFICE, AND NO ONE'S BEEN HELD ACCOUNTABLE FOR THE HUMAN ERROR THAT PUT THEM DOWN.
I SEE.
CHIEF, I NEED YOU TO UNDERSTAND THE **POSITION** I'M IN HERE. I FEEL FOR YOUR **LOSS**, AND I **RESPECT** THE **HELL** OUT OF YOU FOR TAKING ON THIS FIGHT.
PROBLEM IS, I'VE BEEN IN THIS UNIFORM LONG ENOUGH TO RECOGNIZE A MAN WHO'S JUST TAKING A SWING AT ANY GHOST THAT PASSES BY. YOU'RE LOOKING FOR A FIGHT, CHIEF, AND YOU'RE REAL CLOSE TO FINDING ONE THAT YOU CAN'T WIN. I DON'T WANT TO SEE YOU GO DOWN LIKE THAT.
NOW, I'VE DONE A LITTLE DIGGING ON MY OWN IN REGARD TO THIS MATTER, AND I THINK I CAN GET YOU A CHANCE TO TALK TO THE RIGHT PEOPLE...
...BUT THIS IS A CONDITIONAL OFFER. I NEED YOUR WORD THAT YOU'LL ACCEPT THE ANSWERS YOU'RE GIVEN AND PUT THIS MATTER ASIDE. THE MOMENT YOU WALK OUT OF THAT MEETING. YOU GO AGAINST THAT, AND YOU'RE ON YOUR OWN.
ANY ANSWER I CAN GET IS **MORE** THAN I HAVE **NOW**. YOU HAVE MY **WORD**, SIR.

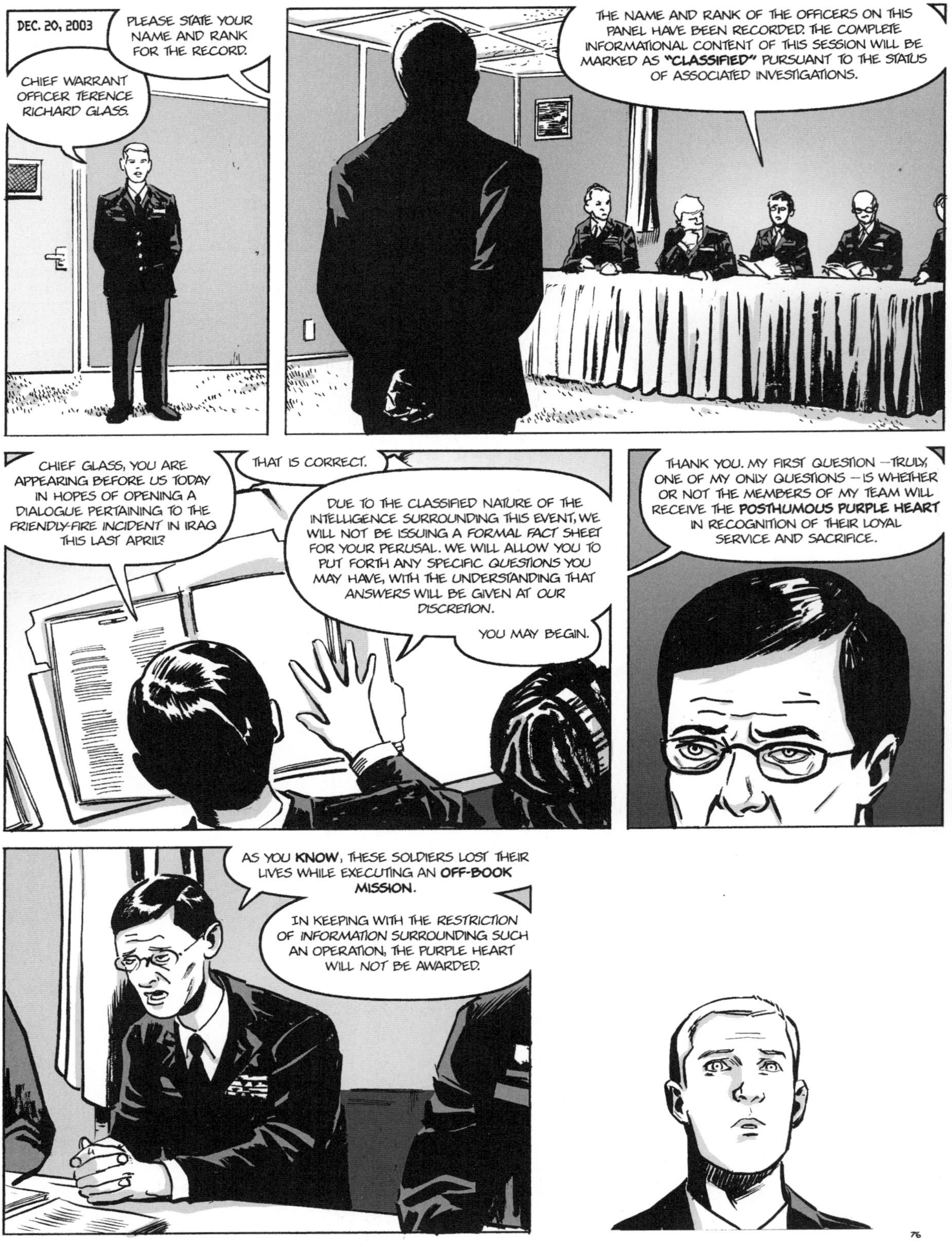
DEC. 20, 2003
PLEASE STATE YOUR NAME AND RANK FOR THE RECORD.
CHIEF WARRANT OFFICER TERENCE RICHARD GLASS.
THE NAME AND RANK OF THE OFFICERS ON THIS PANEL HAVE BEEN RECORDED. THE COMPLETE INFORMATIONAL CONTENT OF THIS SESSION WILL BE MARKED AS "CLASSIFIED" PURSUANT TO THE STATUS OF ASSOCIATED INVESTIGATIONS.
CHIEF GLASS, YOU ARE APPEARING BEFORE US TODAY IN HOPES OF OPENING A DIALOGUE PERTAINING TO THE FRIENDLY-FIRE INCIDENT IN IRAQ THIS LAST APRIL?
THAT IS CORRECT.
DUE TO THE CLASSIFIED NATURE OF THE INTELLIGENCE SURROUNDING THIS EVENT, WE WILL NOT BE ISSUING A FORMAL FACT SHEET FOR YOUR PERUSAL. WE WILL ALLOW YOU TO PUT FORTH ANY SPECIFIC QUESTIONS YOU MAY HAVE, WITH THE UNDERSTANDING THAT ANSWERS WILL BE GIVEN AT OUR DISCRETION.
YOU MAY BEGIN.
THANK YOU. MY FIRST QUESTION -- TRULY, ONE OF MY ONLY QUESTIONS -- IS WHETHER OR NOT THE MEMBERS OF MY TEAM WILL RECEIVE THE POSTHUMOUS PURPLE HEART IN RECOGNITION OF THEIR LOYAL SERVICE AND SACRIFICE.
AS YOU KNOW, THESE SOLDIERS LOST THEIR LIVES WHILE EXECUTING AN OFF-BOOK MISSION.
IN KEEPING WITH THE RESTRICTION OF INFORMATION SURROUNDING SUCH AN OPERATION, THE PURPLE HEART WILL NOT BE AWARDED.

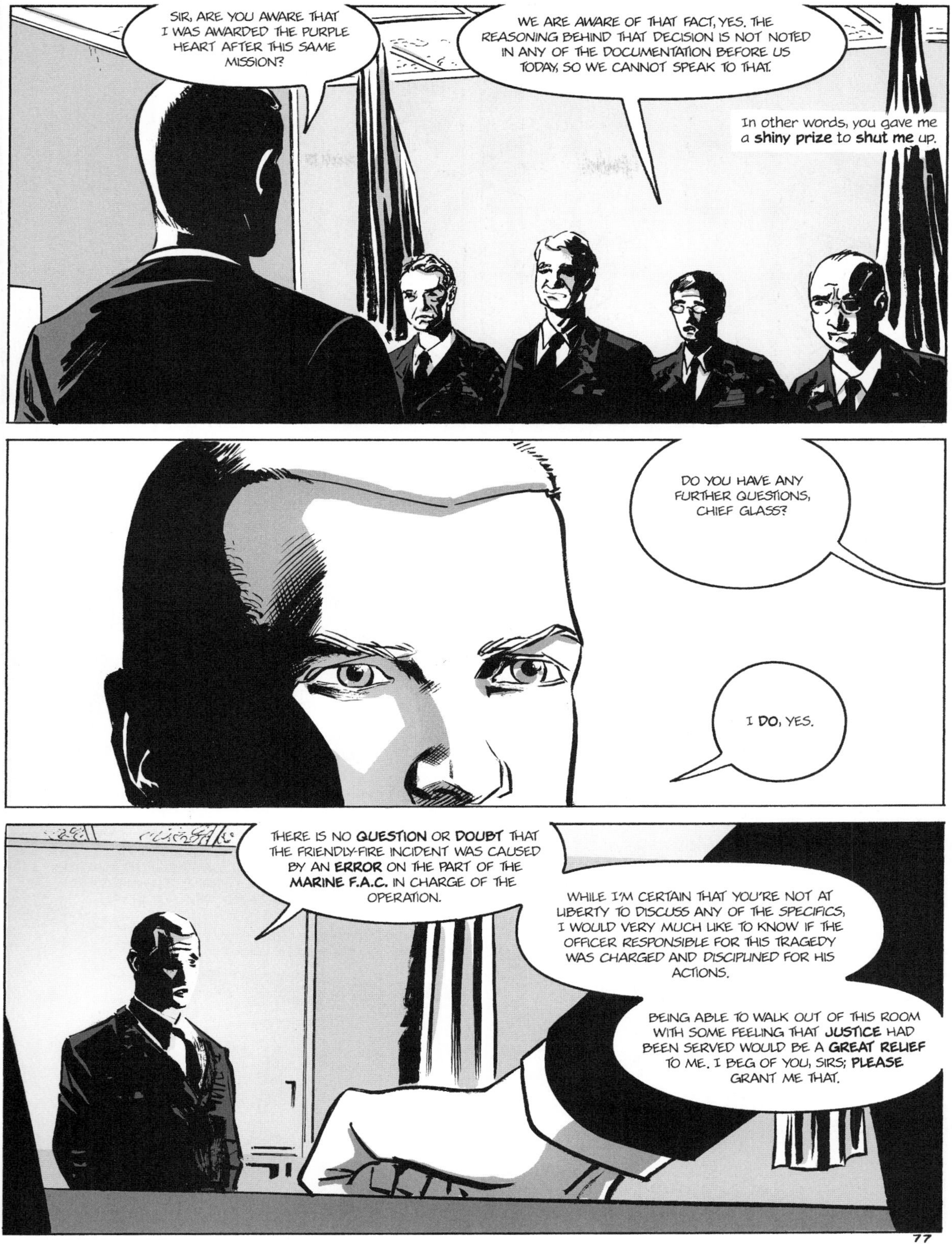
SIR, ARE YOU AWARE THAT I WAS AWARDED THE PURPLE HEART AFTER THIS SAME MISSION?
WE ARE AWARE OF THAT FACT, YES. THE REASONING BEHIND THAT DECISION IS NOT NOTED IN ANY OF THE DOCUMENTATION BEFORE US TODAY, SO WE CANNOT SPEAK TO THAT.
In other words, you gave me a **shiny prize** to **shut me** up.
DO YOU HAVE ANY FURTHER QUESTIONS, CHIEF GLASS?
I **DO**, YES.
THERE IS NO **QUESTION** OR **DOUBT** THAT THE FRIENDLY-FIRE INCIDENT WAS CAUSED BY AN **ERROR** ON THE PART OF THE **MARINE F.A.C.** IN CHARGE OF THE OPERATION.
WHILE I'M CERTAIN THAT YOU'RE NOT AT LIBERTY TO DISCUSS ANY OF THE SPECIFICS, I WOULD VERY MUCH LIKE TO KNOW IF THE OFFICER RESPONSIBLE FOR THIS TRAGEDY WAS CHARGED AND DISCIPLINED FOR HIS ACTIONS.
BEING ABLE TO WALK OUT OF THIS ROOM WITH SOME FEELING THAT **JUSTICE** HAD BEEN SERVED WOULD BE A **GREAT RELIEF** TO ME. I BEG OF YOU, SIRS; **PLEASE** GRANT ME THAT.

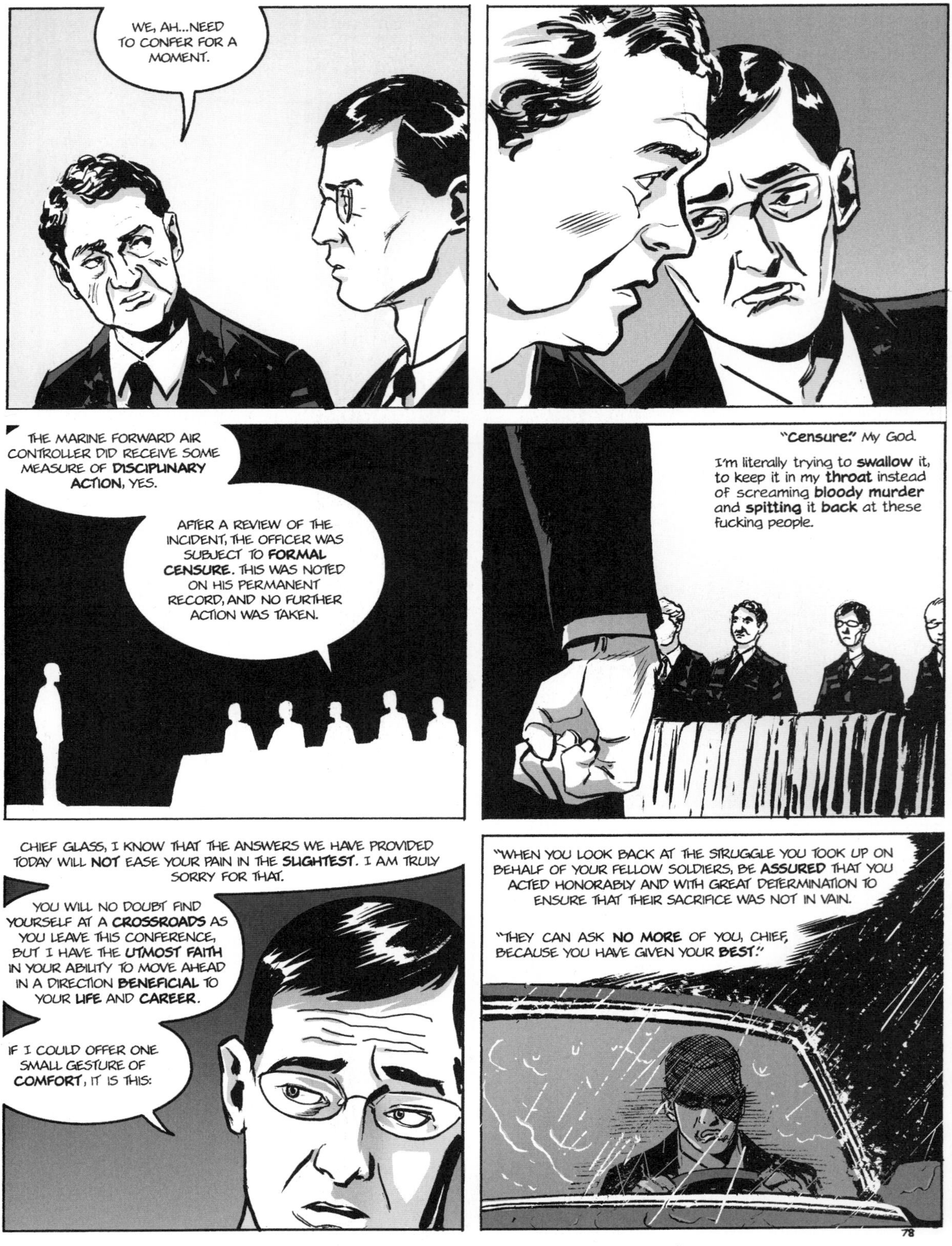
WE, AH...NEED TO CONFER FOR A MOMENT.
THE MARINE FORWARD AIR CONTROLLER DID RECEIVE SOME MEASURE OF **DISCIPLINARY ACTION**, YES.
AFTER A REVIEW OF THE INCIDENT, THE OFFICER WAS SUBJECT TO **FORMAL CENSURE**. THIS WAS NOTED ON HIS PERMANENT RECORD, AND NO FURTHER ACTION WAS TAKEN.
"Censure." My God.
I'm literally trying to **swallow** it, to keep it in my **throat** instead of screaming **bloody murder** and **spitting** it **back** at these fucking people.
CHIEF GLASS, I KNOW THAT THE ANSWERS WE HAVE PROVIDED TODAY WILL **NOT** EASE YOUR PAIN IN THE **SLIGHTEST**. I AM TRULY SORRY FOR THAT.
YOU WILL NO DOUBT FIND YOURSELF AT A **CROSSROADS** AS YOU LEAVE THIS CONFERENCE, BUT I HAVE THE **UTMOST FAITH** IN YOUR ABILITY TO MOVE AHEAD IN A DIRECTION **BENEFICIAL** TO YOUR **LIFE** AND **CAREER**.
IF I COULD OFFER ONE SMALL GESTURE OF **COMFORT**, IT IS THIS:
"WHEN YOU LOOK BACK AT THE STRUGGLE YOU TOOK UP ON BEHALF OF YOUR FELLOW SOLDIERS, BE **ASSURED** THAT YOU ACTED HONORABLY AND WITH GREAT DETERMINATION TO ENSURE THAT THEIR SACRIFICE WAS NOT IN VAIN.
"THEY CAN ASK **NO MORE** OF YOU, CHIEF, BECAUSE YOU HAVE GIVEN YOUR **BEST**."

JANUARY 13, 2004

TERRY... ...I JUST **CAN'T** TAKE ANY **MORE** OF THIS.

WE BARELY MADE IT THROUGH *CHRISTMAS*, AND THINGS ARE JUST GETTING WORSE EVERY DAY. YOU HAVEN'T FOUND A FULL-TIME JOB, YOU CALL IN SICK TO YOUR TEACHING JOB ALL THE TIME—

I **AM** SICK, PATTY.

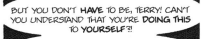

BUT YOU DON'T **HAVE** TO BE, TERRY! CAN'T YOU UNDERSTAND THAT YOU'RE **DOING THIS** TO **YOURSELF**?!

I KNOW THAT THINGS HAVEN'T WORKED OUT THE WAY YOU WANTED THEM TO. IT'S **NOT RIGHT**, AND WE **ALL KNOW** IT...

...BUT IF YOU CAN'T FIND A WAY TO **GET OVER** WHAT HAPPENED TO YOUR FRIENDS, YOU'RE JUST AS DEAD AS THEY ARE.

I'M **ALREADY DEAD!** I'VE BEEN **DEAD** FOR A **LONG** FUCKING **TIME!**

79

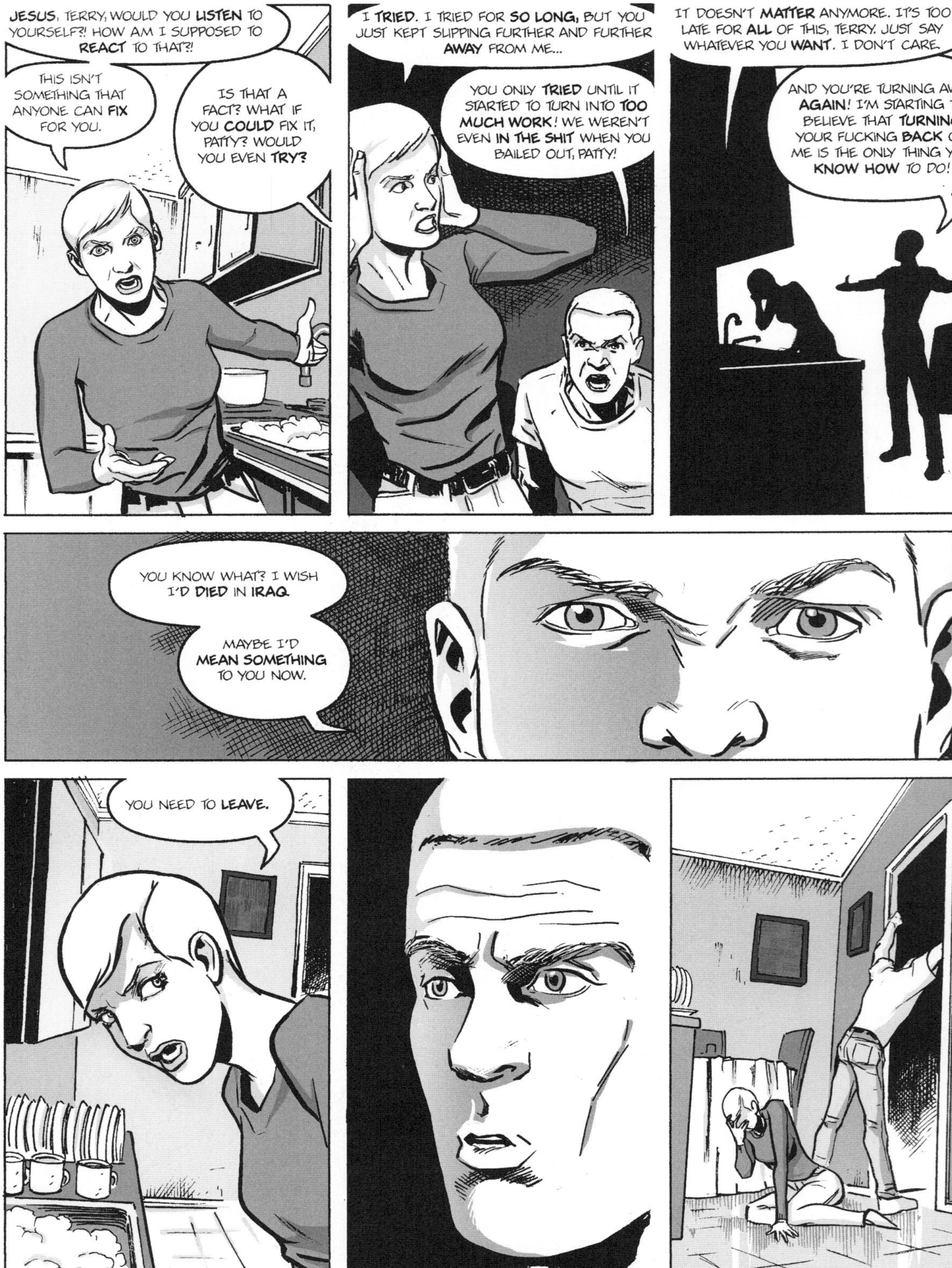
JESUS, TERRY, WOULD YOU LISTEN TO YOURSELF?! HOW AM I SUPPOSED TO REACT TO THAT?!
THIS ISN'T SOMETHING THAT ANYONE CAN FIX FOR YOU.
IS THAT A FACT? WHAT IF YOU COULD FIX IT, PATTY? WOULD YOU EVEN TRY?
I TRIED. I TRIED FOR SO LONG, BUT YOU JUST KEPT SLIPPING FURTHER AND FURTHER AWAY FROM ME...
YOU ONLY TRIED UNTIL IT STARTED TO TURN INTO TOO MUCH WORK! WE WEREN'T EVEN IN THE SHIT WHEN YOU BAILED OUT, PATTY!
IT DOESN'T MATTER ANYMORE. IT'S TOO LATE FOR ALL OF THIS, TERRY. JUST SAY WHATEVER YOU WANT. I DON'T CARE.
AND YOU'RE TURNING AWAY AGAIN! I'M STARTING TO BELIEVE THAT TURNING YOUR FUCKING BACK ON ME IS THE ONLY THING YOU KNOW HOW TO DO!
YOU KNOW WHAT? I WISH I'D DIED IN IRAQ.
MAYBE I'D MEAN SOMETHING TO YOU NOW.
YOU NEED TO LEAVE.

January 22, 2004
Tacoma, Washington
TACOMA TERRACE APARTMENTS
ONE BEDROOM AND STUDIO UNITS NOW RENTING MILITARY DISCOUNTS
Way to go.
Turn every argument into a war. No prisoners, no surrender.
Asshole.
I'M DOING ALL RIGHT. HOW ARE YOU?
THAT'S GOOD.
WELL, I'M NOT REALLY SURE RIGHT NOW. IT'S PROBABLY GOING TO BE A LITTLE WHILE, THOUGH. YOU'LL HAVE TO TRY TO BE PATIENT.
I LOVE YOU, DADDY.
I'LL TALK TO YOU SOON, OKAY?
PUT YOUR MOM ON THE PHONE AGAIN.
I'LL LET YOU KNOW IN ADVANCE IF I CAN GET SOME TIME TO SEE HER.
WHEN I CAN. I'VE BEEN...BUSY WITH SOME WORK THINGS UP HERE.
CWO TERRY GLASS
RETIREMENT PAPERWORK
ATTN: CPT J. VAN METER

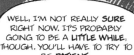

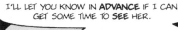

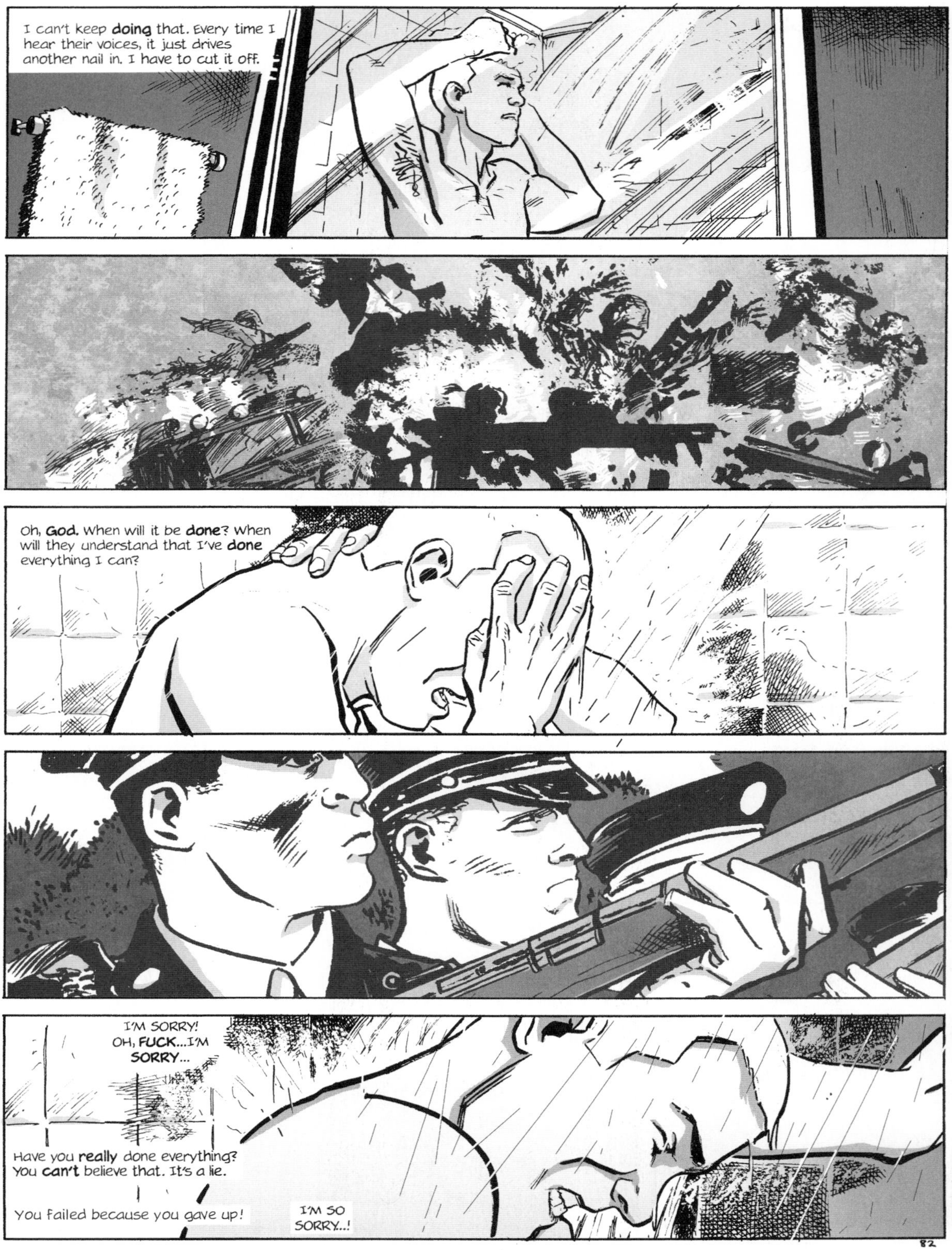
I can't keep **doing** that. Every time I hear their voices, it just drives another nail in. I have to cut it off.
Oh, **God.** When will it be **done**? When will they understand that I've **done** everything I can?
I'M SORRY! OH, **FUCK**...I'M **SORRY**...
Have you **really** done everything? You **can't** believe that. It's a lie.
You failed because you gave up!
I'M SO SORRY...!

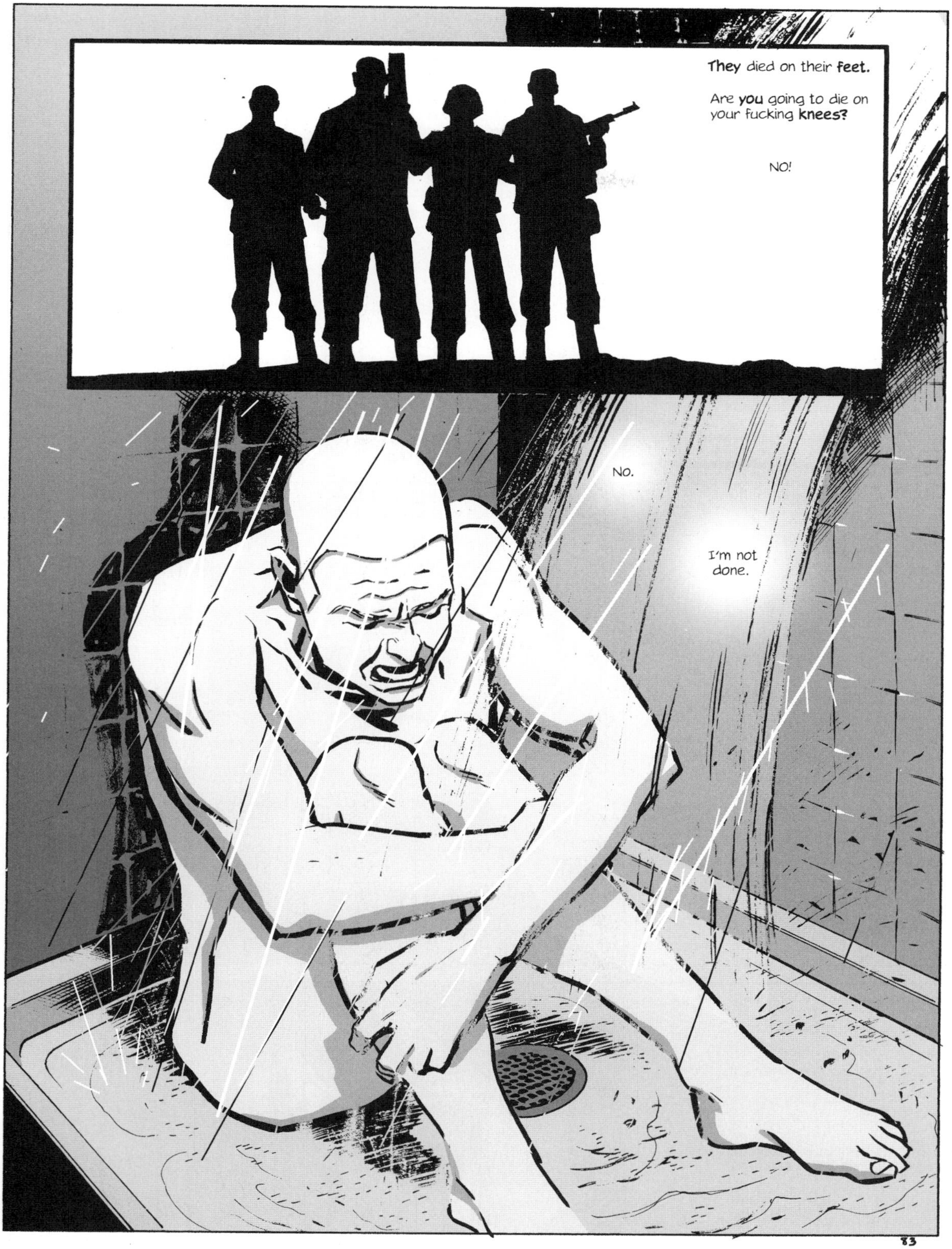

They died on their **feet.**
Are **you** going to die on your fucking **knees?**
NO!
NO.
I'm not done.

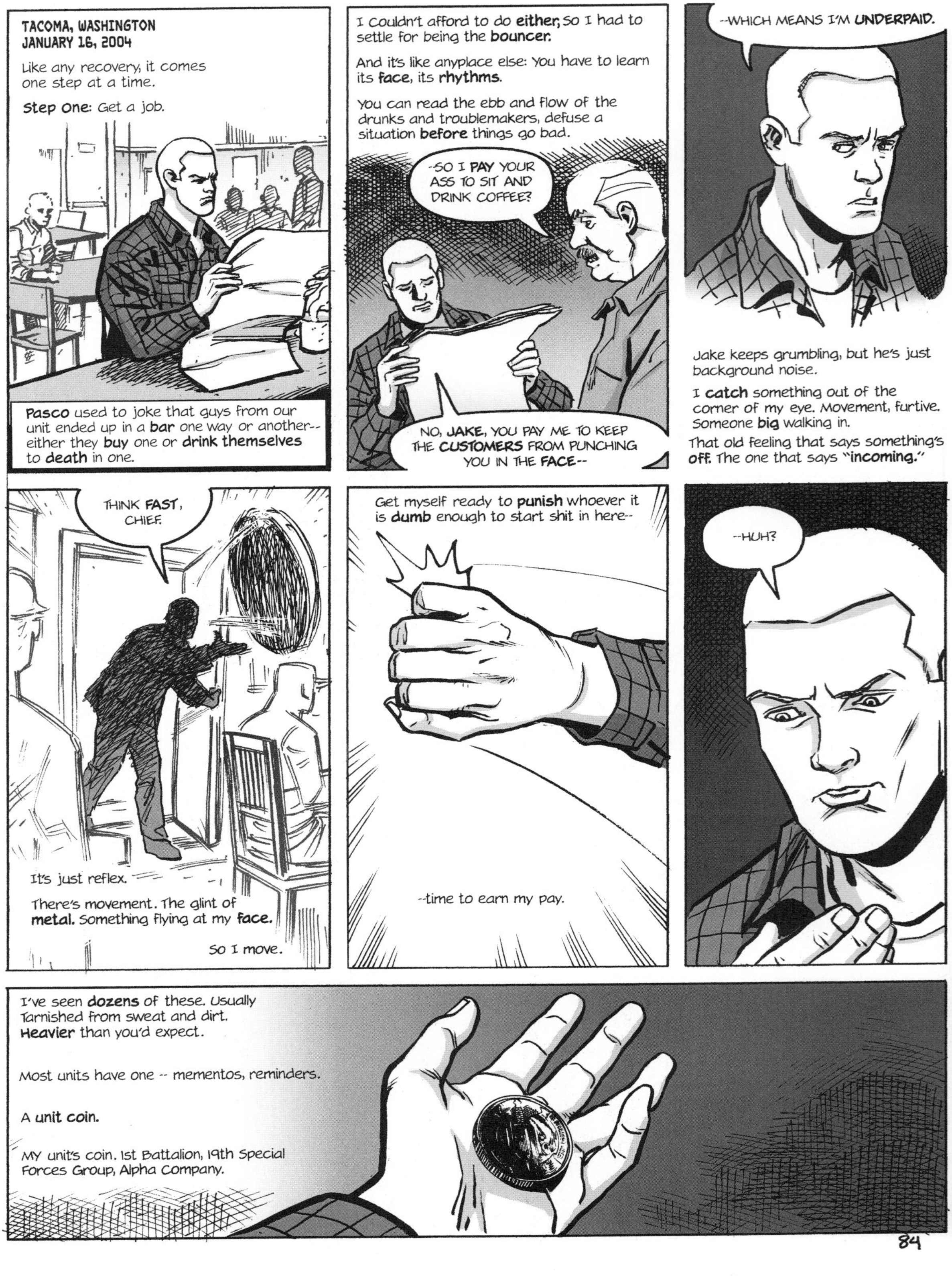

TACOMA, WASHINGTON
JANUARY 16, 2004
Like any recovery, it comes one step at a time.
Step One: Get a job.
Pasco used to joke that guys from our unit ended up in a bar one way or another--either they buy one or drink themselves to death in one.
I couldn't afford to do either, so I had to settle for being the bouncer.
And it's like anyplace else: You have to learn its face, its rhythms.
You can read the ebb and flow of the drunks and troublemakers, defuse a situation before things go bad.
--SO I PAY YOUR ASS TO SIT AND DRINK COFFEE?
NO, JAKE, YOU PAY ME TO KEEP THE CUSTOMERS FROM PUNCHING YOU IN THE FACE--
--WHICH MEANS I'M UNDERPAID.
Jake keeps grumbling, but he's just background noise.
I catch something out of the corner of my eye. Movement, furtive. Someone big walking in.
That old feeling that says something's off. The one that says "incoming."
THINK FAST, CHIEF.
It's just reflex.
There's movement. The glint of metal. Something flying at my face.
So I move.
Get myself ready to punish whoever it is dumb enough to start shit in here--
--time to earn my pay.
--HUH?
I've seen dozens of these. Usually tarnished from sweat and dirt. Heavier than you'd expect.
Most units have one -- mementos, reminders.
A unit coin.
My unit's coin. 1st Battalion, 19th Special Forces Group, Alpha Company.

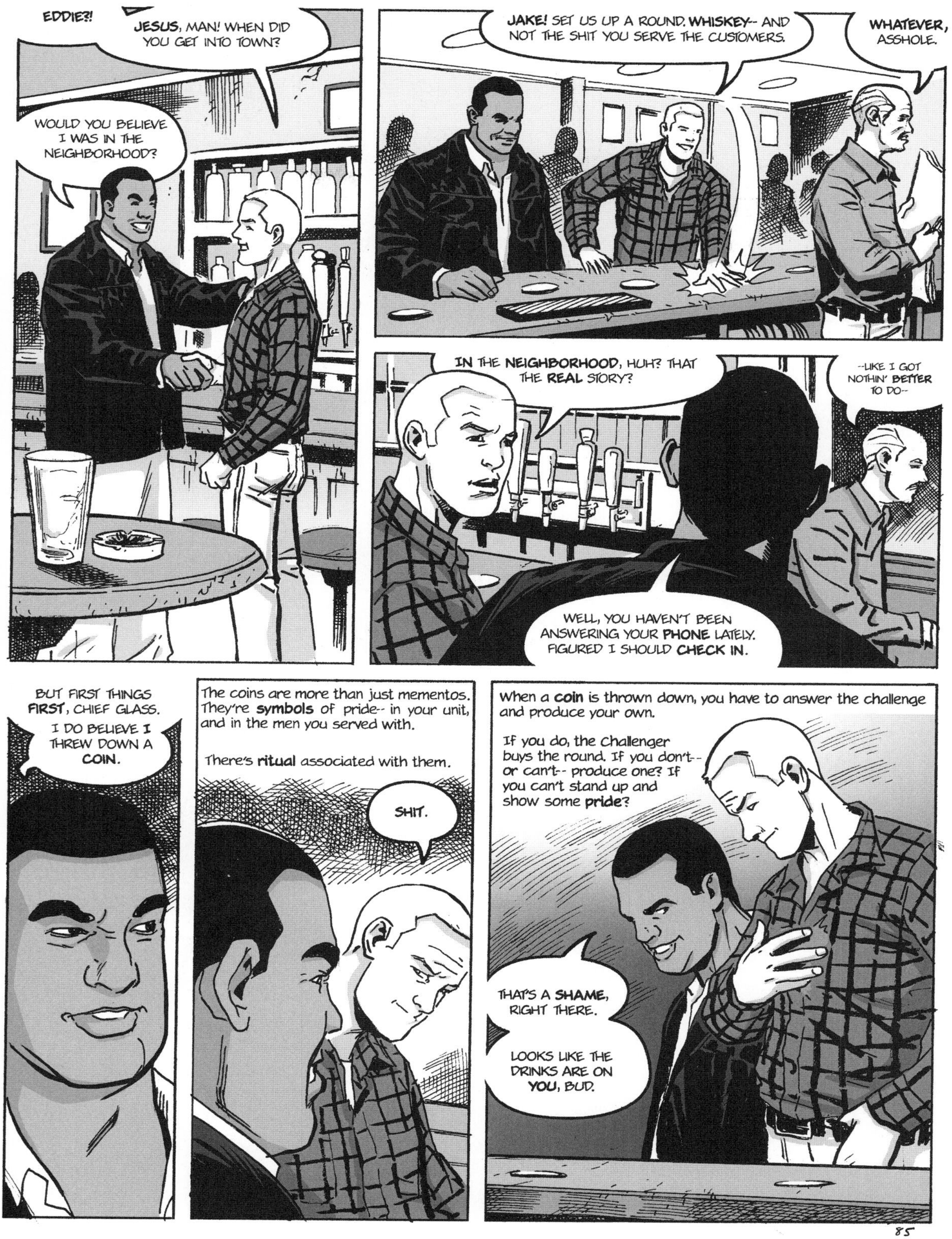

EDDIE?!
JESUS, MAN! WHEN DID YOU GET INTO TOWN?
WOULD YOU BELIEVE I WAS IN THE NEIGHBORHOOD?
JAKE! SET US UP A ROUND. WHISKEY-- AND NOT THE SHIT YOU SERVE THE CUSTOMERS.
WHATEVER, ASSHOLE.
IN THE NEIGHBORHOOD, HUH? THAT THE REAL STORY?
--LIKE I GOT NOTHIN' BETTER TO DO--
WELL, YOU HAVEN'T BEEN ANSWERING YOUR PHONE LATELY. FIGURED I SHOULD CHECK IN.
BUT FIRST THINGS FIRST, CHIEF GLASS.
I DO BELIEVE I THREW DOWN A COIN.
The coins are more than just mementos. They're symbols of pride-- in your unit, and in the men you served with.
There's ritual associated with them.
SHIT.
When a coin is thrown down, you have to answer the challenge and produce your own.
If you do, the challenger buys the round. If you don't-- or can't-- produce one? If you can't stand up and show some pride?
THAT'S A SHAME, RIGHT THERE.
LOOKS LIKE THE DRINKS ARE ON YOU, BUD.

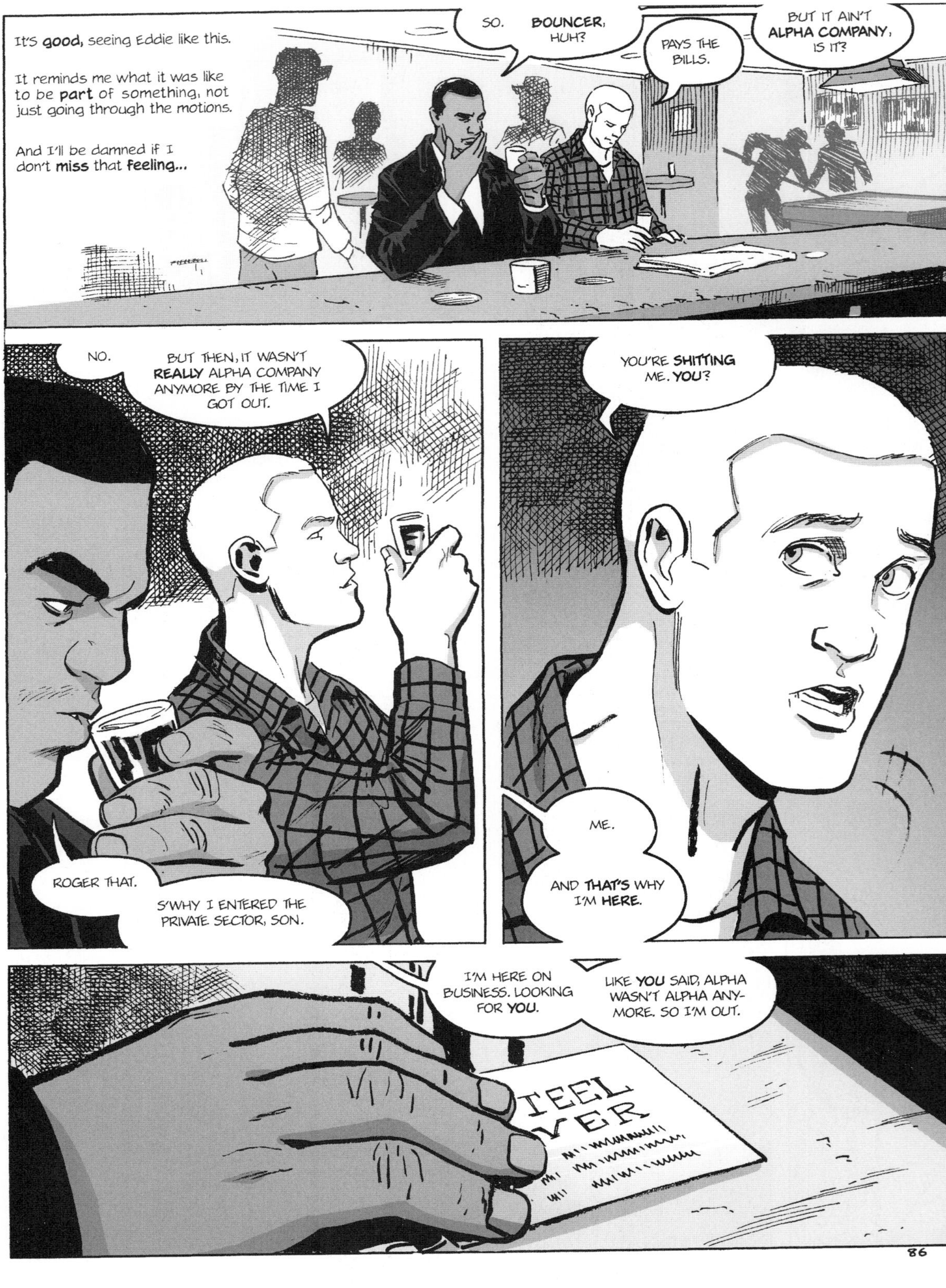

It's **good**, seeing Eddie like this.
It reminds me what it was like to be **part** of something, not just going through the motions.
And I'll be damned if I don't **miss** that **feeling...**
SO. **BOUNCER,** HUH?
PAYS THE BILLS.
BUT IT AIN'T **ALPHA COMPANY,** IS IT?
NO.
BUT THEN, IT WASN'T **REALLY** ALPHA COMPANY ANYMORE BY THE TIME I GOT OUT.
ROGER THAT.
S'WHY I ENTERED THE PRIVATE SECTOR, SON.
YOU'RE **SHITTING** ME. **YOU**?
ME.
AND **THAT'S** WHY I'M **HERE.**
I'M HERE ON BUSINESS. LOOKING FOR **YOU.**
LIKE **YOU** SAID, ALPHA WASN'T ALPHA ANY-MORE. SO I'M OUT.
TEEL
VER

OKAY, NOW I **KNOW** YOU'RE PULLING MY LEG.

I CAN'T BELIEVE YOU SIGNED UP WITH SOME **MERC** OUTFIT. HOW THE FUCK DID **THAT** HAPPEN?

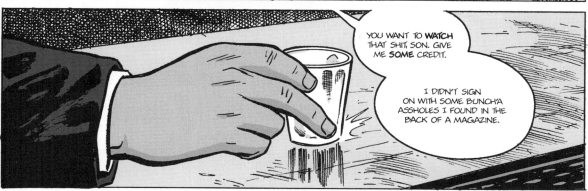

YOU WANT TO **WATCH** THAT SHIT, SON. GIVE ME **SOME** CREDIT.

I DIDN'T SIGN ON WITH SOME BUNCH'A ASSHOLES I FOUND IN THE BACK OF A MAGAZINE.

YOU'VE SEEN THE NEWS. THERE'S A WHOLE NEW **BREED** OF THESE GROUPS, WORKING GOVERNMENT CONTRACTS.

SHIT, I HADDA SIGN A **LOYALTY OATH** TO THE **COUNTRY** AND THE **CONSTITUTION** BEFORE I COULD HOOK UP WITH 'EM.

THERE'S GOOD ONES AND BAD ONES, AND I'M TELLING YOU, NO BULLSHIT, THESE GUYS ARE **TOP SHELF.**

YEAH, WELL, I'VE SEEN A COUPLE OF THE IDIOTS FROM THE **BOTTOM** SHELF.

WE **BOTH** SAW THESE PRIVATE MILITARY GUYS BACK IN THE DESERT. PASCO USED TO CALL 'EM "**RENT-A-WARRIORS.**"

"YOU REMEMBER THAT HALF-ASSED **PISTOL RANGE** WE SET UP TO KILL TIME IN **BAGHDAD**?"

"WE SHARED IT WITH THE LOCAL **FRIENDLIES**. SOMETIMES WE'D GET THE **PRIVATE SECURITY** GUYS, BUT THEY SPENT MORE TIME SHOOTING THE **SHIT** THAN SHOOTING **TARGETS**."

"ALWAYS FELT GOOD, YOU KNOW? SPEND A HALF HOUR, PUNCHING HOLES IN PAPER."

"THERAPEUTIC."

CH-CHK!

"SO, I'VE EMPTIED A COUPLE MAGAZINES. I'M BARELY THERE **FIVE MINUTES**, AND THIS GUY I'D SEEN AROUND A COUPLE TIMES STARTS A CONVERSATION."

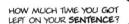

THAT'S SOME NICE **SHOOTING**, SON.

YOU'VE GOT **SKILLS**.

HOW MUCH TIME YOU GOT LEFT ON YOUR **SENTENCE**?

NOT MUCH.

WELL, IF YOU'RE LOOKING FOR **WORK** WHEN YOU GET **FREE**...

...GIVE ME A **CALL**. I COULD **USE** SOMEONE WHO CAN SHOOT AS WELL AS YOU.

FORCE OPS.

"I MEAN, **SERIOUSLY**? THIS GUY SEES ME SHOOT FOR **FIVE MINUTES** AND HE WANTS TO HIRE ME?"

"WHO THE FUCK'D WANT TO BE ON **THAT** TEAM? RIDING INTO A FIREFIGHT WITH A BUNCH OF COWBOYS?"

FAIR ENOUGH. BUT I'LL TELL YOU THIS: I'M IN A **GOOD** OUTFIT, AND IT'S A **GOOD** OFFER.

I TOLD 'EM TO EXPECT YOU--

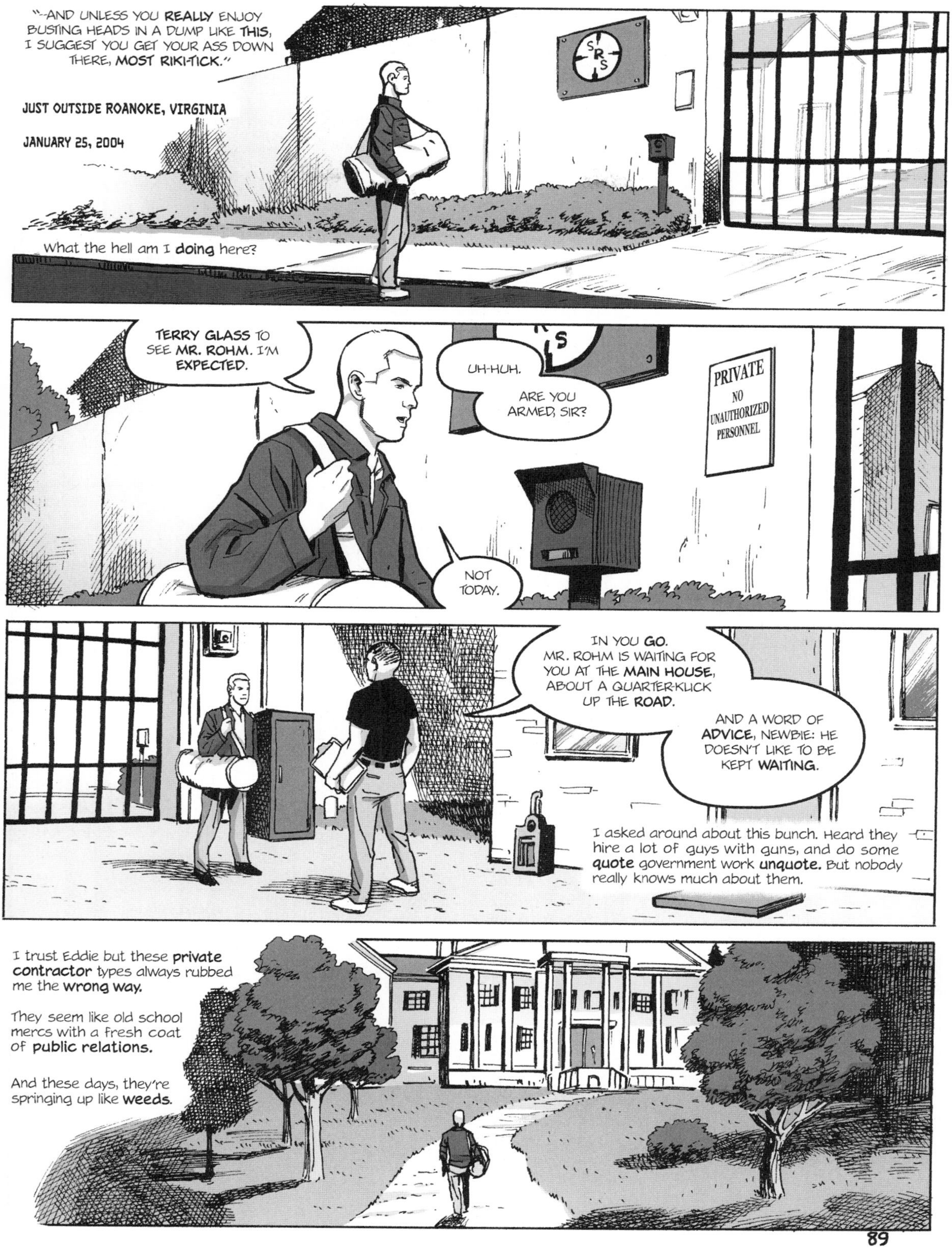
"--AND UNLESS YOU REALLY ENJOY BUSTING HEADS IN A DUMP LIKE THIS, I SUGGEST YOU GET YOUR ASS DOWN THERE, MOST RIKI-TICK."
JUST OUTSIDE ROANOKE, VIRGINIA
JANUARY 25, 2004
What the hell am I doing here?
TERRY GLASS TO SEE MR. ROHM. I'M EXPECTED.
UH-HUH.
ARE YOU ARMED, SIR?
PRIVATE NO UNAUTHORIZED PERSONNEL
NOT TODAY.
IN YOU GO. MR. ROHM IS WAITING FOR YOU AT THE MAIN HOUSE, ABOUT A QUARTER-KLICK UP THE ROAD.
AND A WORD OF ADVICE, NEWBIE: HE DOESN'T LIKE TO BE KEPT WAITING.
I asked around about this bunch. Heard they hire a lot of guys with guns, and do some quote government work unquote. But nobody really knows much about them.
I trust Eddie but these private contractor types always rubbed me the wrong way.
They seem like old school mercs with a fresh coat of public relations.
And these days, they're springing up like weeds.

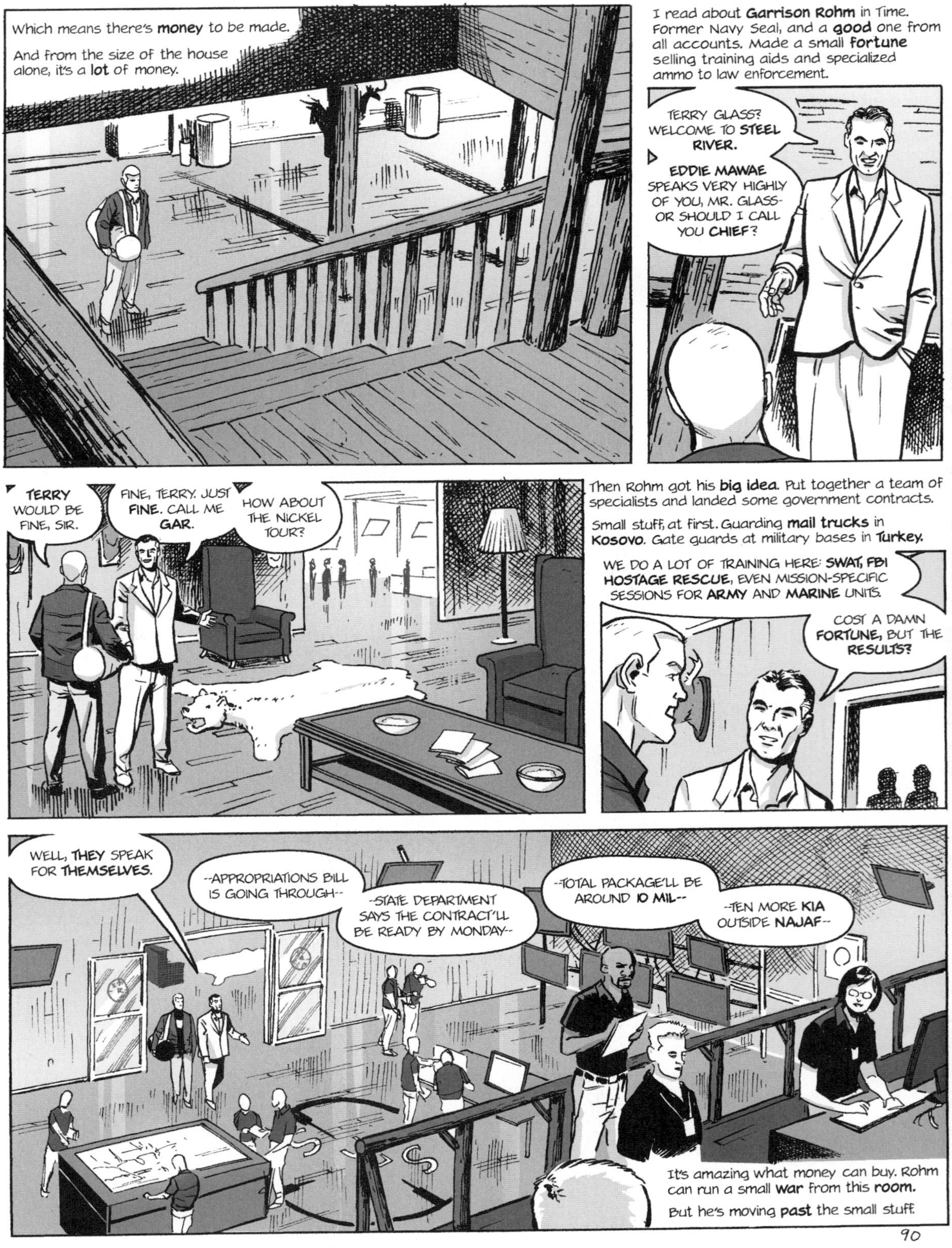

Which means there's **money** to be made.
And from the size of the house alone, it's a **lot** of money.
I read about **Garrison Rohm** in Time. Former Navy Seal, and a **good** one from all accounts. Made a small **fortune** selling training aids and specialized ammo to law enforcement.
TERRY GLASS? WELCOME TO **STEEL RIVER.**
EDDIE MAWAE SPEAKS VERY HIGHLY OF YOU, MR. GLASS-OR SHOULD I CALL YOU **CHIEF**?
TERRY WOULD BE FINE, SIR.
FINE, TERRY. JUST **FINE**. CALL ME **GAR**.
HOW ABOUT THE NICKEL TOUR?
Then Rohm got his **big idea**. Put together a team of specialists and landed some government contracts.
Small stuff, at first. Guarding **mail trucks** in **Kosovo**. Gate guards at military bases in **Turkey**.
WE DO A LOT OF TRAINING HERE: **SWAT, FBI HOSTAGE RESCUE**, EVEN MISSION-SPECIFIC SESSIONS FOR **ARMY** AND **MARINE** UNITS.
COST A DAMN **FORTUNE**, BUT THE **RESULTS**?
WELL, **THEY** SPEAK FOR **THEMSELVES**.
--APPROPRIATIONS BILL IS GOING THROUGH--
--STATE DEPARTMENT SAYS THE CONTRACT'LL BE READY BY MONDAY--
--TOTAL PACKAGE'LL BE AROUND **10 MIL**--
--TEN MORE **KIA** OUTSIDE **NAJAF**--
It's amazing what money can buy. Rohm can run a small **war** from this **room**.
But he's moving **past** the small stuff.

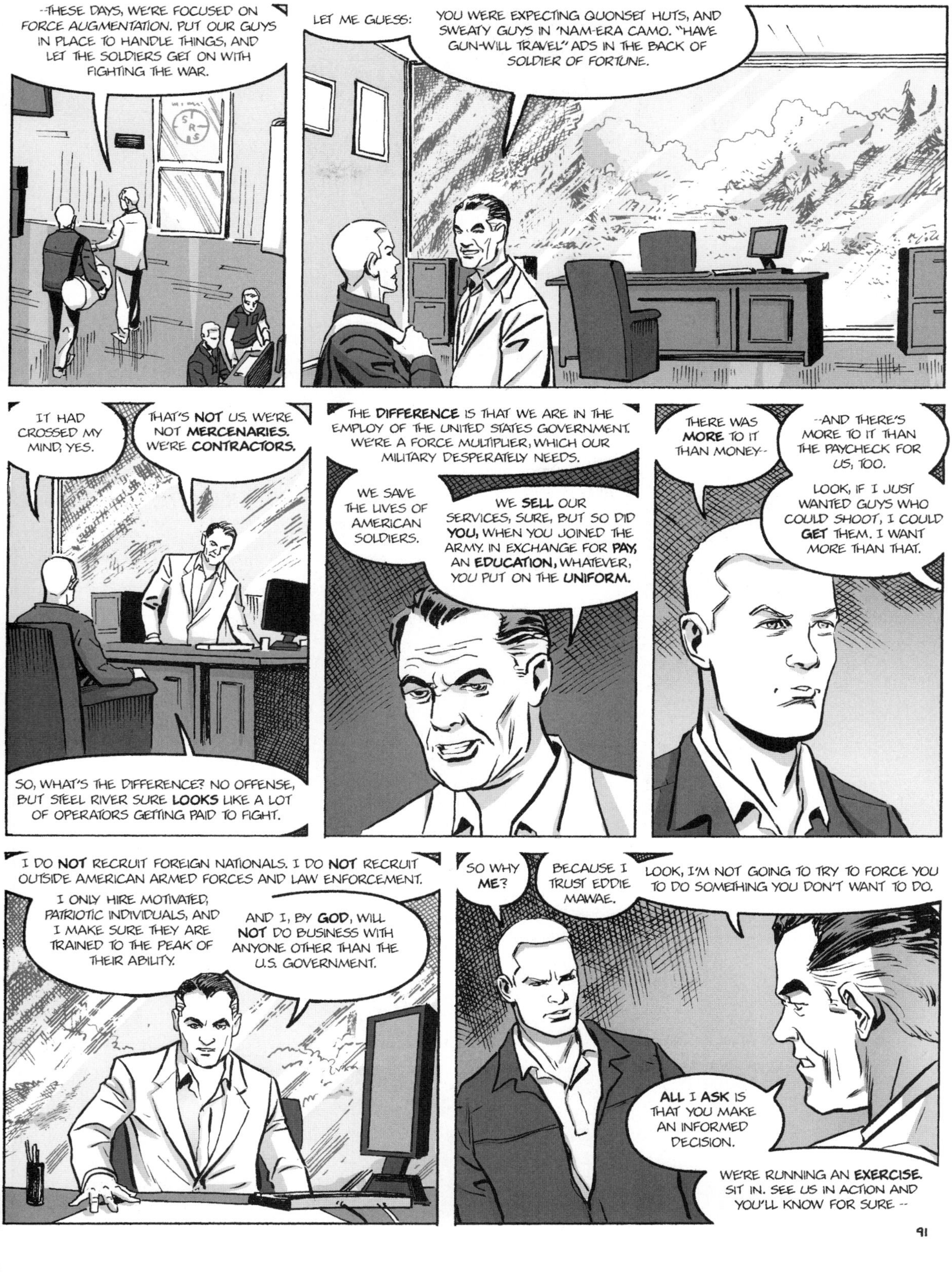
--THESE DAYS, WE'RE FOCUSED ON FORCE AUGMENTATION. PUT OUR GUYS IN PLACE TO HANDLE THINGS, AND LET THE SOLDIERS GET ON WITH FIGHTING THE WAR.
LET ME GUESS:
YOU WERE EXPECTING QUONSET HUTS, AND SWEATY GUYS IN 'NAM-ERA CAMO. "HAVE GUN-WILL TRAVEL" ADS IN THE BACK OF SOLDIER OF FORTUNE.
IT HAD CROSSED MY MIND, YES.
THAT'S NOT US. WE'RE NOT MERCENARIES. WE'RE CONTRACTORS.
SO, WHAT'S THE DIFFERENCE? NO OFFENSE, BUT STEEL RIVER SURE LOOKS LIKE A LOT OF OPERATORS GETTING PAID TO FIGHT.
THE DIFFERENCE IS THAT WE ARE IN THE EMPLOY OF THE UNITED STATES GOVERNMENT. WE'RE A FORCE MULTIPLIER, WHICH OUR MILITARY DESPERATELY NEEDS.
WE SAVE THE LIVES OF AMERICAN SOLDIERS.
WE SELL OUR SERVICES, SURE, BUT SO DID YOU, WHEN YOU JOINED THE ARMY. IN EXCHANGE FOR PAY, AN EDUCATION, WHATEVER, YOU PUT ON THE UNIFORM.
THERE WAS MORE TO IT THAN MONEY--
--AND THERE'S MORE TO IT THAN THE PAYCHECK FOR US, TOO.
LOOK, IF I JUST WANTED GUYS WHO COULD SHOOT, I COULD GET THEM. I WANT MORE THAN THAT.
I DO NOT RECRUIT FOREIGN NATIONALS. I DO NOT RECRUIT OUTSIDE AMERICAN ARMED FORCES AND LAW ENFORCEMENT.
I ONLY HIRE MOTIVATED, PATRIOTIC INDIVIDUALS, AND I MAKE SURE THEY ARE TRAINED TO THE PEAK OF THEIR ABILITY.
AND I, BY GOD, WILL NOT DO BUSINESS WITH ANYONE OTHER THAN THE U.S. GOVERNMENT.
SO WHY ME?
BECAUSE I TRUST EDDIE MAWAE.
LOOK, I'M NOT GOING TO TRY TO FORCE YOU TO DO SOMETHING YOU DON'T WANT TO DO.
ALL I ASK IS THAT YOU MAKE AN INFORMED DECISION.
WE'RE RUNNING AN EXERCISE. SIT IN. SEE US IN ACTION AND YOU'LL KNOW FOR SURE --

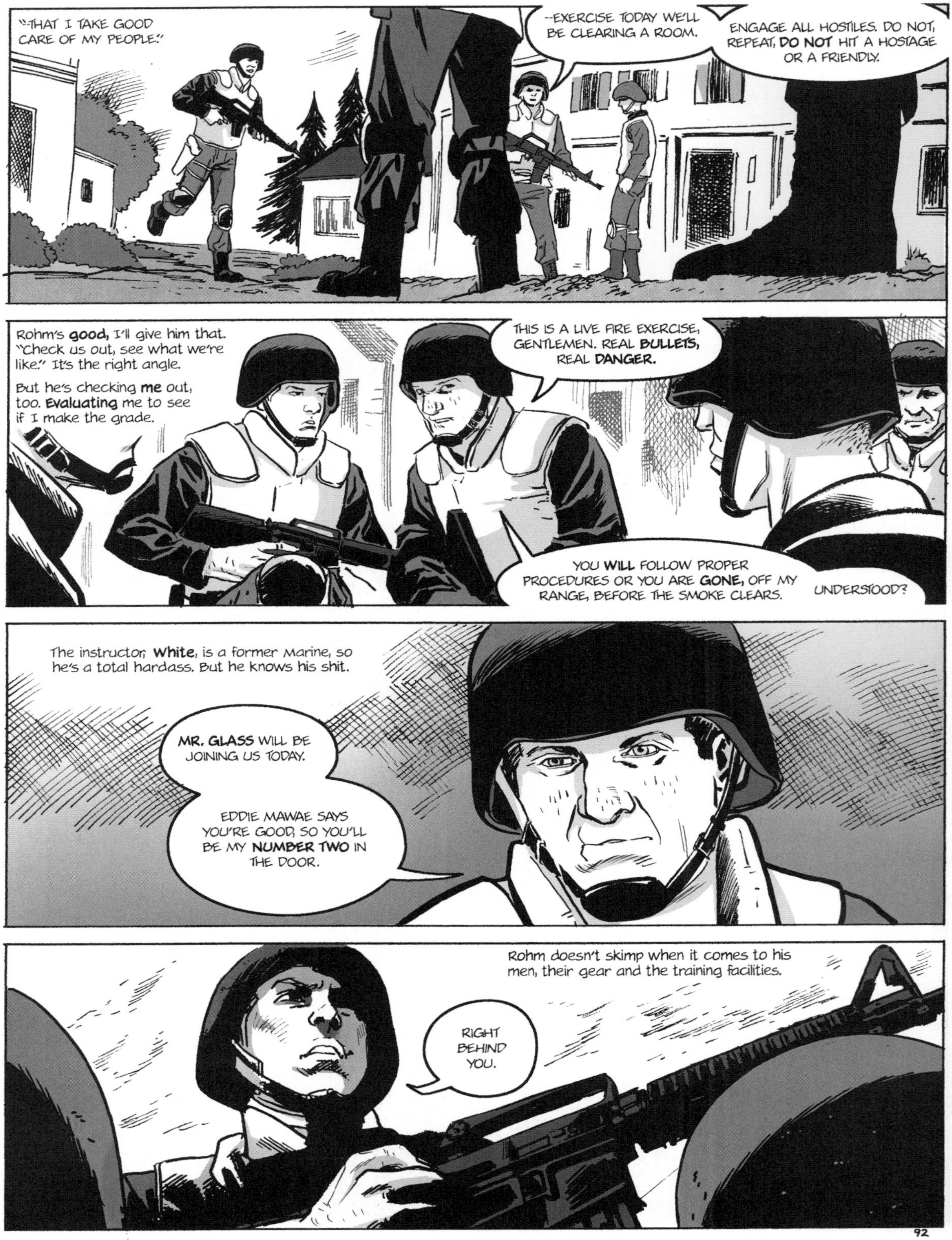
"--THAT I TAKE GOOD CARE OF MY PEOPLE."
--EXERCISE TODAY WE'LL BE CLEARING A ROOM.
ENGAGE ALL HOSTILES. DO NOT, REPEAT, DO NOT HIT A HOSTAGE OR A FRIENDLY.
Rohm's good, I'll give him that. "Check us out, see what we're like." It's the right angle.
But he's checking me out, too. Evaluating me to see if I make the grade.
THIS IS A LIVE FIRE EXERCISE, GENTLEMEN. REAL BULLETS, REAL DANGER.
YOU WILL FOLLOW PROPER PROCEDURES OR YOU ARE GONE, OFF MY RANGE, BEFORE THE SMOKE CLEARS.
UNDERSTOOD?
The instructor, White, is a former Marine, so he's a total hardass. But he knows his shit.
MR. GLASS WILL BE JOINING US TODAY.
EDDIE MAWAE SAYS YOU'RE GOOD, SO YOU'LL BE MY NUMBER TWO IN THE DOOR.
Rohm doesn't skimp when it comes to his men, their gear and the training facilities.
RIGHT BEHIND YOU.

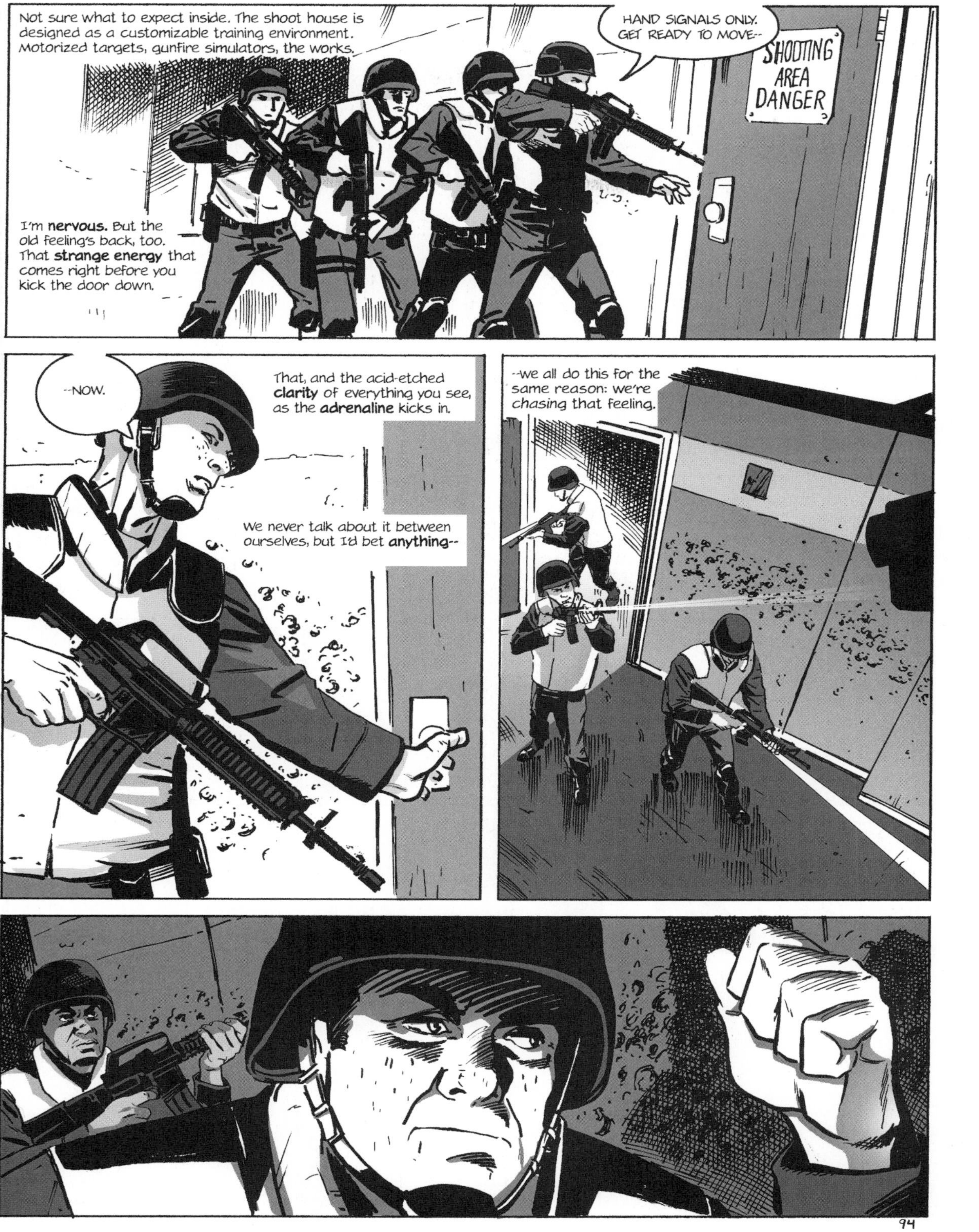
Not sure what to expect inside. The shoot house is designed as a customizable training environment. Motorized targets, gunfire simulators, the works.
HAND SIGNALS ONLY. GET READY TO MOVE--
SHOOTING AREA DANGER
I'm nervous. But the old feeling's back, too. That strange energy that comes right before you kick the door down.
--NOW.
That, and the acid-etched clarity of everything you see, as the adrenaline kicks in.
We never talk about it between ourselves, but I'd bet anything--
--we all do this for the same reason: we're chasing that feeling.

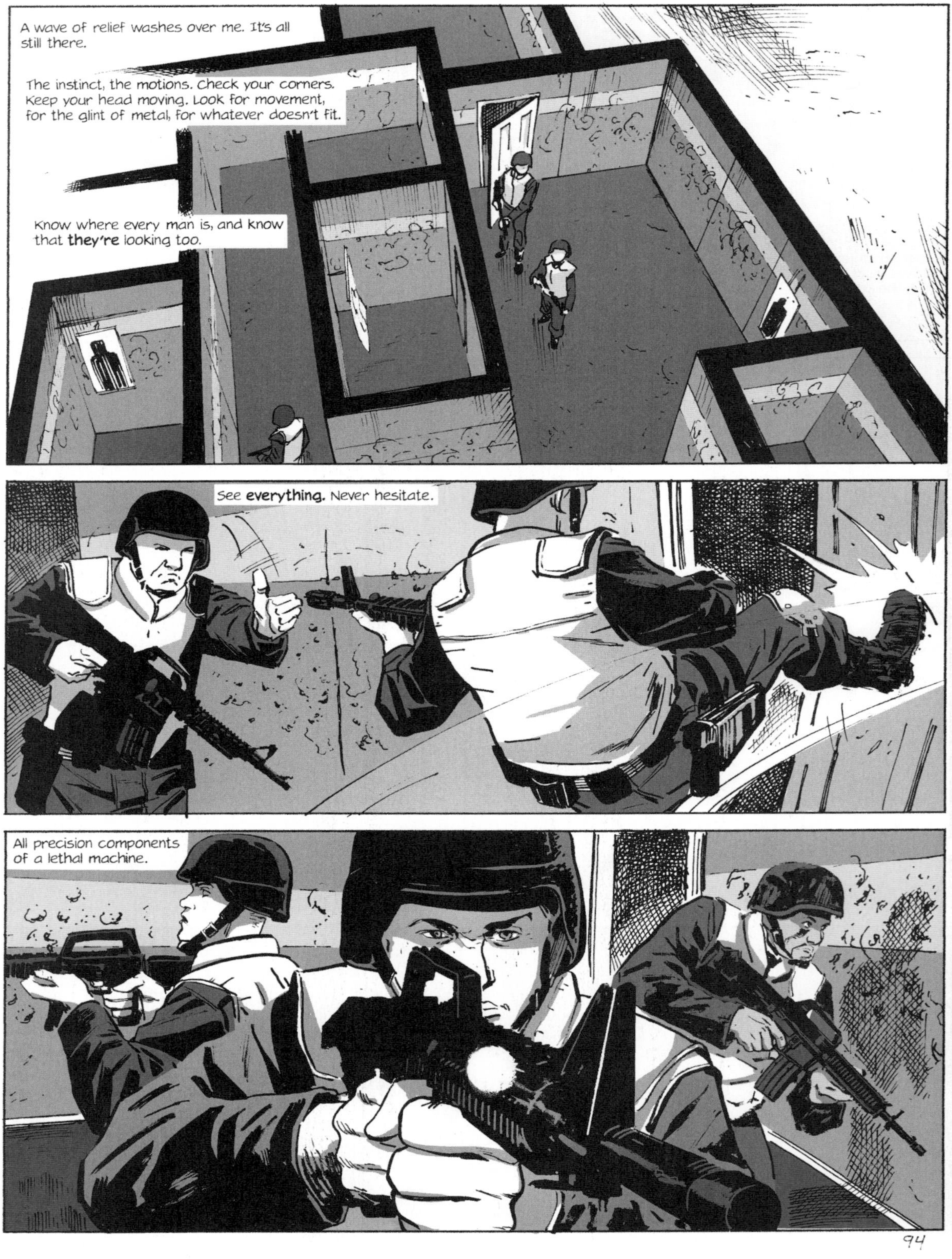
A wave of relief washes over me. It's all still there.
The instinct, the motions. Check your corners. Keep your head moving. Look for movement, for the glint of metal, for whatever doesn't fit.
Know where every man is, and know that **they're** looking too.
See **everything.** Never hesitate.
All precision components of a lethal machine.

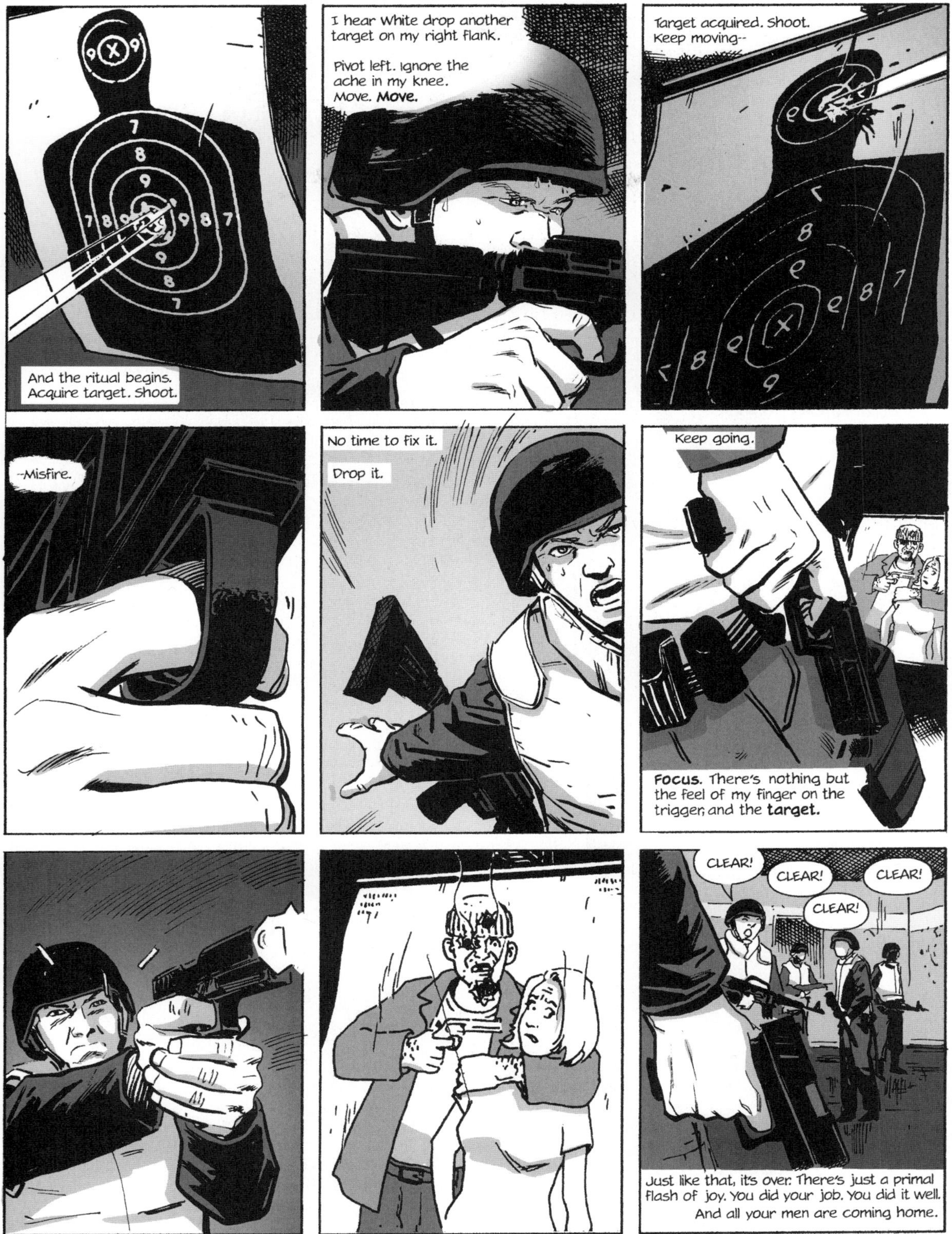

And the ritual begins. Acquire target. Shoot.
I hear White drop another target on my right flank.
Pivot left. Ignore the ache in my knee. Move. **Move.**
Target acquired. Shoot. Keep moving--
--Misfire.
No time to fix it.
Drop it.
Keep going.
Focus. There's nothing but the feel of my finger on the trigger, and the **target.**
CLEAR!
CLEAR!
CLEAR!
CLEAR!
Just like that, it's over. There's just a primal flash of joy. You did your job. You did it well. And all your men are coming home.

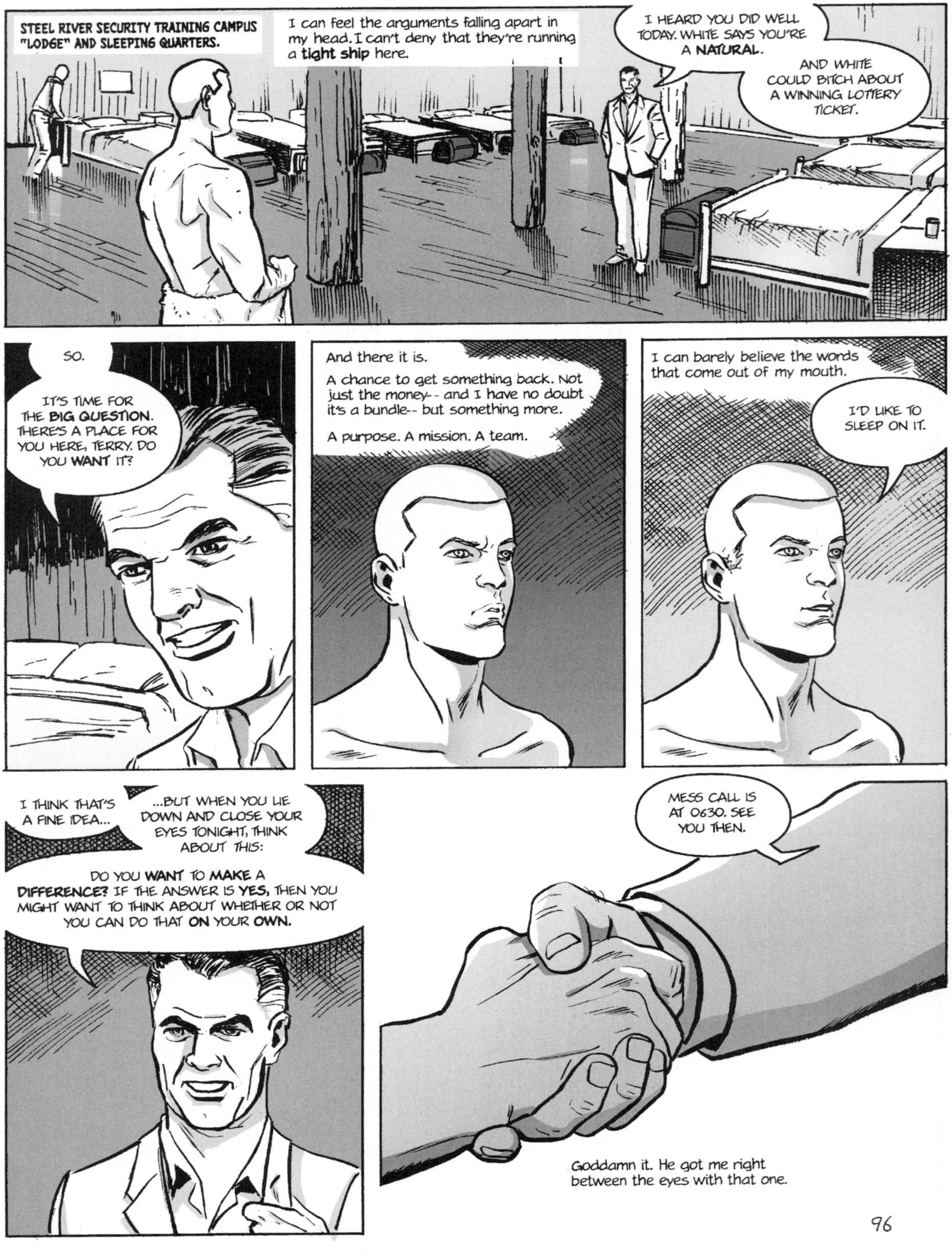
STEEL RIVER SECURITY TRAINING CAMPUS "LODGE" AND SLEEPING QUARTERS.
I can feel the arguments falling apart in my head. I can't deny that they're running a tight ship here.
I HEARD YOU DID WELL TODAY. WHITE SAYS YOU'RE A NATURAL.
AND WHITE COULD BITCH ABOUT A WINNING LOTTERY TICKET.
SO.
IT'S TIME FOR THE BIG QUESTION. THERE'S A PLACE FOR YOU HERE, TERRY. DO YOU WANT IT?
And there it is.
A chance to get something back. Not just the money-- and I have no doubt it's a bundle-- but something more.
A purpose. A mission. A team.
I can barely believe the words that come out of my mouth.
I'D LIKE TO SLEEP ON IT.
I THINK THAT'S A FINE IDEA...
...BUT WHEN YOU LIE DOWN AND CLOSE YOUR EYES TONIGHT, THINK ABOUT THIS:
DO YOU WANT TO MAKE A DIFFERENCE? IF THE ANSWER IS YES, THEN YOU MIGHT WANT TO THINK ABOUT WHETHER OR NOT YOU CAN DO THAT ON YOUR OWN.
MESS CALL IS AT 0630. SEE YOU THEN.
Goddamn it. He got me right between the eyes with that one.

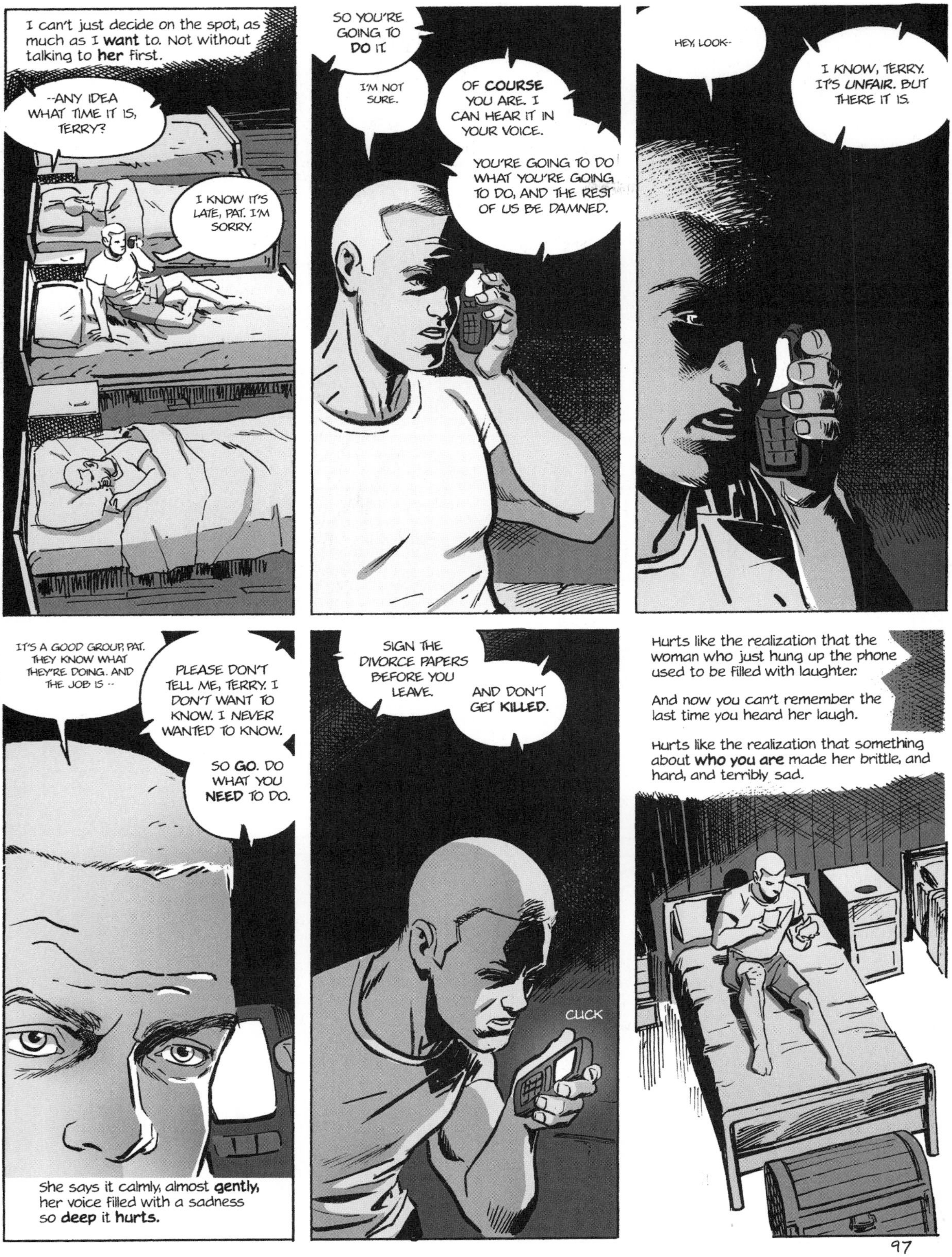
I can't just decide on the spot, as much as I **want** to. Not without talking to **her** first.
--ANY IDEA WHAT TIME IT IS, TERRY?
I KNOW IT'S LATE, PAT. I'M SORRY.
SO YOU'RE GOING TO **DO** IT.
I'M NOT SURE.
OF **COURSE** YOU ARE. I CAN HEAR IT IN YOUR VOICE.
YOU'RE GOING TO DO WHAT YOU'RE GOING TO DO, AND THE REST OF US BE DAMNED.
HEY, LOOK--
I KNOW, TERRY. IT'S **UNFAIR**. BUT THERE IT IS.
IT'S A *GOOD* GROUP, PAT. THEY KNOW WHAT THEY'RE DOING. AND THE JOB IS --
PLEASE DON'T TELL ME, TERRY. I DON'T WANT TO KNOW. I NEVER WANTED TO KNOW.
SO **GO**. DO WHAT YOU **NEED** TO DO.
She says it calmly, almost **gently**, her voice filled with a sadness so **deep** it **hurts.**
SIGN THE DIVORCE PAPERS BEFORE YOU LEAVE.
AND DON'T GET **KILLED**.
CLICK
Hurts like the realization that the woman who just hung up the phone used to be filled with laughter.
And now you can't remember the last time you heard her laugh.
Hurts like the realization that something about **who you are** made her brittle, and hard, and terribly sad.

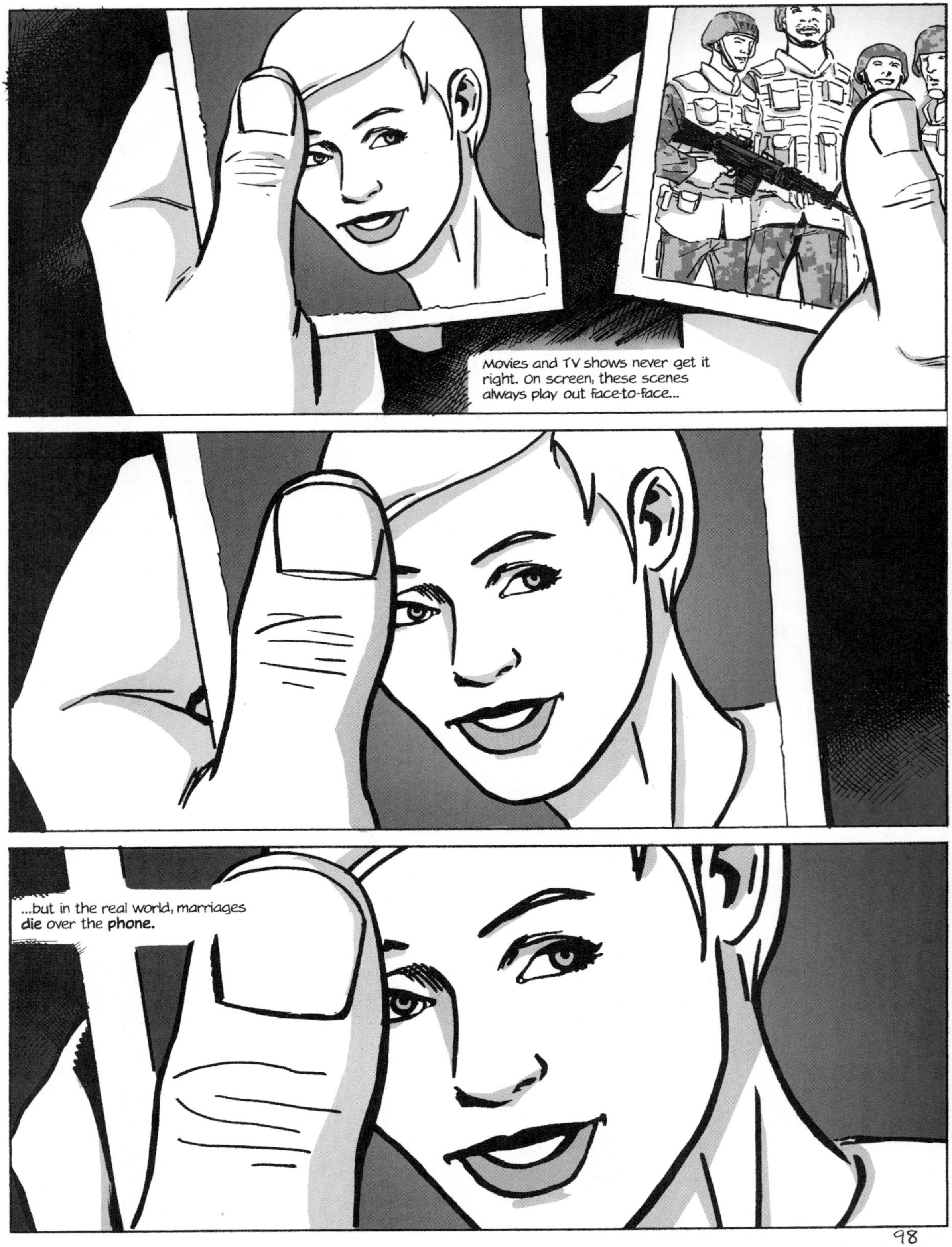
Movies and TV shows never get it right. On screen, these scenes always play out face-to-face...
...but in the real world, marriages **die** over the **phone.**

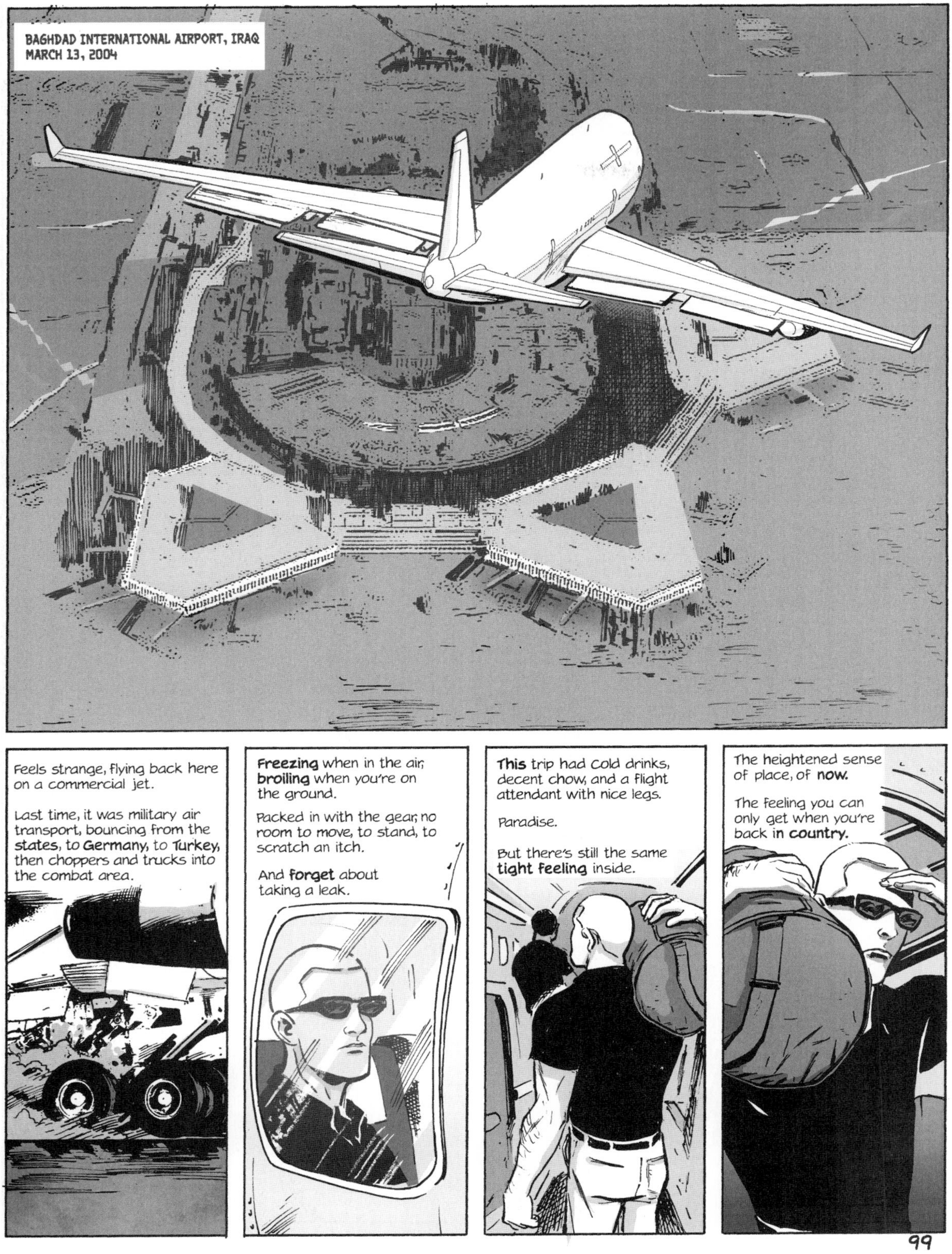
BAGHDAD INTERNATIONAL AIRPORT, IRAQ
MARCH 13, 2004
Feels strange, flying back here on a commercial jet.
Last time, it was military air transport, bouncing from the states, to Germany, to Turkey, then choppers and trucks into the combat area.
Freezing when in the air, broiling when you're on the ground.
Packed in with the gear, no room to move, to stand, to scratch an itch.
And forget about taking a leak.
This trip had cold drinks, decent chow, and a flight attendant with nice legs.
Paradise.
But there's still the same tight feeling inside.
The heightened sense of place, of now.
The feeling you can only get when you're back in country.

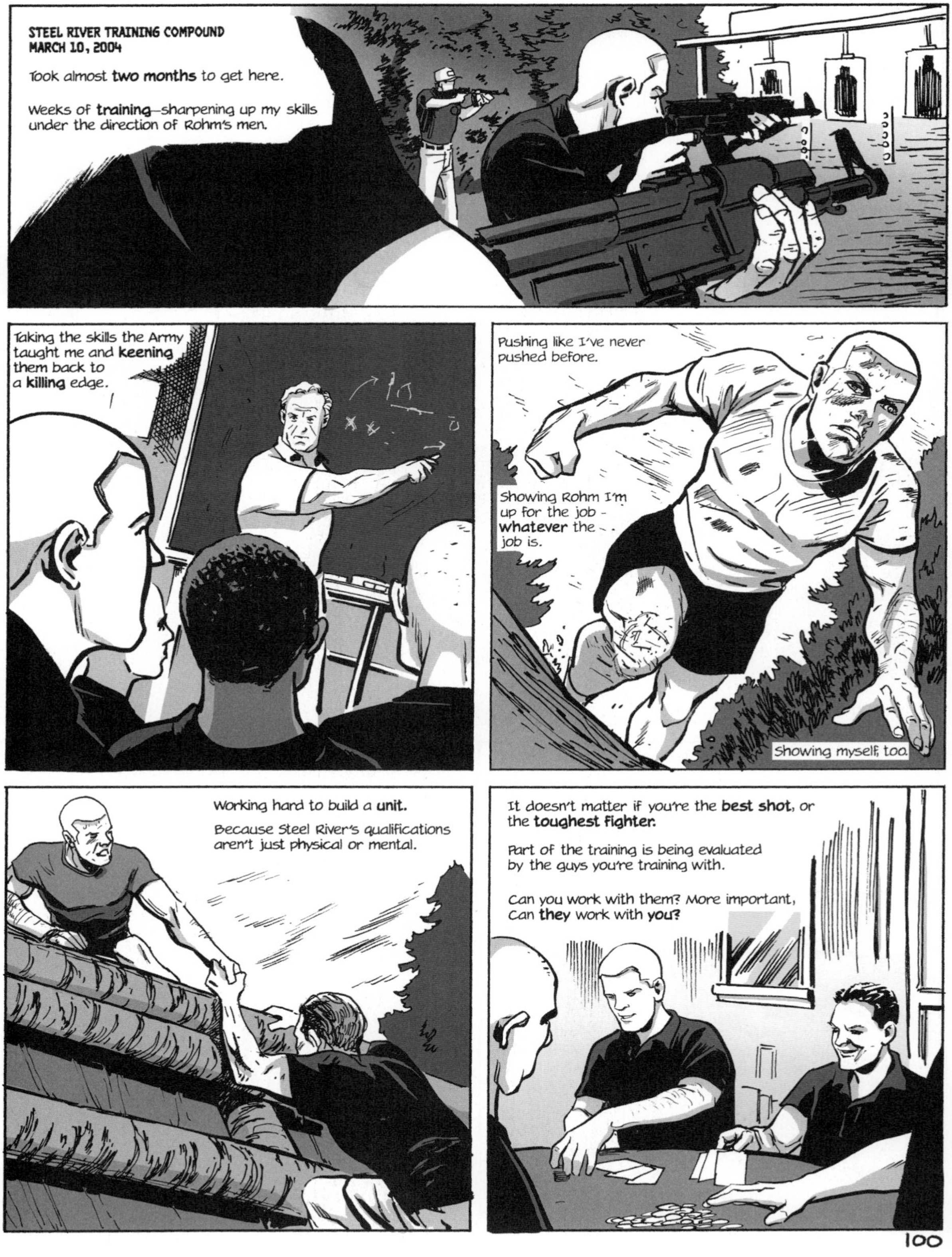
STEEL RIVER TRAINING COMPOUND
MARCH 10, 2004
Took almost **two months** to get here.
Weeks of **training**—sharpening up my skills under the direction of Rohm's men.
Taking the skills the Army taught me and **keening** them back to a **killing** edge.
Pushing like I've never pushed before.
Showing Rohm I'm up for the job - **whatever** the job is.
Showing myself, too.
Working hard to build a **unit.**
Because Steel River's qualifications aren't just physical or mental.
It doesn't matter if you're the **best shot**, or the **toughest fighter.**
Part of the training is being evaluated by the guys you're training with.
Can you work with them? More important, Can **they** work with **you?**

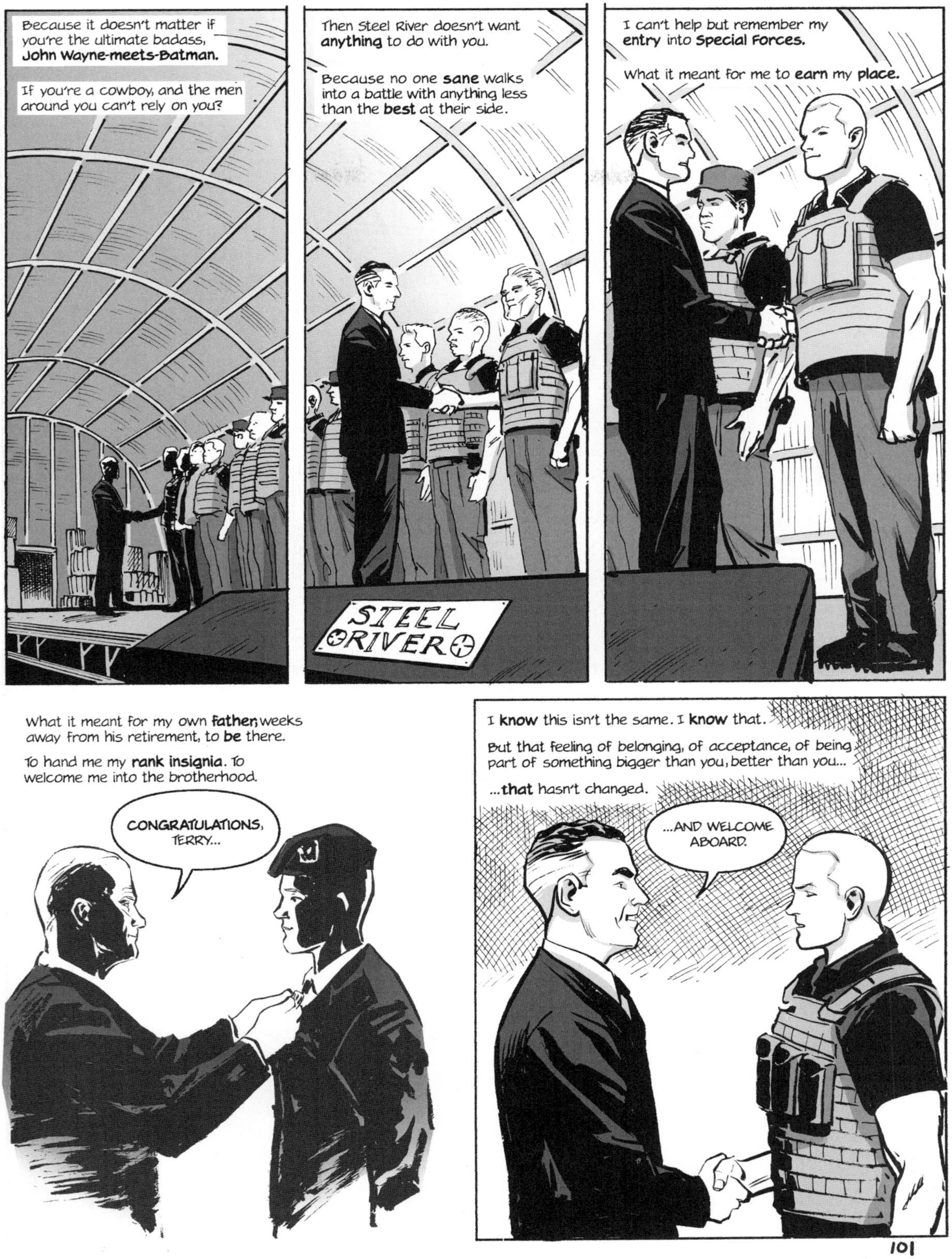
Because it doesn't matter if you're the ultimate badass, **John Wayne-meets-Batman.**
If you're a cowboy, and the men around you can't rely on you?
Then Steel River doesn't want **anything** to do with you.
Because no one **sane** walks into a battle with anything less than the **best** at their side.
STEEL RIVER
I can't help but remember my **entry** into **Special Forces.**
What it meant for me to **earn** my **place.**
What it meant for my own **father,** weeks away from his retirement, to **be** there.
To hand me my **rank insignia**. To welcome me into the brotherhood.
CONGRATULATIONS, TERRY...
I **know** this isn't the same. I **know** that.
But that feeling of belonging, of acceptance, of being part of something bigger than you, better than you...
...**that** hasn't changed.
...AND WELCOME ABOARD.

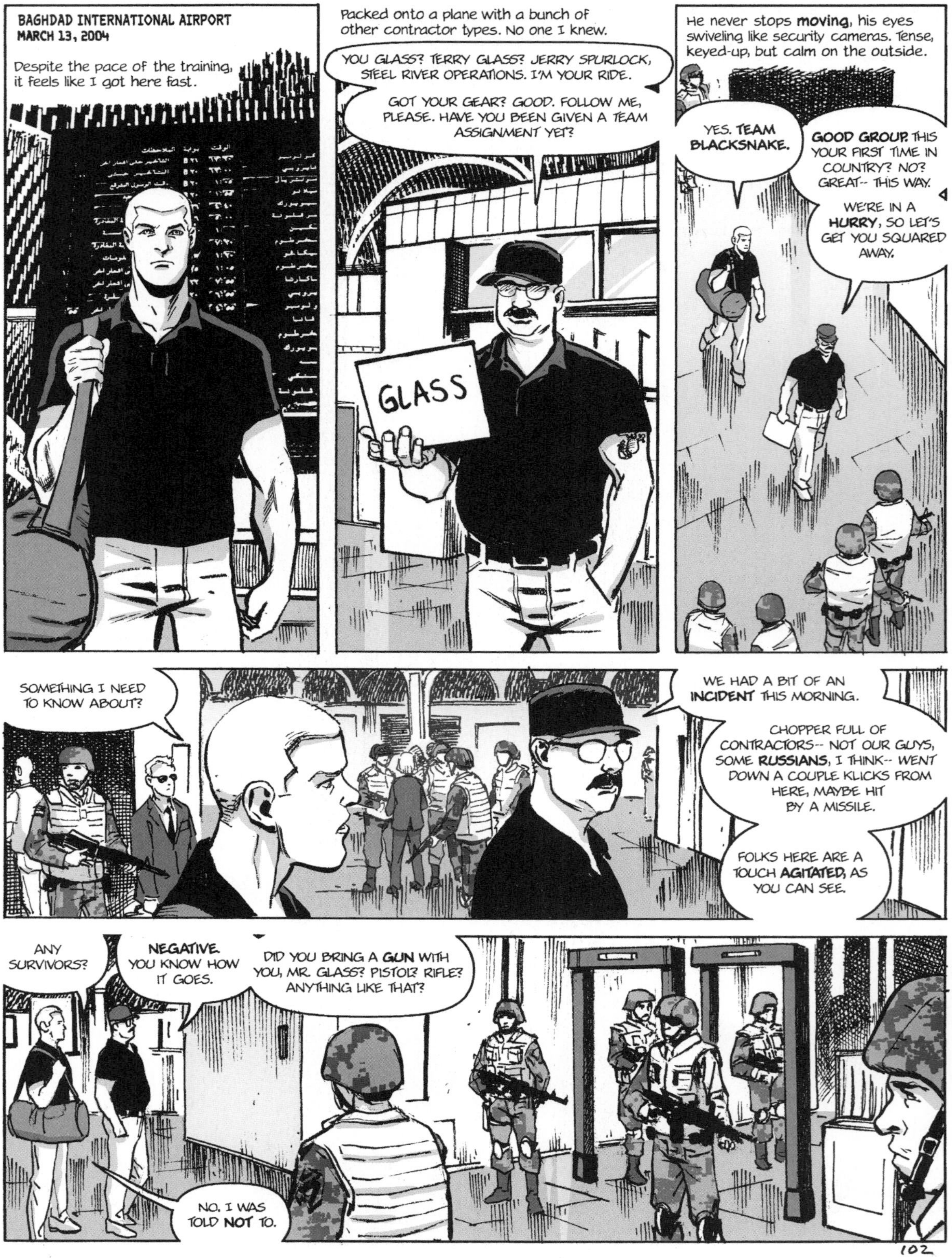
BAGHDAD INTERNATIONAL AIRPORT
MARCH 13, 2004
Despite the pace of the training, it feels like I got here fast.
Packed onto a plane with a bunch of other contractor types. No one I knew.
YOU GLASS? TERRY GLASS? JERRY SPURLOCK, STEEL RIVER OPERATIONS. I'M YOUR RIDE.
GOT YOUR GEAR? GOOD. FOLLOW ME, PLEASE. HAVE YOU BEEN GIVEN A TEAM ASSIGNMENT YET?
GLASS
He never stops **moving**, his eyes swiveling like security cameras. Tense, keyed-up, but calm on the outside.
YES. **TEAM BLACKSNAKE.**
GOOD GROUP. THIS YOUR FIRST TIME IN COUNTRY? NO? GREAT-- THIS WAY.
WE'RE IN A **HURRY**, SO LET'S GET YOU SQUARED AWAY.
SOMETHING I NEED TO KNOW ABOUT?
WE HAD A BIT OF AN **INCIDENT** THIS MORNING.
CHOPPER FULL OF CONTRACTORS-- NOT OUR GUYS, SOME **RUSSIANS**, I THINK-- WENT DOWN A COUPLE KLICKS FROM HERE, MAYBE HIT BY A MISSILE.
FOLKS HERE ARE A TOUCH **AGITATED**, AS YOU CAN SEE.
ANY SURVIVORS?
NEGATIVE. YOU KNOW HOW IT GOES.
DID YOU BRING A **GUN** WITH YOU, MR. GLASS? PISTOL? RIFLE? ANYTHING LIKE THAT?
NO. I WAS TOLD **NOT** TO.

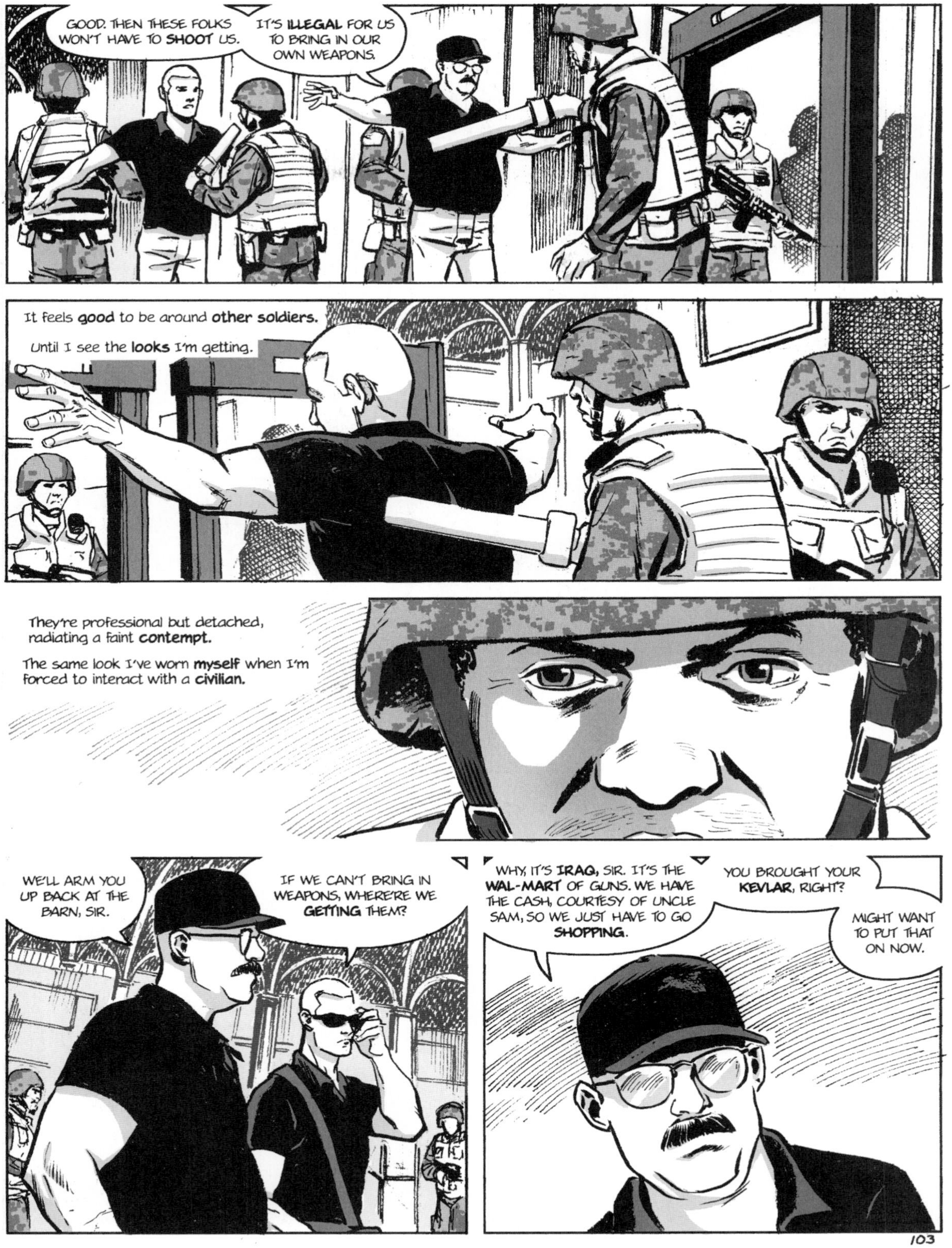
GOOD. THEN THESE FOLKS WON'T HAVE TO SHOOT US.
IT'S ILLEGAL FOR US TO BRING IN OUR OWN WEAPONS.
It feels good to be around other soldiers.
Until I see the looks I'm getting.
They're professional but detached, radiating a faint contempt.
The same look I've worn myself when I'm forced to interact with a civilian.
IF WE CAN'T BRING IN WEAPONS, WHERE'RE WE GETTING THEM?
WE'LL ARM YOU UP BACK AT THE BARN, SIR.
WHY, IT'S IRAQ, SIR. IT'S THE WAL-MART OF GUNS. WE HAVE THE CASH, COURTESY OF UNCLE SAM, SO WE JUST HAVE TO GO SHOPPING.
YOU BROUGHT YOUR KEVLAR, RIGHT?
MIGHT WANT TO PUT THAT ON NOW.

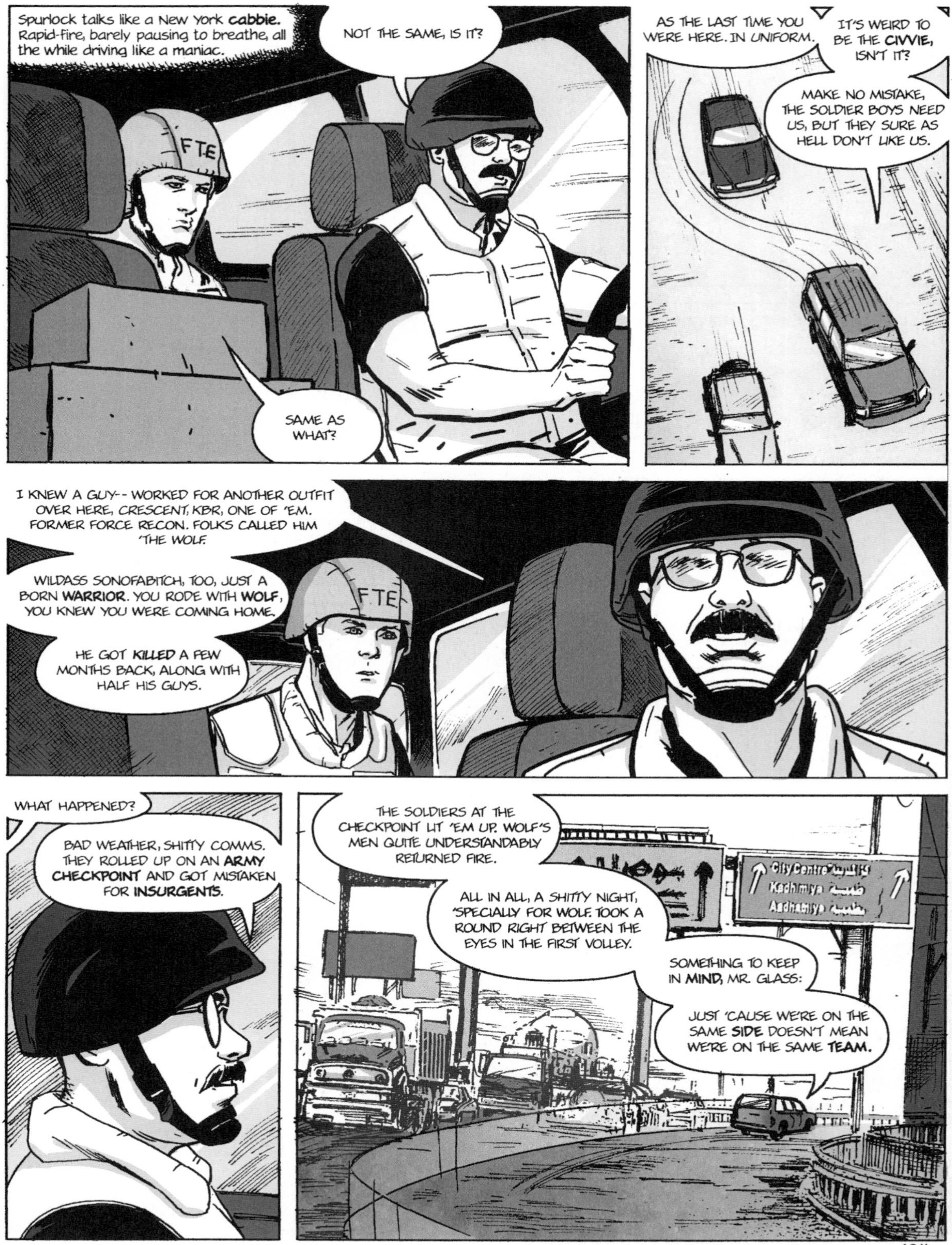

Spurlock talks like a New York **cabbie.** Rapid-fire, barely pausing to breathe, all the while driving like a maniac.
NOT THE SAME, IS IT?
SAME AS WHAT?
AS THE LAST TIME YOU WERE HERE. IN UNIFORM.
IT'S WEIRD TO BE THE **CIVVIE,** ISN'T IT?
MAKE NO MISTAKE, THE SOLDIER BOYS NEED US, BUT THEY SURE AS HELL DON'T LIKE US.
I KNEW A GUY-- WORKED FOR ANOTHER OUTFIT OVER HERE, CRESCENT, KBR, ONE OF 'EM. FORMER FORCE RECON. FOLKS CALLED HIM 'THE WOLF.'
WILDASS SONOFABITCH, TOO, JUST A BORN **WARRIOR**. YOU RODE WITH **WOLF**, YOU KNEW YOU WERE COMING HOME.
HE GOT **KILLED** A FEW MONTHS BACK, ALONG WITH HALF HIS GUYS.
FTE
WHAT HAPPENED?
BAD WEATHER, SHITTY COMMS. THEY ROLLED UP ON AN **ARMY CHECKPOINT** AND GOT MISTAKEN FOR **INSURGENTS**.
THE SOLDIERS AT THE CHECKPOINT LIT 'EM UP. WOLF'S MEN QUITE UNDERSTANDABLY RETURNED FIRE.
ALL IN ALL, A SHITTY NIGHT, 'SPECIALLY FOR WOLF. TOOK A ROUND RIGHT BETWEEN THE EYES IN THE FIRST VOLLEY.
SOMETHING TO KEEP IN **MIND**, MR. GLASS:
JUST 'CAUSE WE'RE ON THE SAME **SIDE** DOESN'T MEAN WE'RE ON THE SAME **TEAM.**
City Centre
Kadhimiya
Aadhamiya

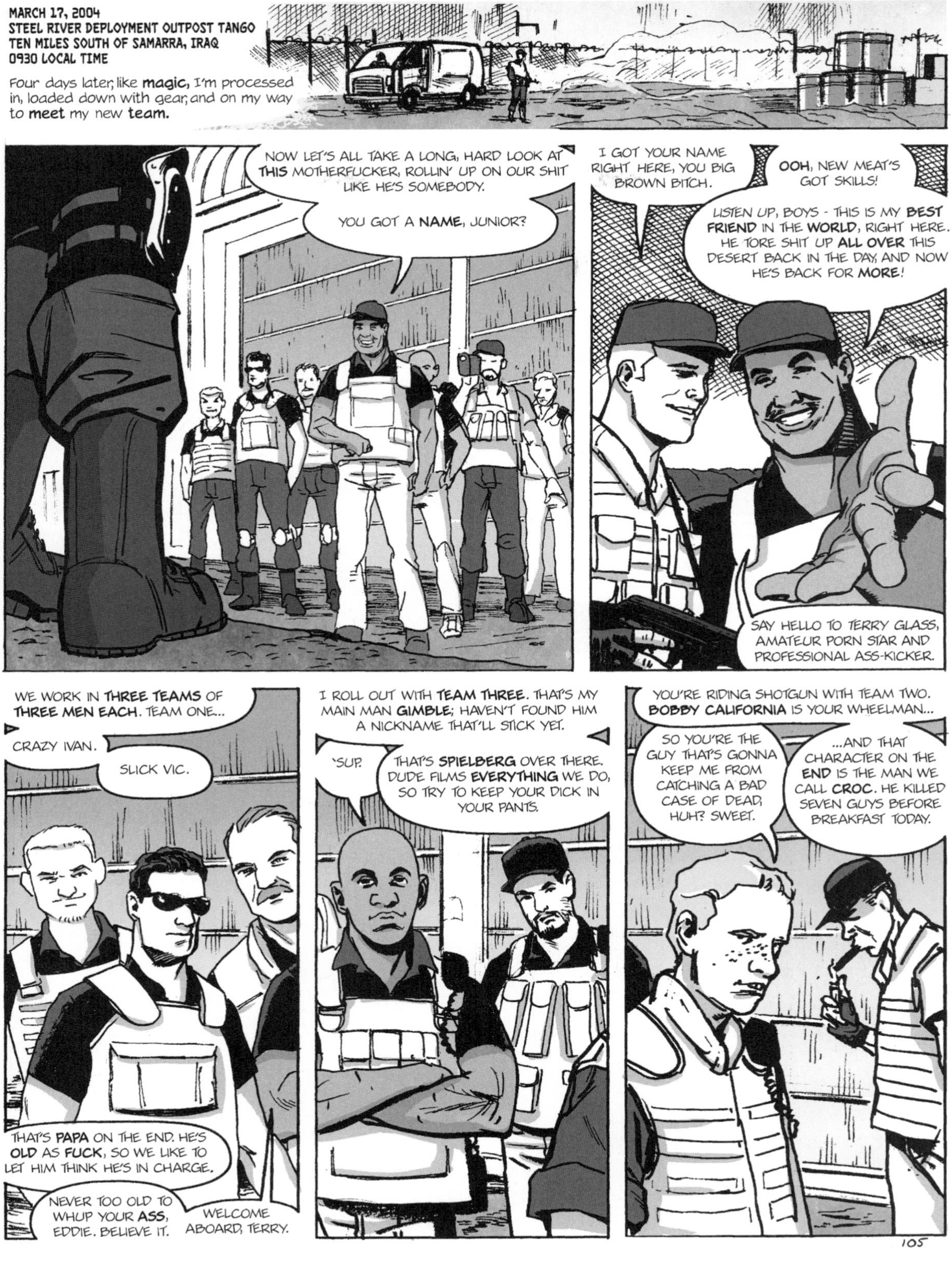

MARCH 17, 2004
STEEL RIVER DEPLOYMENT OUTPOST TANGO
TEN MILES SOUTH OF SAMARRA, IRAQ
0930 LOCAL TIME
Four days later, like magic, I'm processed in, loaded down with gear, and on my way to meet my new team.
NOW LET'S ALL TAKE A LONG, HARD LOOK AT THIS MOTHERFUCKER, ROLLIN' UP ON OUR SHIT LIKE HE'S SOMEBODY.
YOU GOT A NAME, JUNIOR?
I GOT YOUR NAME RIGHT HERE, YOU BIG BROWN BITCH.
OOH, NEW MEAT'S GOT SKILLS!
LISTEN UP, BOYS - THIS IS MY BEST FRIEND IN THE WORLD, RIGHT HERE. HE TORE SHIT UP ALL OVER THIS DESERT BACK IN THE DAY, AND NOW HE'S BACK FOR MORE!
SAY HELLO TO TERRY GLASS, AMATEUR PORN STAR AND PROFESSIONAL ASS-KICKER.
WE WORK IN THREE TEAMS OF THREE MEN EACH. TEAM ONE...
CRAZY IVAN.
SLICK VIC.
THAT'S PAPA ON THE END. HE'S OLD AS FUCK, SO WE LIKE TO LET HIM THINK HE'S IN CHARGE.
NEVER TOO OLD TO WHUP YOUR ASS, EDDIE. BELIEVE IT.
WELCOME ABOARD, TERRY.
I ROLL OUT WITH TEAM THREE. THAT'S MY MAIN MAN GIMBLE; HAVEN'T FOUND HIM A NICKNAME THAT'LL STICK YET.
'SUP.
THAT'S SPIELBERG OVER THERE. DUDE FILMS EVERYTHING WE DO, SO TRY TO KEEP YOUR DICK IN YOUR PANTS.
YOU'RE RIDING SHOTGUN WITH TEAM TWO. BOBBY CALIFORNIA IS YOUR WHEELMAN...
SO YOU'RE THE GUY THAT'S GONNA KEEP ME FROM CATCHING A BAD CASE OF DEAD, HUH? SWEET.
...AND THAT CHARACTER ON THE END IS THE MAN WE CALL CROC. HE KILLED SEVEN GUYS BEFORE BREAKFAST TODAY.

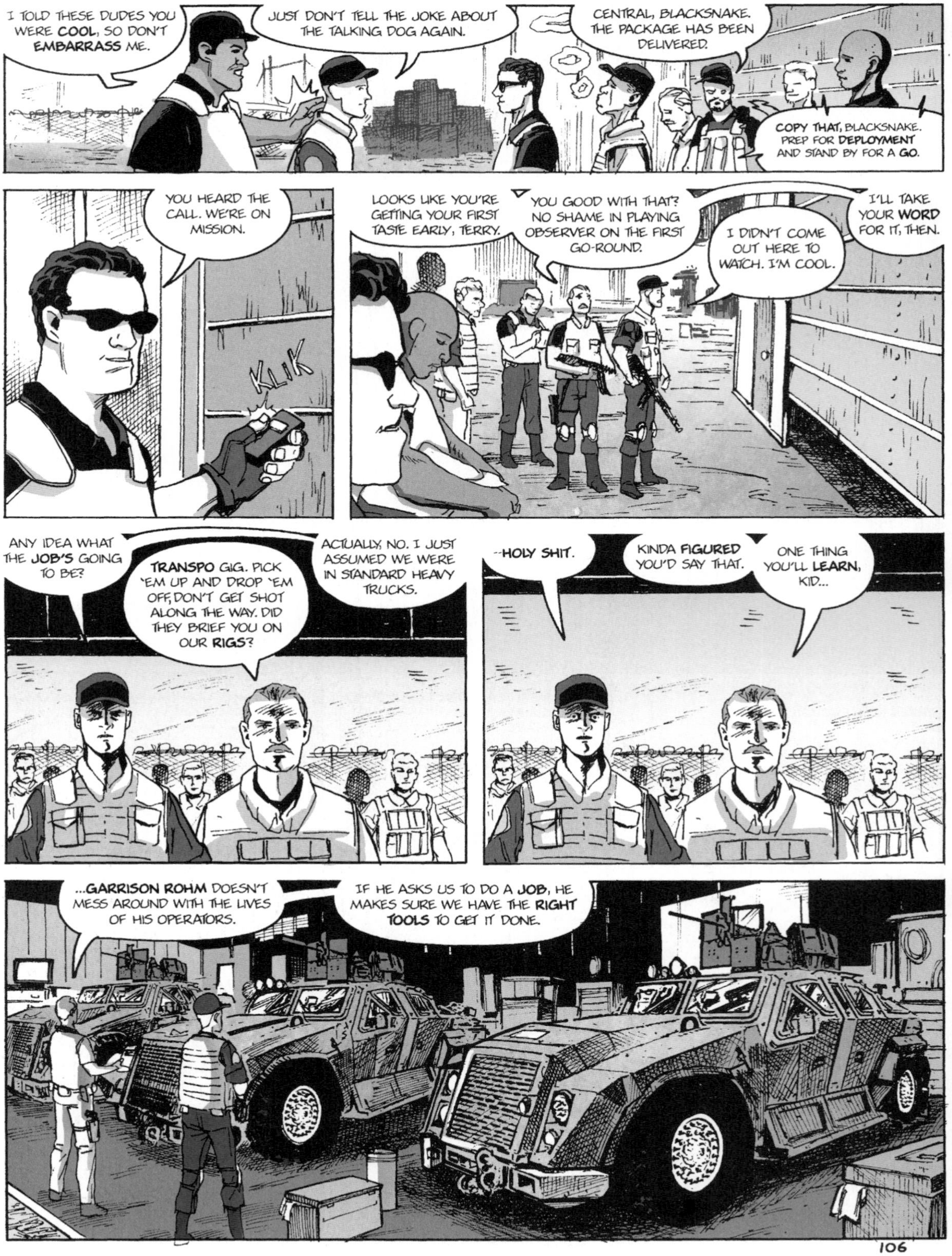
I TOLD THESE DUDES YOU WERE COOL, SO DON'T EMBARRASS ME.
JUST DON'T TELL THE JOKE ABOUT THE TALKING DOG AGAIN.
CENTRAL, BLACKSNAKE. THE PACKAGE HAS BEEN DELIVERED.
COPY THAT, BLACKSNAKE. PREP FOR DEPLOYMENT AND STAND BY FOR A GO.
YOU HEARD THE CALL. WE'RE ON MISSION.
KLIK
LOOKS LIKE YOU'RE GETTING YOUR FIRST TASTE EARLY, TERRY.
YOU GOOD WITH THAT? NO SHAME IN PLAYING OBSERVER ON THE FIRST GO-ROUND.
I DIDN'T COME OUT HERE TO WATCH. I'M COOL.
I'LL TAKE YOUR WORD FOR IT, THEN.
ANY IDEA WHAT THE JOB'S GOING TO BE?
TRANSPO GIG. PICK 'EM UP AND DROP 'EM OFF, DON'T GET SHOT ALONG THE WAY. DID THEY BRIEF YOU ON OUR RIGS?
ACTUALLY, NO. I JUST ASSUMED WE WERE IN STANDARD HEAVY TRUCKS.
--HOLY SHIT.
KINDA FIGURED YOU'D SAY THAT.
ONE THING YOU'LL LEARN, KID...
...GARRISON ROHM DOESN'T MESS AROUND WITH THE LIVES OF HIS OPERATORS.
IF HE ASKS US TO DO A JOB, HE MAKES SURE WE HAVE THE RIGHT TOOLS TO GET IT DONE.

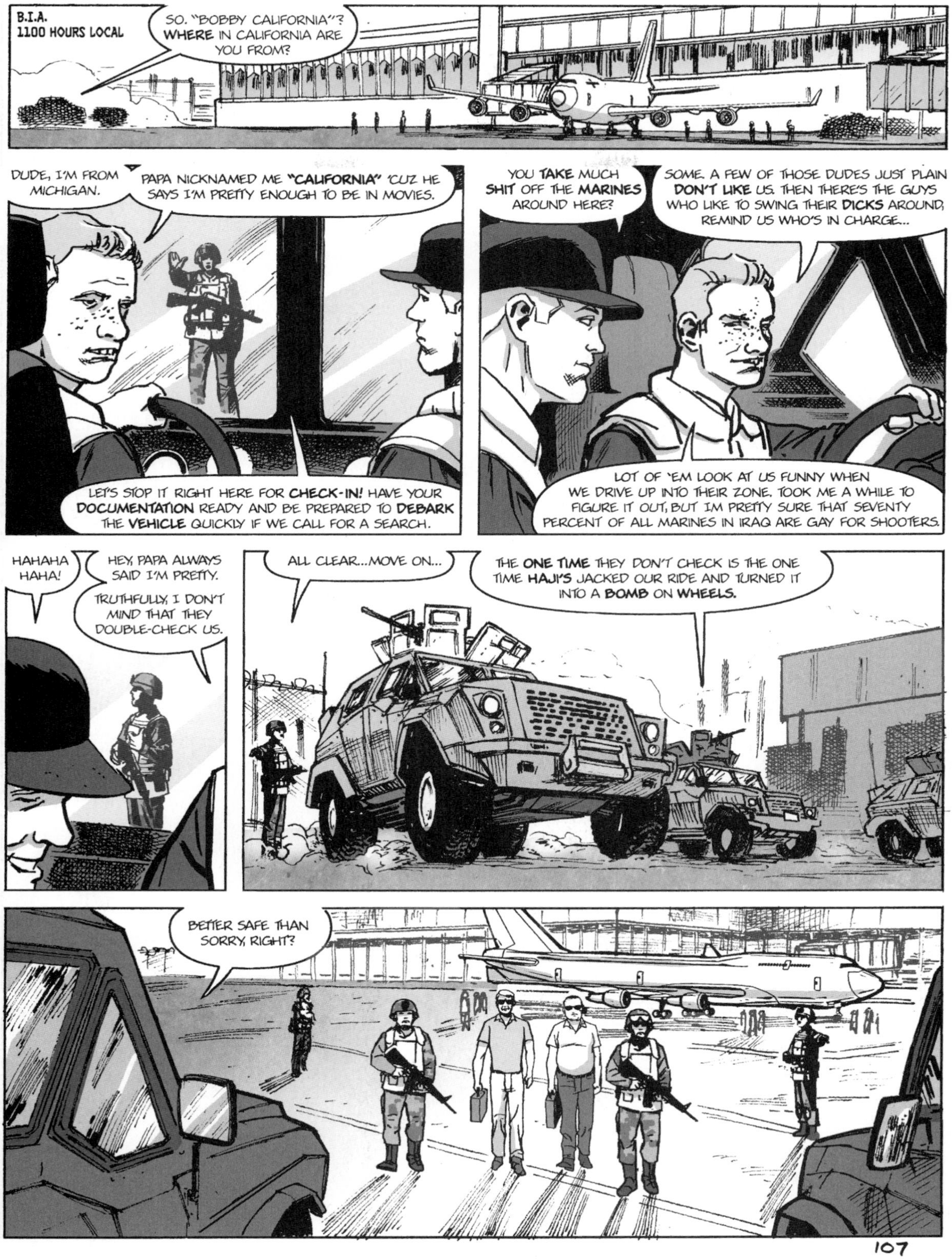
B.I.A.
1100 HOURS LOCAL
SO. "BOBBY CALIFORNIA"? WHERE IN CALIFORNIA ARE YOU FROM?
DUDE, I'M FROM MICHIGAN.
PAPA NICKNAMED ME "CALIFORNIA" 'CUZ HE SAYS I'M PRETTY ENOUGH TO BE IN MOVIES.
LET'S STOP IT RIGHT HERE FOR CHECK-IN! HAVE YOUR DOCUMENTATION READY AND BE PREPARED TO DEBARK THE VEHICLE QUICKLY IF WE CALL FOR A SEARCH.
YOU TAKE MUCH SHIT OFF THE MARINES AROUND HERE?
SOME. A FEW OF THOSE DUDES JUST PLAIN DON'T LIKE US. THEN THERE'S THE GUYS WHO LIKE TO SWING THEIR DICKS AROUND, REMIND US WHO'S IN CHARGE...
LOT OF 'EM LOOK AT US FUNNY WHEN WE DRIVE UP INTO THEIR ZONE. TOOK ME A WHILE TO FIGURE IT OUT, BUT IM PRETTY SURE THAT SEVENTY PERCENT OF ALL MARINES IN IRAQ ARE GAY FOR SHOOTERS.
HAHAHA HAHA!
HEY, PAPA ALWAYS SAID I'M PRETTY.
TRUTHFULLY, I DON'T MIND THAT THEY DOUBLE-CHECK US.
ALL CLEAR...MOVE ON...
THE ONE TIME THEY DON'T CHECK IS THE ONE TIME HAJI'S JACKED OUR RIDE AND TURNED IT INTO A BOMB ON WHEELS.
BETTER SAFE THAN SORRY, RIGHT?

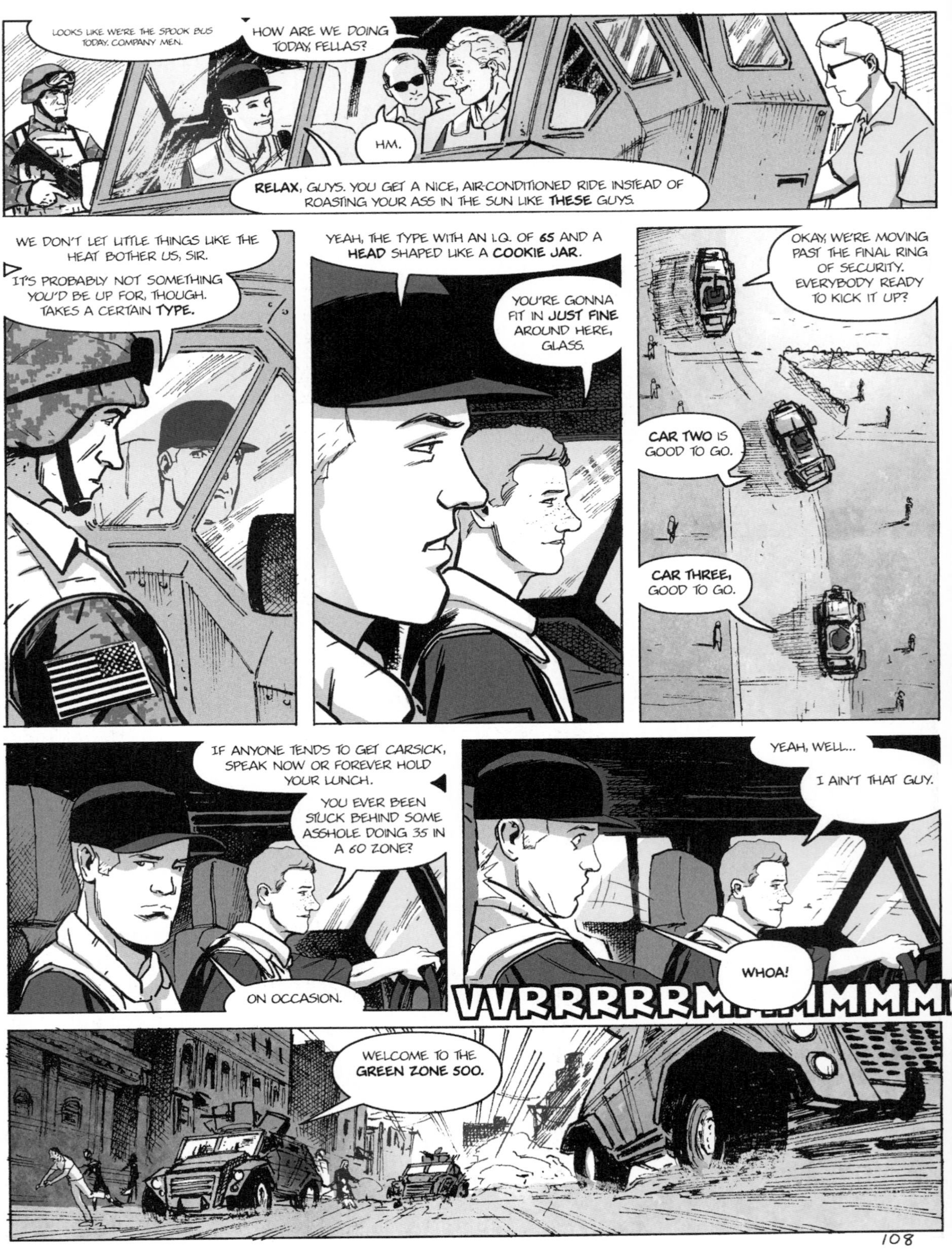
LOOKS LIKE WE'RE THE SPOOK BUS TODAY. COMPANY MEN.
HOW ARE WE DOING TODAY, FELLAS?
HM.
RELAX, GUYS. YOU GET A NICE, AIR-CONDITIONED RIDE INSTEAD OF ROASTING YOUR ASS IN THE SUN LIKE THESE GUYS.
WE DON'T LET LITTLE THINGS LIKE THE HEAT BOTHER US, SIR.
IT'S PROBABLY NOT SOMETHING YOU'D BE UP FOR, THOUGH. TAKES A CERTAIN TYPE.
YEAH, THE TYPE WITH AN I.Q. OF 65 AND A HEAD SHAPED LIKE A COOKIE JAR.
YOU'RE GONNA FIT IN JUST FINE AROUND HERE, GLASS.
OKAY, WE'RE MOVING PAST THE FINAL RING OF SECURITY. EVERYBODY READY TO KICK IT UP?
CAR TWO IS GOOD TO GO.
CAR THREE, GOOD TO GO.
IF ANYONE TENDS TO GET CARSICK, SPEAK NOW OR FOREVER HOLD YOUR LUNCH.
YOU EVER BEEN STUCK BEHIND SOME ASSHOLE DOING 35 IN A 60 ZONE?
ON OCCASION.
YEAH, WELL...
I AIN'T THAT GUY.
WHOA!
VVRRRRRMMMMMM
WELCOME TO THE GREEN ZONE 500.

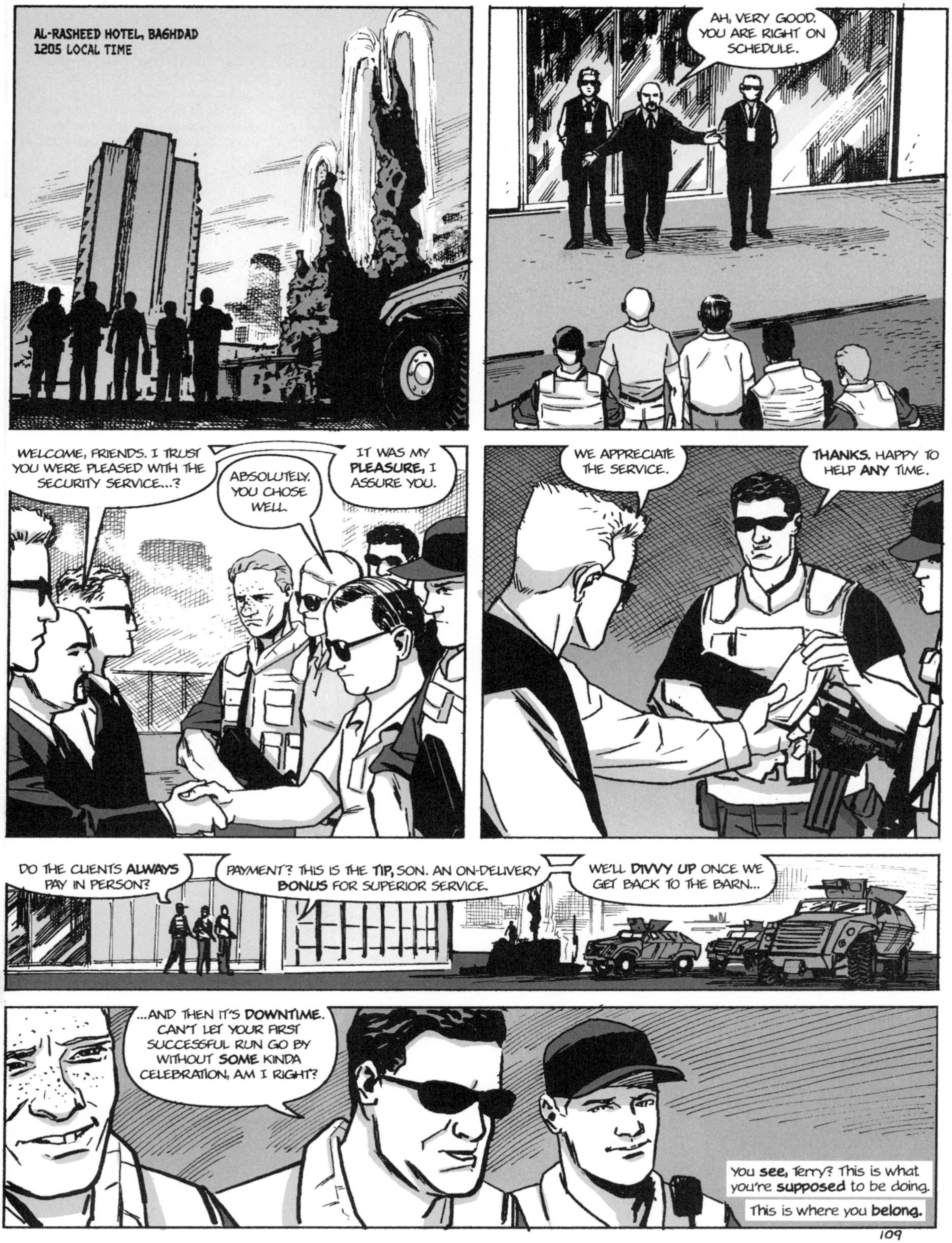

AL-RASHEED HOTEL, BAGHDAD
1205 LOCAL TIME
AH, VERY GOOD. YOU ARE RIGHT ON SCHEDULE.
WELCOME, FRIENDS. I TRUST YOU WERE PLEASED WITH THE SECURITY SERVICE...?
ABSOLUTELY. YOU CHOSE WELL.
IT WAS MY PLEASURE, I ASSURE YOU.
WE APPRECIATE THE SERVICE.
THANKS. HAPPY TO HELP ANY TIME.
DO THE CLIENTS ALWAYS PAY IN PERSON?
PAYMENT? THIS IS THE TIP, SON. AN ON-DELIVERY BONUS FOR SUPERIOR SERVICE.
WE'LL DIVVY UP ONCE WE GET BACK TO THE BARN...
...AND THEN IT'S DOWNTIME. CAN'T LET YOUR FIRST SUCCESSFUL RUN GO BY WITHOUT SOME KINDA CELEBRATION, AM I RIGHT?
You see, Terry? This is what you're supposed to be doing.
This is where you belong.

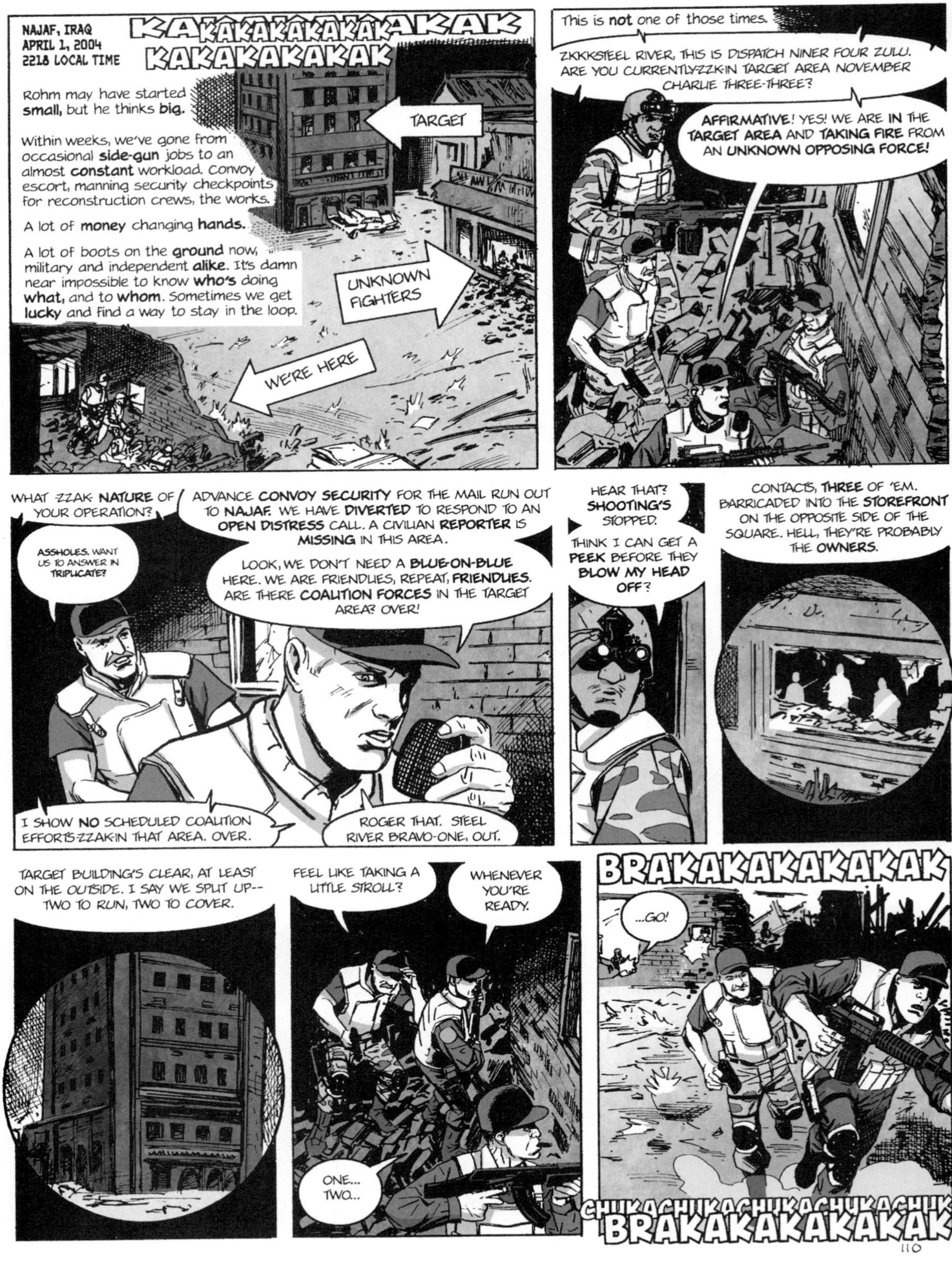
NAJAF, IRAQ
APRIL 1, 2004
2218 LOCAL TIME
KAKAKAKAKAKAKAKAK
KAKAKAKAKAK
Rohm may have started small, but he thinks big.
Within weeks, we've gone from occasional side-gun jobs to an almost constant workload. Convoy escort, manning security checkpoints for reconstruction crews, the works.
A lot of money changing hands.
A lot of boots on the ground now, military and independent alike. It's damn near impossible to know who's doing what, and to whom. Sometimes we get lucky and find a way to stay in the loop.
TARGET
UNKNOWN FIGHTERS
WE'RE HERE
This is not one of those times.
ZKKKSTEEL RIVER, THIS IS DISPATCH NINER FOUR ZULU. ARE YOU CURRENTLY-ZZK-IN TARGET AREA NOVEMBER CHARLIE THREE-THREE?
AFFIRMATIVE! YES! WE ARE IN THE TARGET AREA AND TAKING FIRE FROM AN UNKNOWN OPPOSING FORCE!
WHAT -ZZAK- NATURE OF YOUR OPERATION?
ADVANCE CONVOY SECURITY FOR THE MAIL RUN OUT TO NAJAF. WE HAVE DIVERTED TO RESPOND TO AN OPEN DISTRESS CALL. A CIVILIAN REPORTER IS MISSING IN THIS AREA.
ASSHOLES. WANT US TO ANSWER IN TRIPLICATE?
LOOK, WE DON'T NEED A BLUE-ON-BLUE HERE. WE ARE FRIENDLIES, REPEAT, FRIENDLIES. ARE THERE COALITION FORCES IN THE TARGET AREA? OVER!
I SHOW NO SCHEDULED COALITION EFFORTS-ZZAK-IN THAT AREA. OVER.
ROGER THAT. STEEL RIVER BRAVO-ONE, OUT.
HEAR THAT? SHOOTING'S STOPPED.
THINK I CAN GET A PEEK BEFORE THEY BLOW MY HEAD OFF?
CONTACTS, THREE OF 'EM. BARRICADED INTO THE STOREFRONT ON THE OPPOSITE SIDE OF THE SQUARE. HELL, THEY'RE PROBABLY THE OWNERS.
TARGET BUILDING'S CLEAR, AT LEAST ON THE OUTSIDE. I SAY WE SPLIT UP-- TWO TO RUN, TWO TO COVER.
FEEL LIKE TAKING A LITTLE STROLL?
WHENEVER YOU'RE READY.
ONE... TWO...
BRAKAKAKAKAKAK
...GO!
CHUKACHUKACHUKACHUKACHUK
BRAKAKAKAKAKAK

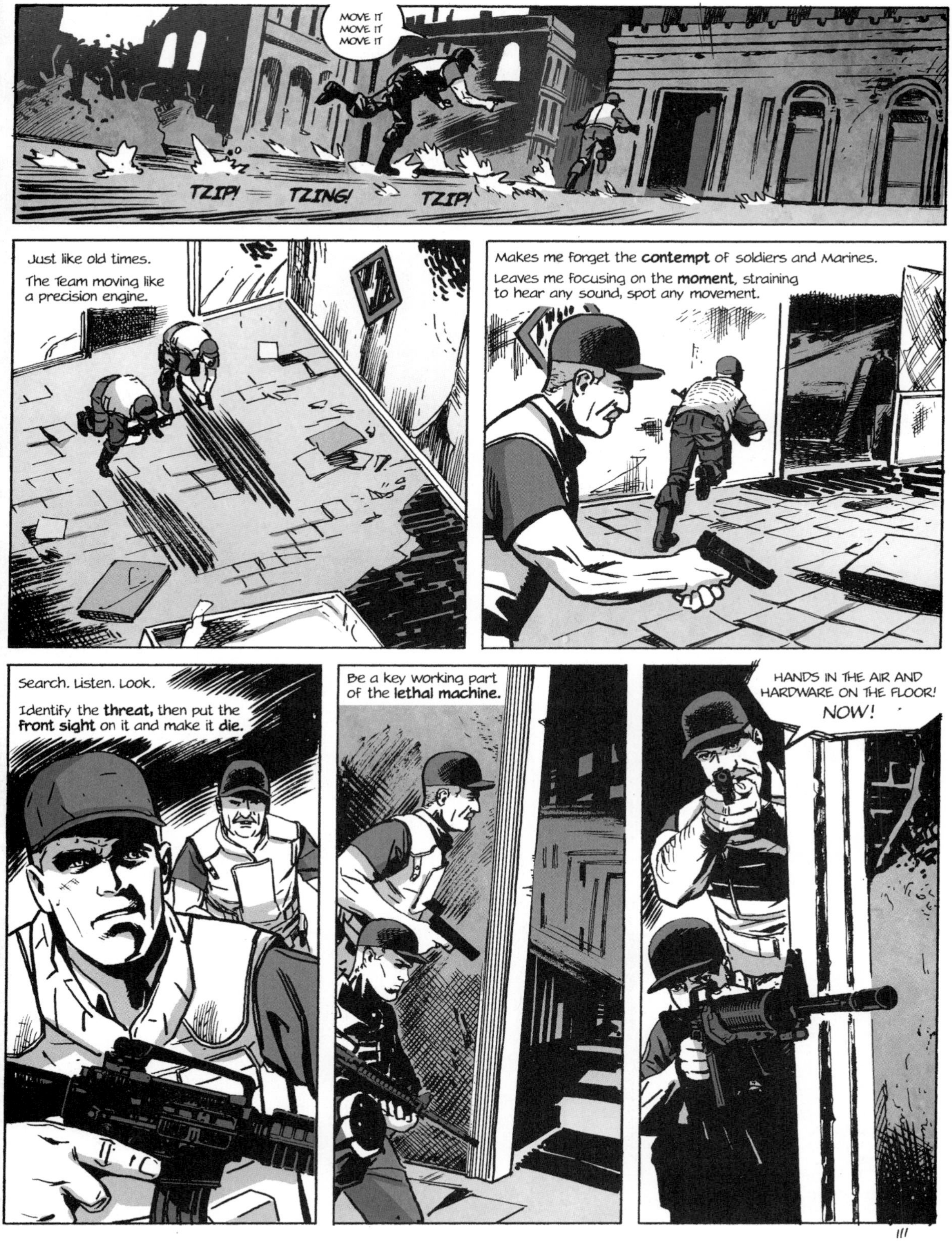

MOVE IT
MOVE IT
MOVE IT
TZIP!
TZING!
TZIP!
Just like old times.
The Team moving like a precision engine.
Makes me forget the **contempt** of soldiers and Marines.
Leaves me focusing on the **moment**, straining to hear any sound, spot any movement.
Search. Listen. Look.
Identify the **threat,** then put the **front sight** on it and make it **die.**
Be a key working part of the **lethal machine.**
HANDS IN THE AIR AND HARDWARE ON THE FLOOR!
NOW!

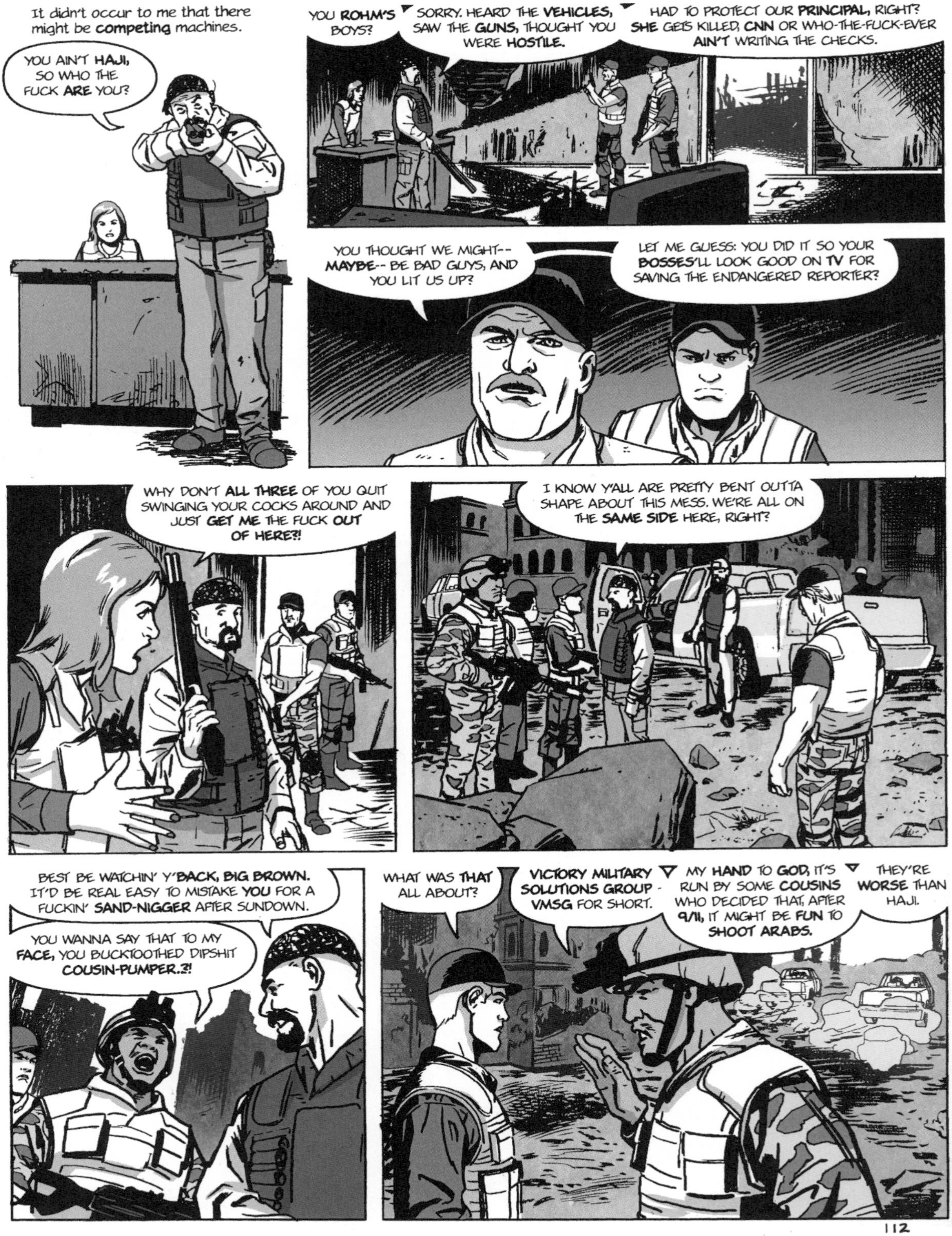

It didn't occur to me that there might be competing machines.
YOU AIN'T HAJI, SO WHO THE FUCK ARE YOU?
YOU ROHM'S BOYS?
SORRY. HEARD THE VEHICLES, SAW THE GUNS, THOUGHT YOU WERE HOSTILE.
HAD TO PROTECT OUR PRINCIPAL, RIGHT? SHE GETS KILLED, CNN OR WHO-THE-FUCK-EVER AIN'T WRITING THE CHECKS.
YOU THOUGHT WE MIGHT-- MAYBE-- BE BAD GUYS, AND YOU LIT US UP?
LET ME GUESS: YOU DID IT SO YOUR BOSSES'LL LOOK GOOD ON TV FOR SAVING THE ENDANGERED REPORTER?
WHY DON'T ALL THREE OF YOU QUIT SWINGING YOUR COCKS AROUND AND JUST GET ME THE FUCK OUT OF HERE?!
I KNOW Y'ALL ARE PRETTY BENT OUTTA SHAPE ABOUT THIS MESS. WE'RE ALL ON THE SAME SIDE HERE, RIGHT?
BEST BE WATCHIN' Y'BACK, BIG BROWN. IT'D BE REAL EASY TO MISTAKE YOU FOR A FUCKIN' SAND-NIGGER AFTER SUNDOWN.
YOU WANNA SAY THAT TO MY FACE, YOU BUCKTOOTHED DIPSHIT COUSIN-PUMPER..?!
WHAT WAS THAT ALL ABOUT?
VICTORY MILITARY SOLUTIONS GROUP - VMSG FOR SHORT.
MY HAND TO GOD, IT'S RUN BY SOME COUSINS WHO DECIDED THAT, AFTER 9/11, IT MIGHT BE FUN TO SHOOT ARABS.
THEY'RE WORSE THAN HAJI.

MAY 12TH, 2004
OUTPOST TANGO
1700 HOURS

Two **months** in-country and it still feels good. We're making a **difference** here, and I'm sending a big **check** home every two weeks.

I can usually swing a **phone** call every **Sunday**. It's always **Emily** who answers. We talk for **ten minutes** and then she hands me off to **Patty**; it's **awkward**, but at least we're not arguing.

The **divorce** was clean and quick, and Patty was **cool** about handling the **money** in private. I'm guessing it makes it **easier** for her to accept cash from **this job** if she feels like I'm not being **forced** to give it to her.

I don't know how things are going to play out when I'm **done** here, but I don't expect a **fight** if it comes down to figuring out **custody**. I'm secretly hoping it **won't**.

My **Dad's** been carrying the torch for my old unit, **digging** around where he can. Turns out the Marine F.A.C. ended up in the **State Department** after the Corps declined to push him up the ladder.

I just pray State sticks his dumb ass behind a desk where he can't kill anyone else.

I'd managed to put the guy's **name** and **face** out of my mind until now. I need to **forget** he ever **existed**.

Sometimes **reality** can be every bit as **ugly** as **war**. Right now, I feel like I might have a slim chance of surviving **both** if I can keep looking **forward** and stop looking **back**.

BAGHDAD, IRAQ
JUNE 4, 2004
1155 LOCAL TIME

The work is **varied**, that's for sure. No time to get **bored**.

Take **Aban** here, for instance. Five minutes ago, I knew him as a friendly market vendor who always gave us fresh fruit when we'd pass by his stall.

You can imagine my **surprise** when I saw him accepting a "**gift**" from a key **local militia** member. That messenger bag he's carrying? If it's not packed with explosives, I'll kiss your ass.

We made **eye contact**. He started **running**.

OUT OF THE WAY! MOVE!

This asshole **grew up** on these streets, dodging Saddam's **spies** and corrupt **police**.

Guys like this know where to **hide** in here. How to **kill us** in here.

BLACKSNAKE NINE TO **ALL OPERATORS**! I'M IN PURSUIT OF A SINGLE HOSTILE, HEADING **NORTH** THROUGH THE ALLEYS PAST THE **MARKETPLACE**!

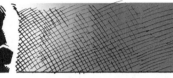

113

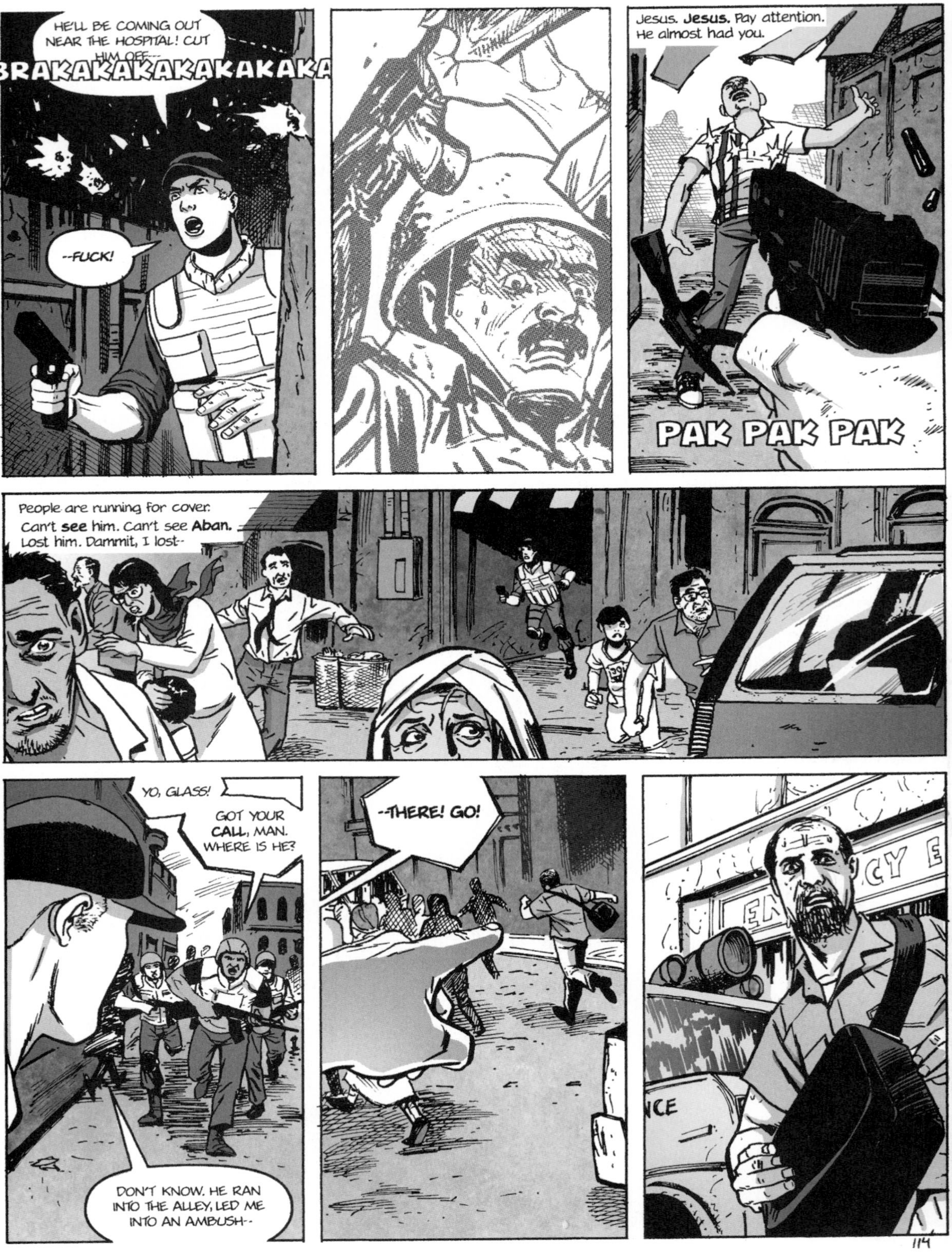
HE'LL BE COMING OUT NEAR THE HOSPITAL! CUT HIM OFF---
BRAKAKAKAKAKAKAKAKA
--FUCK!
Jesus. **Jesus.** Pay attention. He almost had you.
PAK PAK PAK
People are running for cover.
Can't **see** him. Can't see **Aban.** Lost him. Dammit, I lost-
YO, GLASS!
GOT YOUR **CALL**, MAN. WHERE IS HE?
DON'T KNOW. HE RAN INTO THE ALLEY, LED ME INTO AN AMBUSH--
--THERE! GO!

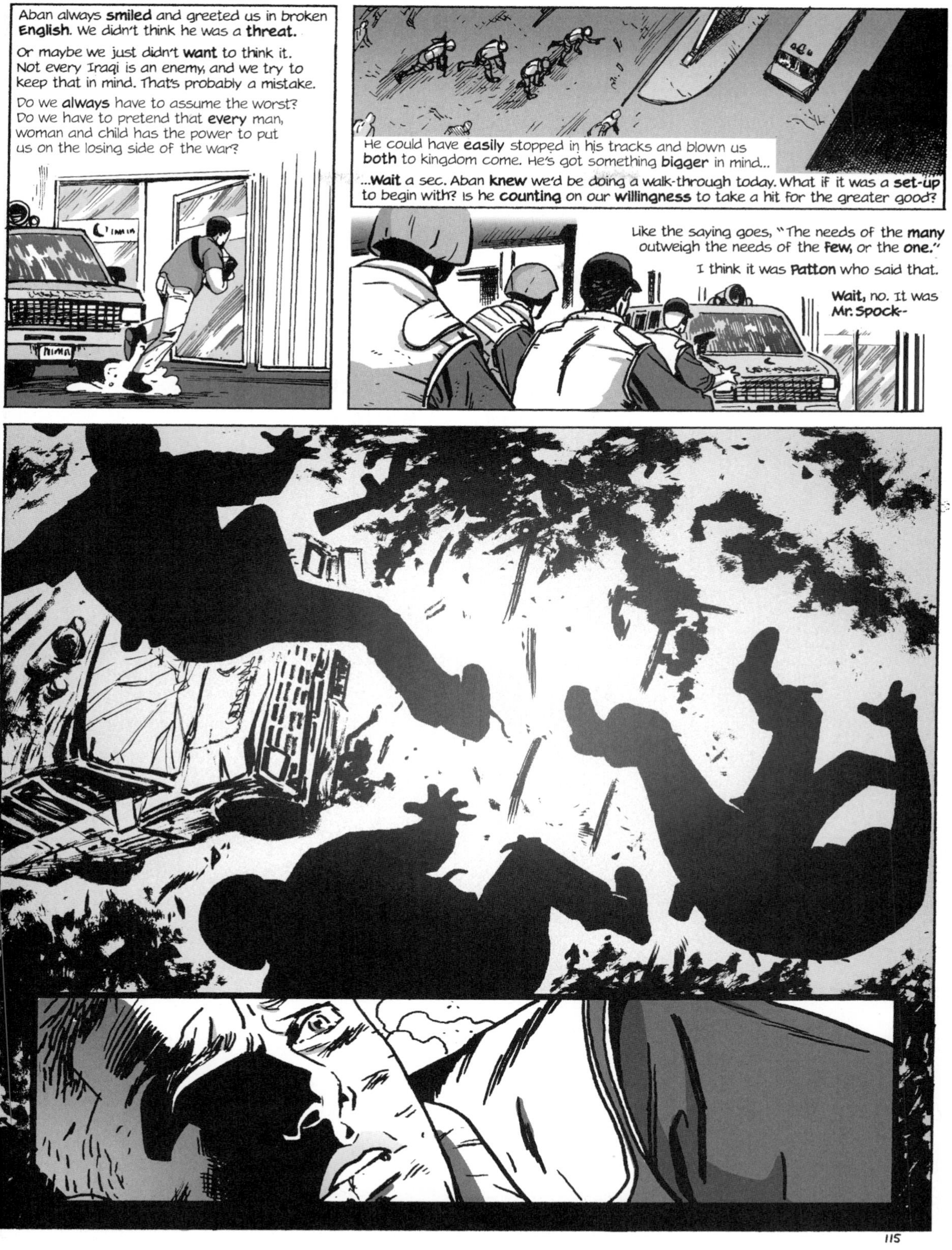
Aban always smiled and greeted us in broken English. We didn't think he was a threat.
Or maybe we just didn't want to think it. Not every Iraqi is an enemy, and we try to keep that in mind. That's probably a mistake.
Do we always have to assume the worst? Do we have to pretend that every man, woman and child has the power to put us on the losing side of the war?
He could have easily stopped in his tracks and blown us both to kingdom come. He's got something bigger in mind...
...Wait a sec. Aban knew we'd be doing a walk-through today. What if it was a set-up to begin with? Is he counting on our willingness to take a hit for the greater good?
Like the saying goes, "The needs of the many outweigh the needs of the few, or the one."
I think it was Patton who said that.
Wait, no. It was Mr. Spock-

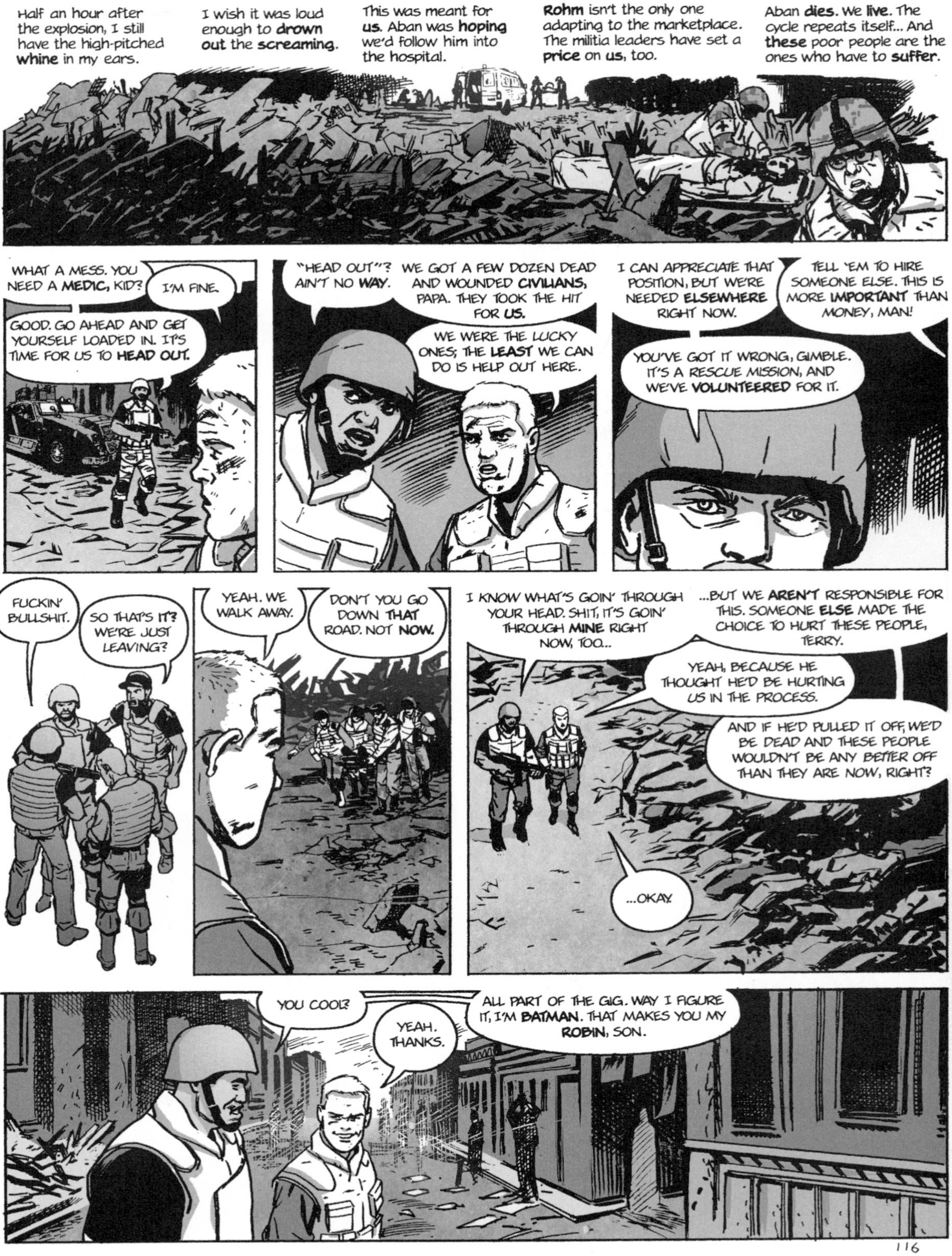

Half an hour after the explosion, I still have the high-pitched **whine** in my ears.
I wish it was loud enough to **drown out** the **screaming**.
This was meant for **us**. Aban was **hoping** we'd follow him into the hospital.
Rohm isn't the only one adapting to the marketplace. The militia leaders have set a **price** on **us**, too.
Aban **dies**. We **live**. The cycle repeats itself... And **these** poor people are the ones who have to **suffer**.
WHAT A MESS. YOU NEED A **MEDIC**, KID?
I'M FINE.
GOOD. GO AHEAD AND GET YOURSELF LOADED IN. IT'S TIME FOR US TO **HEAD OUT**.
"HEAD OUT"? AIN'T NO **WAY**.
WE GOT A FEW DOZEN DEAD AND WOUNDED **CIVILIANS**, PAPA. THEY TOOK THE HIT FOR **US**.
WE WERE THE *LUCKY* ONES; THE **LEAST** WE CAN DO IS HELP OUT HERE.
I CAN APPRECIATE THAT POSITION, BUT WE'RE NEEDED **ELSEWHERE** RIGHT NOW.
TELL 'EM TO HIRE SOMEONE ELSE. THIS IS MORE **IMPORTANT** THAN MONEY, MAN!
YOU'VE GOT IT WRONG, GIMBLE. IT'S A RESCUE MISSION, AND WE'VE **VOLUNTEERED** FOR IT.
FUCKIN' BULLSHIT.
SO THAT'S **IT?** WE'RE JUST LEAVING?
YEAH. WE WALK AWAY.
DON'T YOU GO DOWN **THAT** ROAD. NOT **NOW**.
I KNOW WHAT'S GOIN' THROUGH YOUR HEAD. SHIT, IT'S GOIN' THROUGH **MINE** RIGHT NOW, TOO...
...BUT WE **AREN'T** RESPONSIBLE FOR THIS. SOMEONE **ELSE** MADE THE CHOICE TO HURT THESE PEOPLE, TERRY.
YEAH, BECAUSE HE THOUGHT HE'D BE HURTING US IN THE PROCESS.
AND IF HE'D PULLED IT OFF, WE'D BE DEAD AND THESE PEOPLE WOULDN'T BE ANY *BETTER OFF* THAN THEY ARE NOW, RIGHT?
...OKAY.
YOU COOL?
YEAH. THANKS.
ALL PART OF THE GIG. WAY I FIGURE IT, I'M **BATMAN**. THAT MAKES YOU MY **ROBIN**, SON.

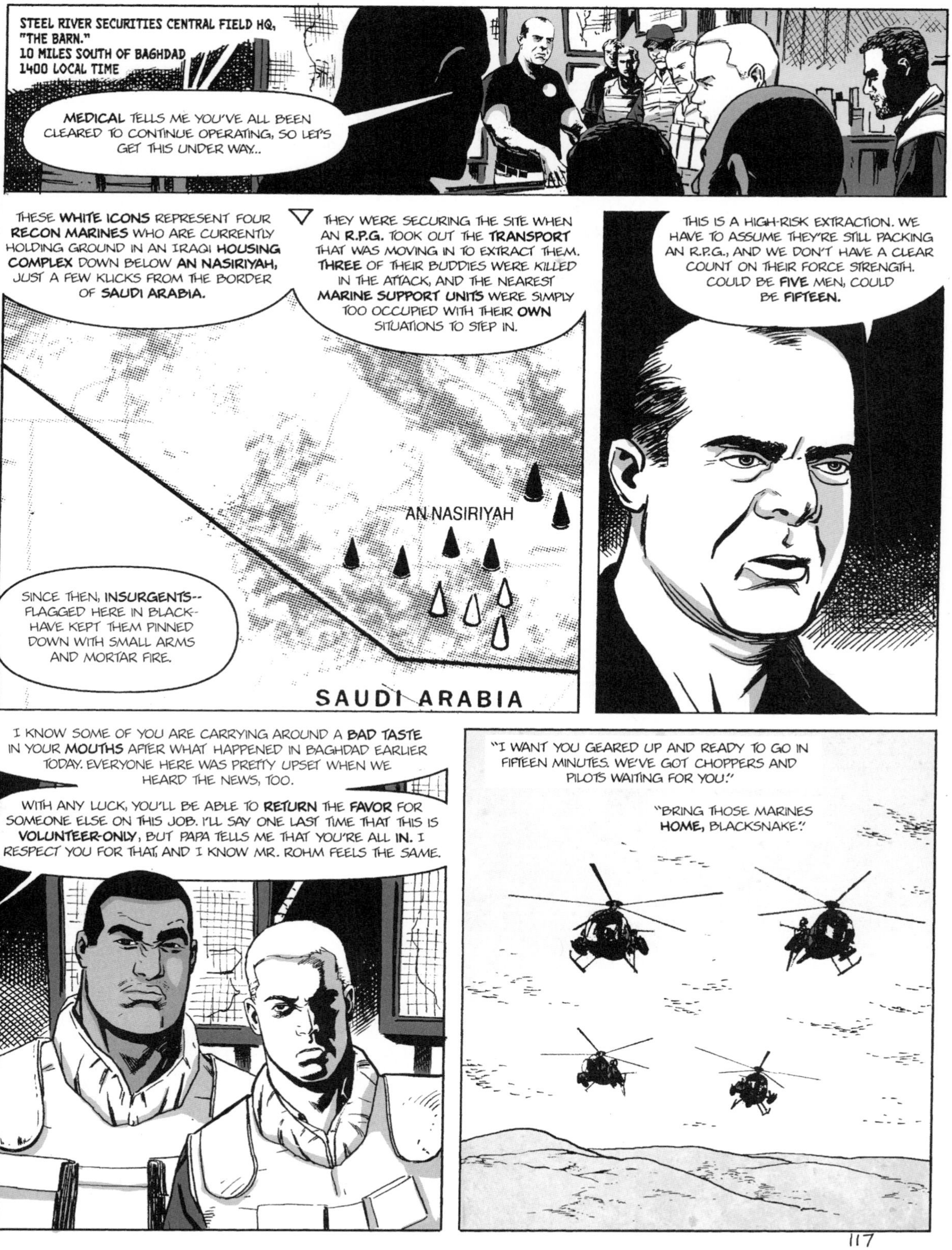
STEEL RIVER SECURITIES CENTRAL FIELD HQ, "THE BARN." 10 MILES SOUTH OF BAGHDAD 1400 LOCAL TIME
MEDICAL TELLS ME YOU'VE ALL BEEN CLEARED TO CONTINUE OPERATING, SO LET'S GET THIS UNDER WAY...
THESE WHITE ICONS REPRESENT FOUR RECON MARINES WHO ARE CURRENTLY HOLDING GROUND IN AN IRAQI HOUSING COMPLEX DOWN BELOW AN NASIRIYAH, JUST A FEW KLICKS FROM THE BORDER OF SAUDI ARABIA.
THEY WERE SECURING THE SITE WHEN AN R.P.G. TOOK OUT THE TRANSPORT THAT WAS MOVING IN TO EXTRACT THEM. THREE OF THEIR BUDDIES WERE KILLED IN THE ATTACK, AND THE NEAREST MARINE SUPPORT UNITS WERE SIMPLY TOO OCCUPIED WITH THEIR OWN SITUATIONS TO STEP IN.
AN NASIRIYAH
SINCE THEN, INSURGENTS--FLAGGED HERE IN BLACK--HAVE KEPT THEM PINNED DOWN WITH SMALL ARMS AND MORTAR FIRE.
SAUDI ARABIA
THIS IS A HIGH-RISK EXTRACTION. WE HAVE TO ASSUME THEY'RE STILL PACKING AN R.P.G., AND WE DON'T HAVE A CLEAR COUNT ON THEIR FORCE STRENGTH. COULD BE FIVE MEN, COULD BE FIFTEEN.
I KNOW SOME OF YOU ARE CARRYING AROUND A BAD TASTE IN YOUR MOUTHS AFTER WHAT HAPPENED IN BAGHDAD EARLIER TODAY. EVERYONE HERE WAS PRETTY UPSET WHEN WE HEARD THE NEWS, TOO.
WITH ANY LUCK, YOU'LL BE ABLE TO RETURN THE FAVOR FOR SOMEONE ELSE ON THIS JOB. I'LL SAY ONE LAST TIME THAT THIS IS VOLUNTEER-ONLY, BUT PAPA TELLS ME THAT YOU'RE ALL IN. I RESPECT YOU FOR THAT, AND I KNOW MR. ROHM FEELS THE SAME.
"I WANT YOU GEARED UP AND READY TO GO IN FIFTEEN MINUTES. WE'VE GOT CHOPPERS AND PILOTS WAITING FOR YOU."
"BRING THOSE MARINES HOME, BLACKSNAKE."

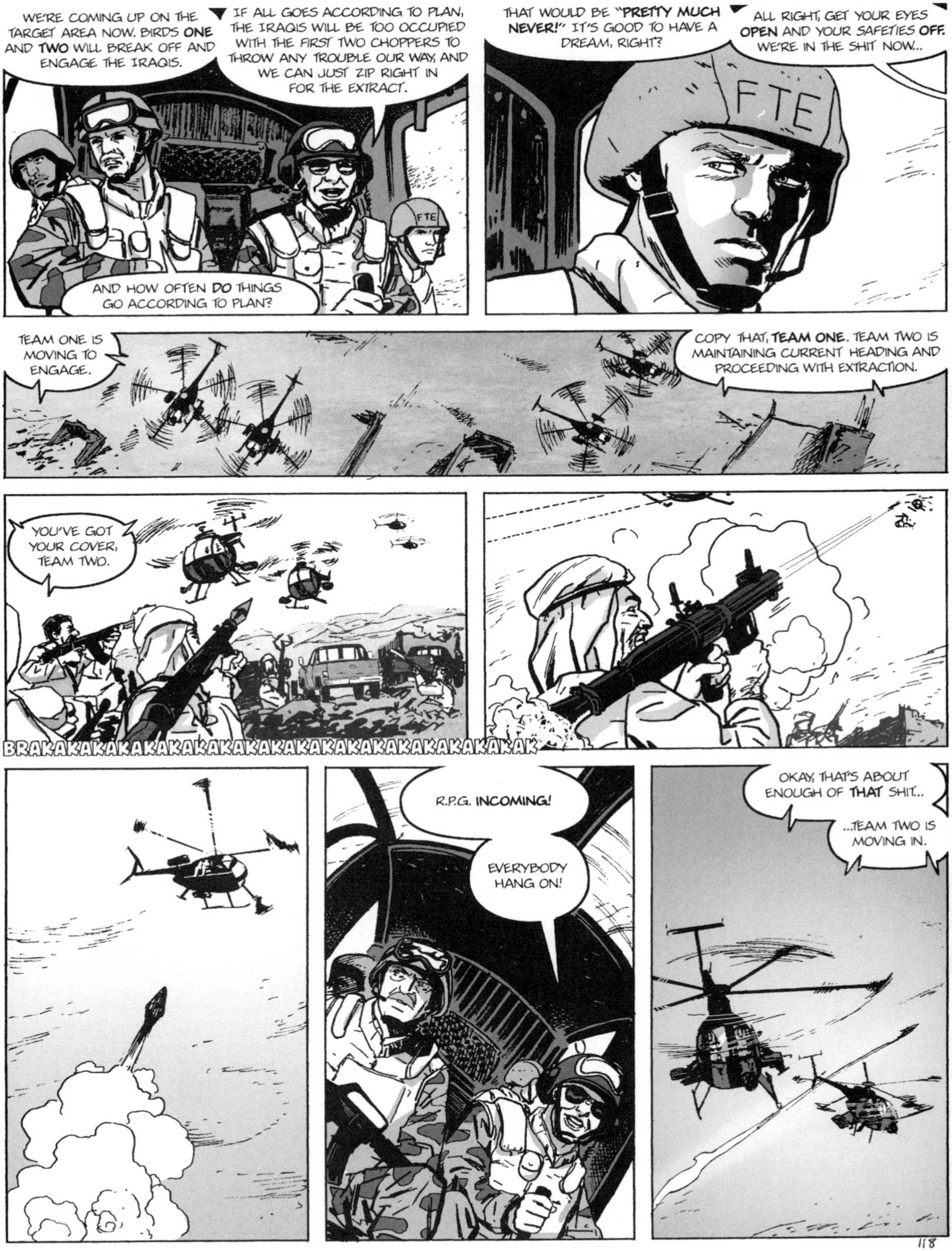
WE'RE COMING UP ON THE TARGET AREA NOW. BIRDS ONE AND TWO WILL BREAK OFF AND ENGAGE THE IRAQIS.
IF ALL GOES ACCORDING TO PLAN, THE IRAQIS WILL BE TOO OCCUPIED WITH THE FIRST TWO CHOPPERS TO THROW ANY TROUBLE OUR WAY, AND WE CAN JUST ZIP RIGHT IN FOR THE EXTRACT.
AND HOW OFTEN DO THINGS GO ACCORDING TO PLAN?
THAT WOULD BE "PRETTY MUCH NEVER!" IT'S GOOD TO HAVE A DREAM, RIGHT?
ALL RIGHT, GET YOUR EYES OPEN AND YOUR SAFETIES OFF. WE'RE IN THE SHIT NOW...
FTE
TEAM ONE IS MOVING TO ENGAGE.
COPY THAT, TEAM ONE. TEAM TWO IS MAINTAINING CURRENT HEADING AND PROCEEDING WITH EXTRACTION.
YOU'VE GOT YOUR COVER, TEAM TWO.
BRAKAKAKAKAKAKAKAKAKAKAKAKAKAKAKAKAKAKAKAK
R.P.G. INCOMING!
EVERYBODY HANG ON!
OKAY, THAT'S ABOUT ENOUGH OF THAT SHIT...
...TEAM TWO IS MOVING IN.

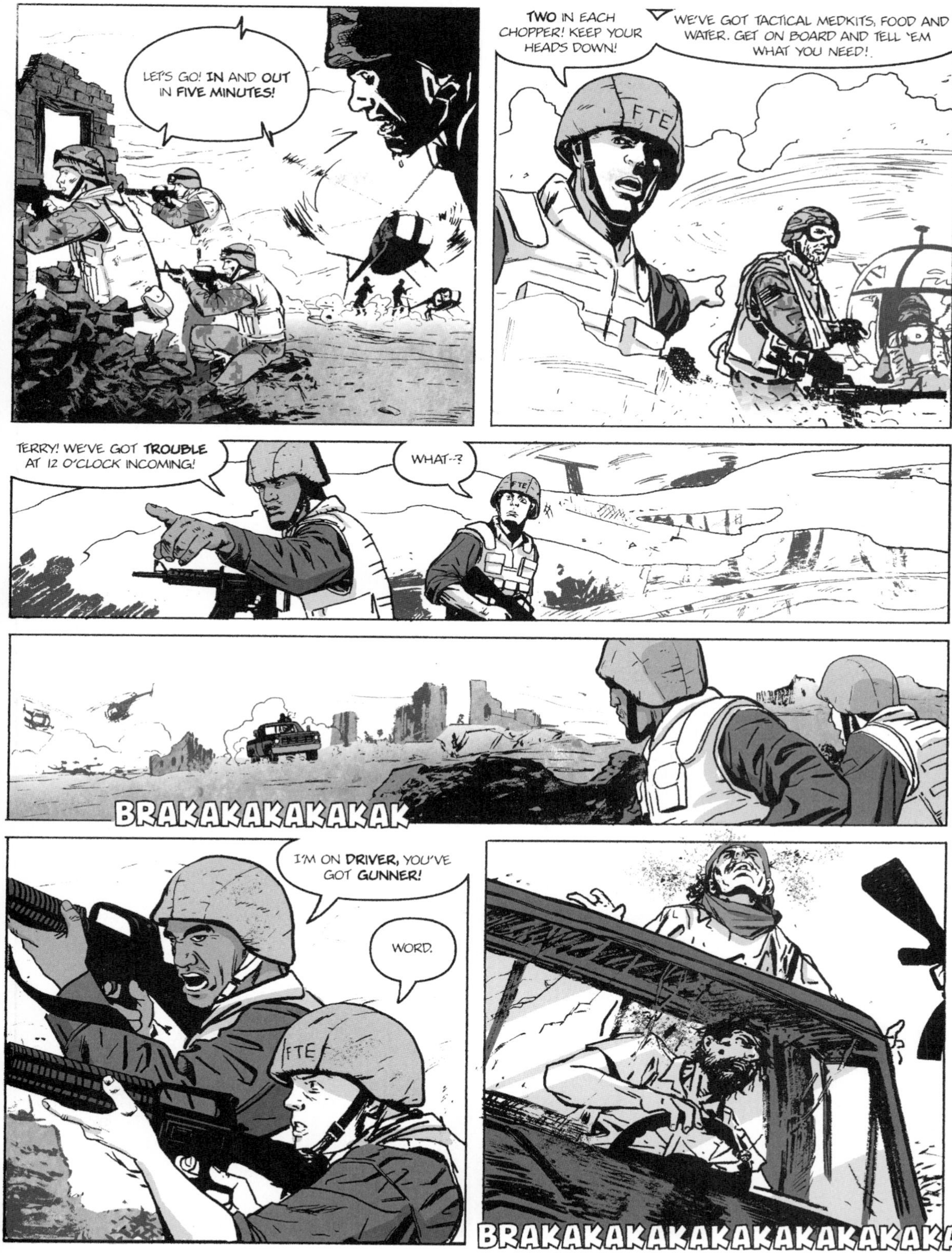
LET'S GO! IN AND OUT IN FIVE MINUTES!
TWO IN EACH CHOPPER! KEEP YOUR HEADS DOWN!
WE'VE GOT TACTICAL MEDKITS, FOOD AND WATER. GET ON BOARD AND TELL 'EM WHAT YOU NEED!
FTE
TERRY! WE'VE GOT TROUBLE AT 12 O'CLOCK INCOMING!
WHAT--?
BRAKAKAKAKAKAKAK
I'M ON DRIVER, YOU'VE GOT GUNNER!
WORD.
BRAKAKAKAKAKAKAKAKAKAKAKAKA

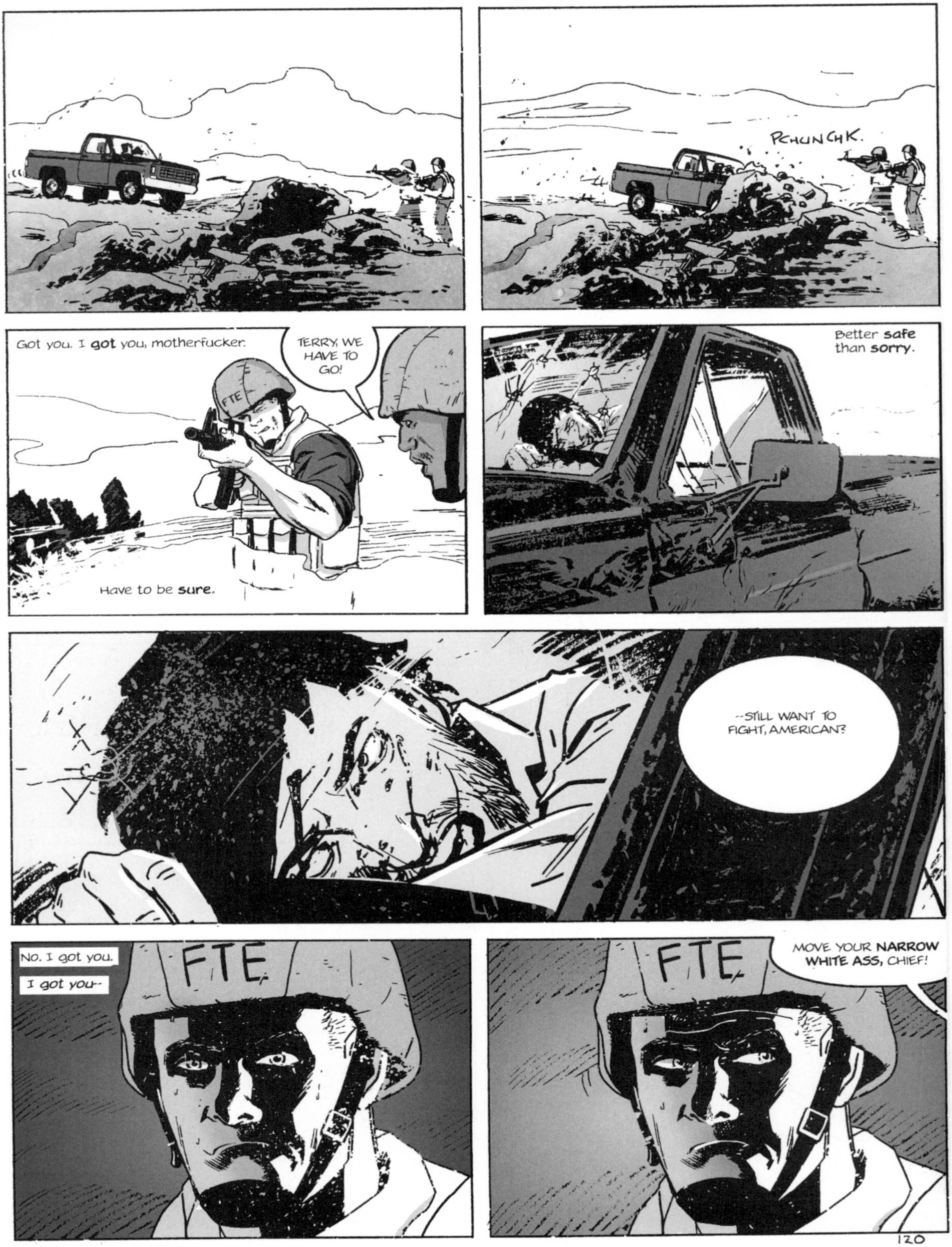
PCHUNCHK.
Got you. I got you, motherfucker.
TERRY, WE HAVE TO GO!
Have to be sure.
Better safe than sorry.
--STILL WANT TO FIGHT, AMERICAN?
No. I got you.
I got you--
MOVE YOUR NARROW WHITE ASS, CHIEF!

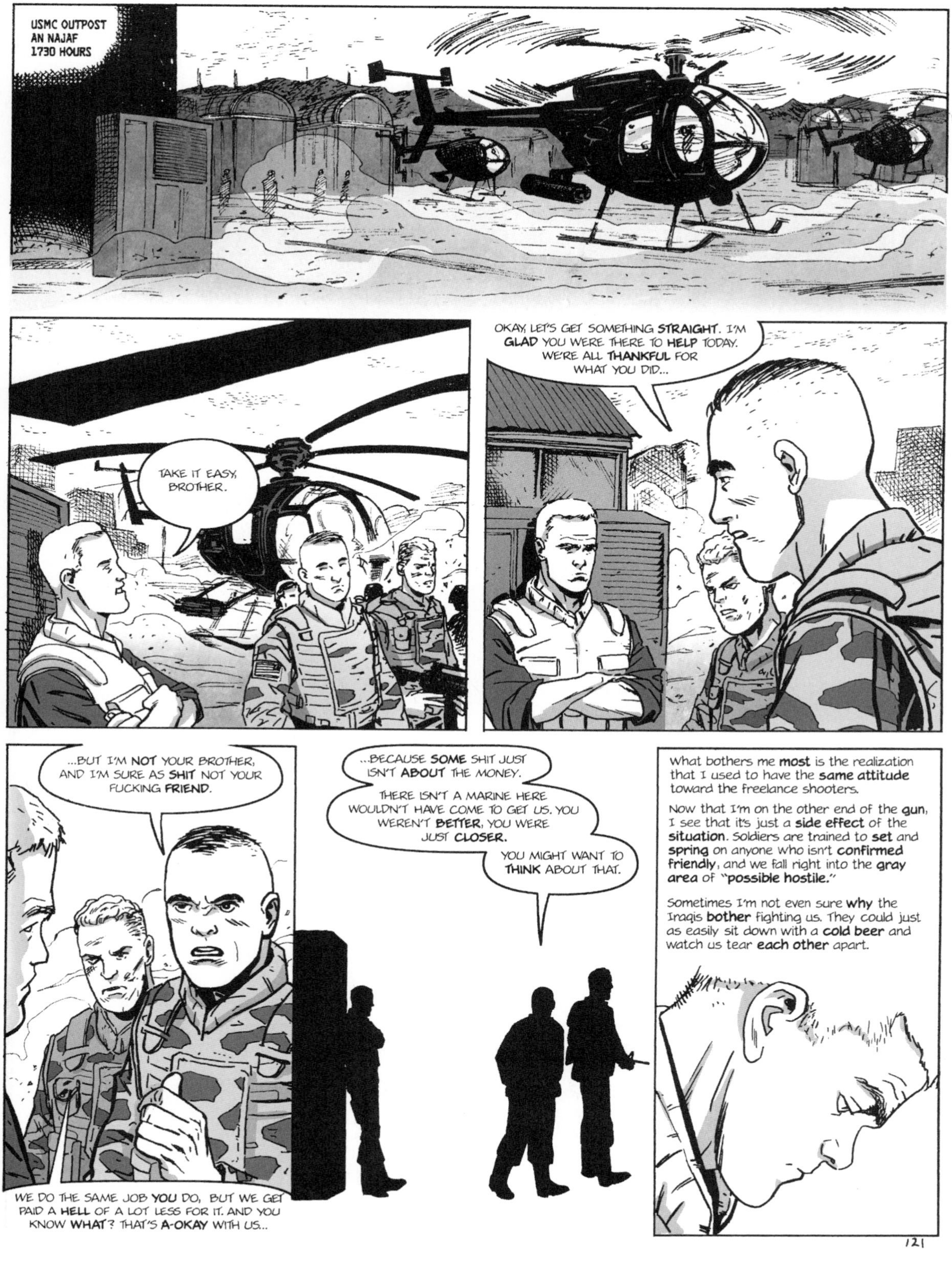
USMC OUTPOST AN NAJAF 1730 HOURS
TAKE IT EASY, BROTHER.
OKAY, LET'S GET SOMETHING STRAIGHT. I'M GLAD YOU WERE THERE TO HELP TODAY. WE'RE ALL THANKFUL FOR WHAT YOU DID...
...BUT I'M NOT YOUR BROTHER, AND I'M SURE AS SHIT NOT YOUR FUCKING FRIEND.
WE DO THE SAME JOB YOU DO, BUT WE GET PAID A HELL OF A LOT LESS FOR IT. AND YOU KNOW WHAT? THAT'S A-OKAY WITH US...
...BECAUSE SOME SHIT JUST ISN'T ABOUT THE MONEY.
THERE ISN'T A MARINE HERE WOULDN'T HAVE COME TO GET US. YOU WEREN'T BETTER, YOU WERE JUST CLOSER.
YOU MIGHT WANT TO THINK ABOUT THAT.
What bothers me most is the realization that I used to have the same attitude toward the freelance shooters.
Now that I'm on the other end of the gun, I see that it's just a side effect of the situation. Soldiers are trained to set and spring on anyone who isn't confirmed friendly, and we fall right into the gray area of "possible hostile."
Sometimes I'm not even sure why the Iraqis bother fighting us. They could just as easily sit down with a cold beer and watch us tear each other apart.

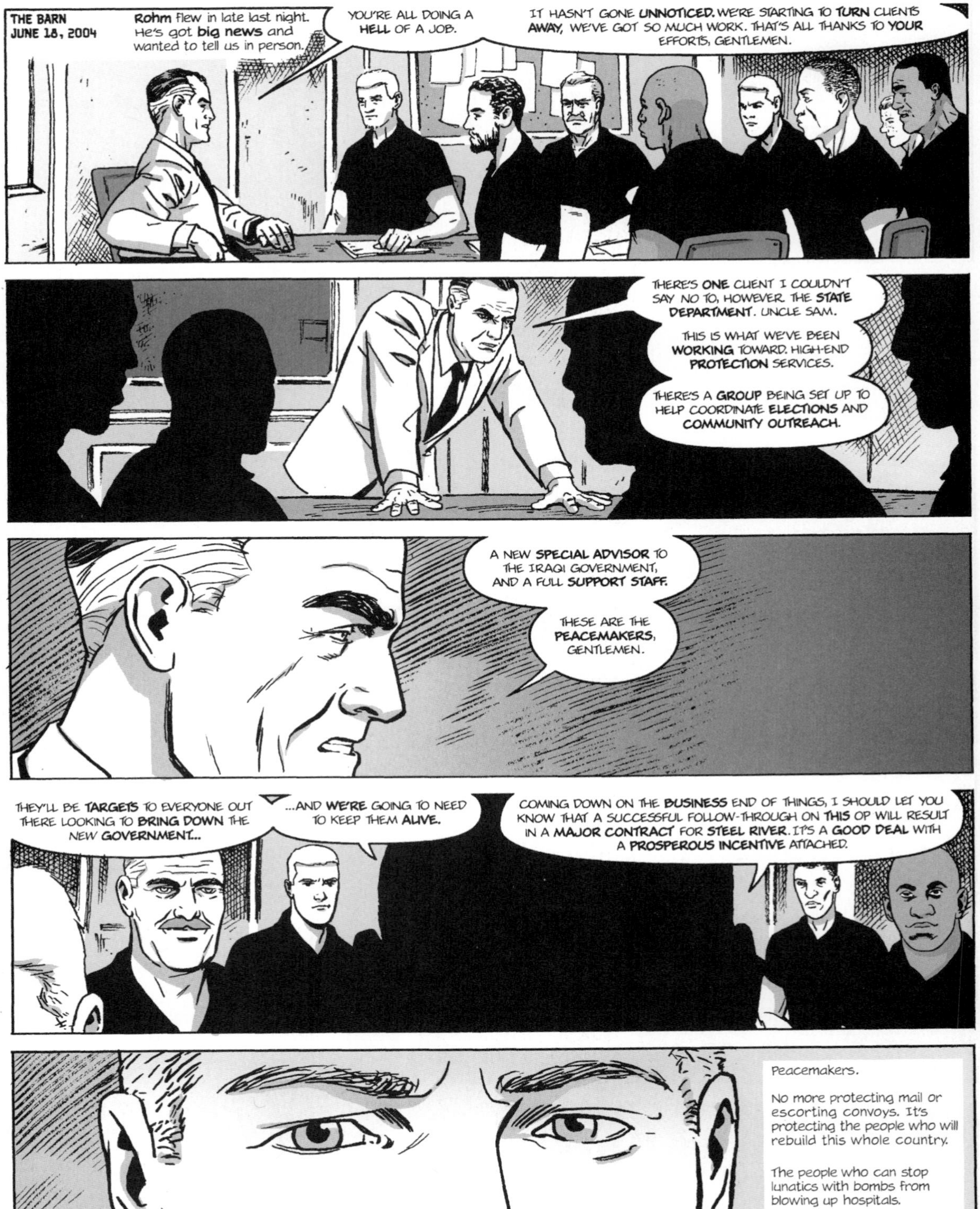
THE BARN
JUNE 18, 2004
Rohm flew in late last night. He's got big news and wanted to tell us in person.
YOU'RE ALL DOING A HELL OF A JOB.
IT HASN'T GONE UNNOTICED. WE'RE STARTING TO TURN CLIENTS AWAY, WE'VE GOT SO MUCH WORK. THAT'S ALL THANKS TO YOUR EFFORTS, GENTLEMEN.
THERE'S ONE CLIENT I COULDN'T SAY NO TO, HOWEVER. THE STATE DEPARTMENT. UNCLE SAM.
THIS IS WHAT WE'VE BEEN WORKING TOWARD. HIGH-END PROTECTION SERVICES.
THERE'S A GROUP BEING SET UP TO HELP COORDINATE ELECTIONS AND COMMUNITY OUTREACH.
A NEW SPECIAL ADVISOR TO THE IRAQI GOVERNMENT, AND A FULL SUPPORT STAFF.
THESE ARE THE PEACEMAKERS, GENTLEMEN.
THEY'LL BE TARGETS TO EVERYONE OUT THERE LOOKING TO BRING DOWN THE NEW GOVERNMENT...
...AND WE'RE GOING TO NEED TO KEEP THEM ALIVE.
COMING DOWN ON THE BUSINESS END OF THINGS, I SHOULD LET YOU KNOW THAT A SUCCESSFUL FOLLOW-THROUGH ON THIS OP WILL RESULT IN A MAJOR CONTRACT FOR STEEL RIVER. IT'S A GOOD DEAL WITH A PROSPEROUS INCENTIVE ATTACHED.
Peacemakers.
No more protecting mail or escorting convoys. It's protecting the people who will rebuild this whole country.
The people who can stop lunatics with bombs from blowing up hospitals.
Work that matters.

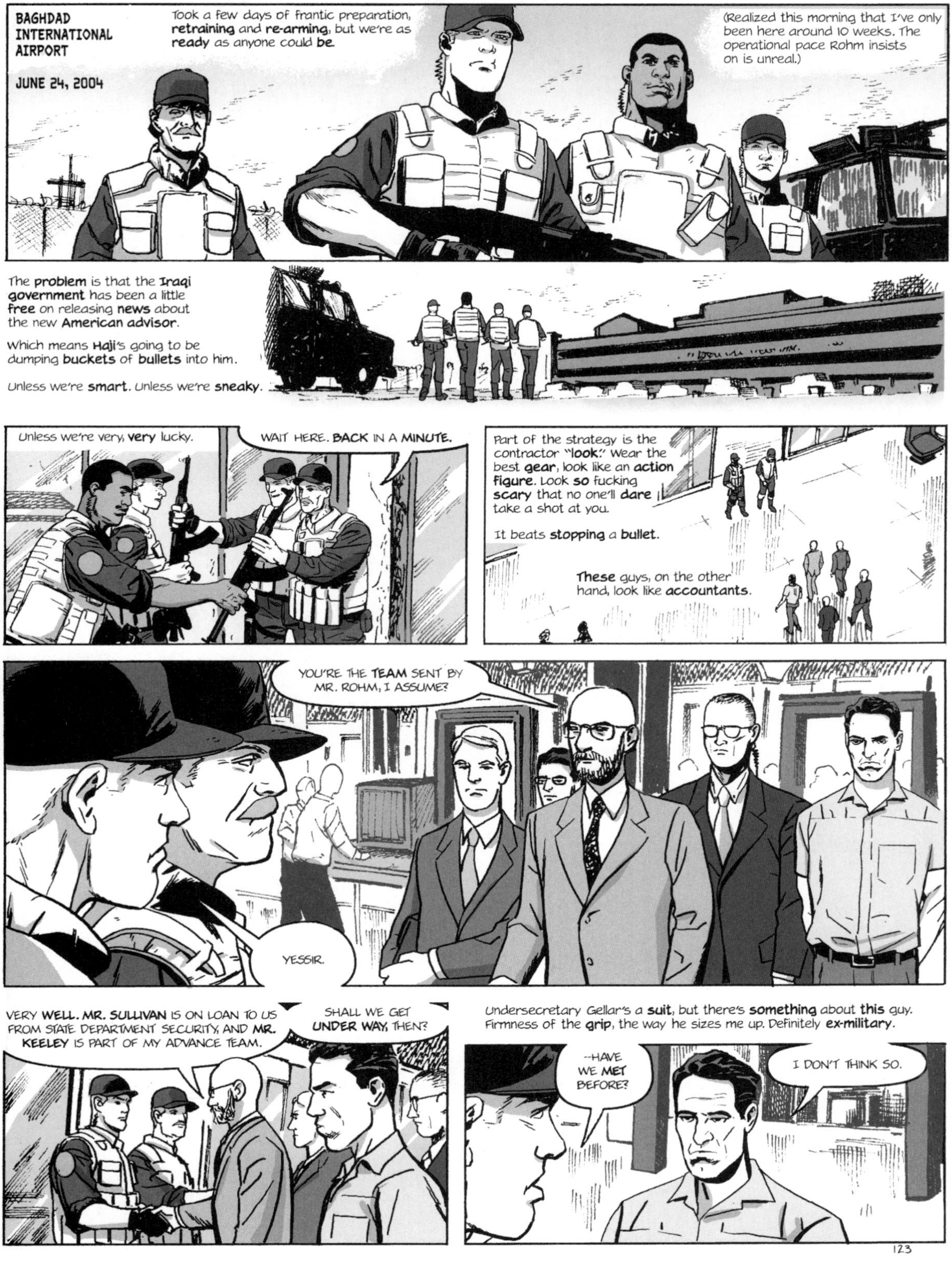
BAGHDAD INTERNATIONAL AIRPORT
JUNE 24, 2004
Took a few days of frantic preparation, retraining and re-arming, but we're as ready as anyone could be.
(Realized this morning that I've only been here around 10 weeks. The operational pace Rohm insists on is unreal.)
The problem is that the Iraqi government has been a little free on releasing news about the new American advisor.
Which means Haji's going to be dumping buckets of bullets into him.
Unless we're smart. Unless we're sneaky.
Unless we're very, very lucky.
WAIT HERE. BACK IN A MINUTE.
Part of the strategy is the contractor "look." Wear the best gear, look like an action figure. Look so fucking scary that no one'll dare take a shot at you.
It beats stopping a bullet.
These guys, on the other hand, look like accountants.
YOU'RE THE TEAM SENT BY MR. ROHM, I ASSUME?
YESSIR.
VERY WELL. MR. SULLIVAN IS ON LOAN TO US FROM STATE DEPARTMENT SECURITY, AND MR. KEELEY IS PART OF MY ADVANCE TEAM.
SHALL WE GET UNDER WAY, THEN?
Undersecretary Gellar's a suit, but there's something about this guy. Firmness of the grip, the way he sizes me up. Definitely ex-military.
--HAVE WE MET BEFORE?
I DON'T THINK SO.

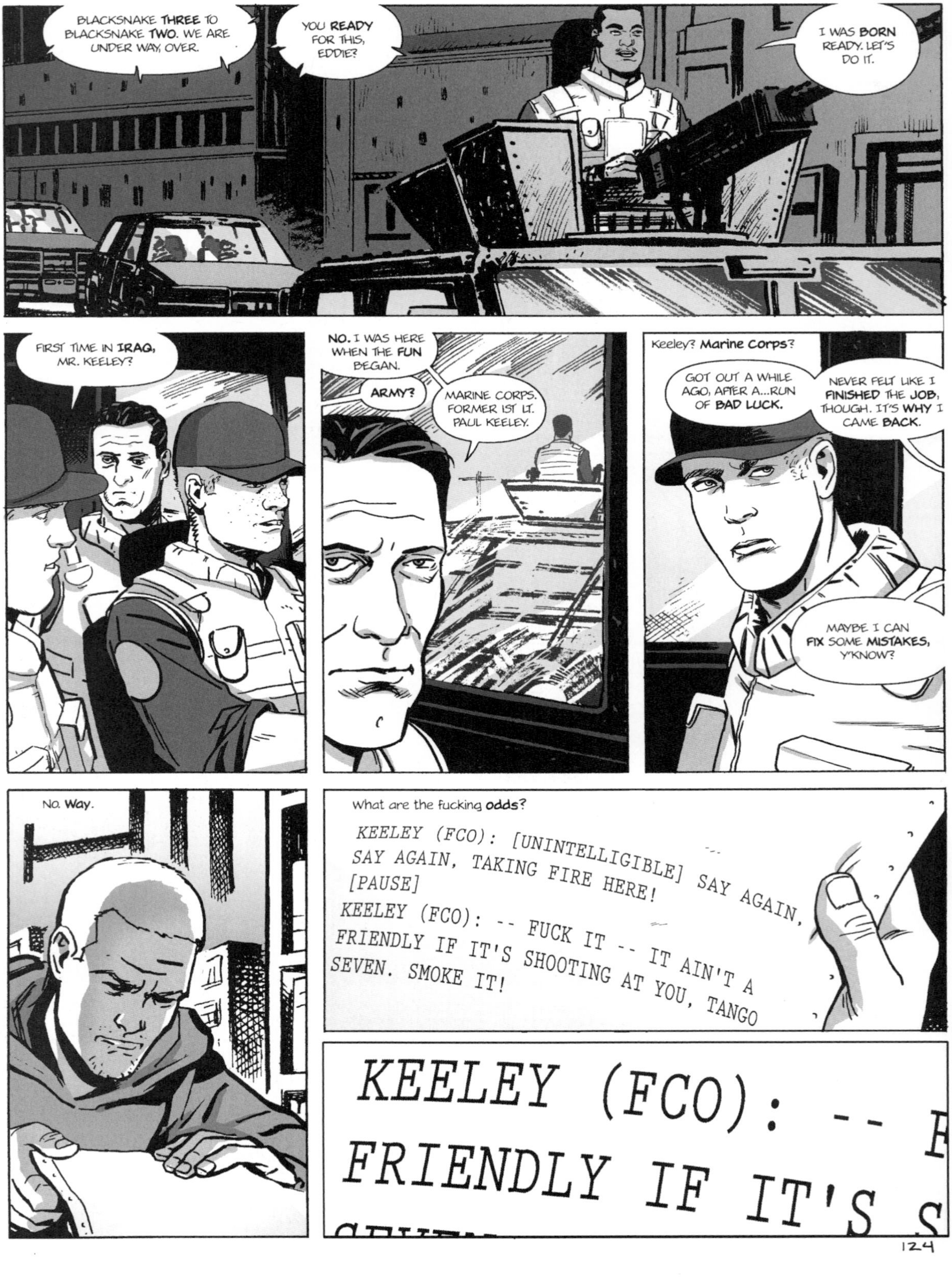
BLACKSNAKE THREE TO BLACKSNAKE TWO. WE ARE UNDER WAY, OVER.
YOU READY FOR THIS, EDDIE?
I WAS BORN READY. LET'S DO IT.
FIRST TIME IN IRAQ, MR. KEELEY?
NO. I WAS HERE WHEN THE FUN BEGAN.
ARMY?
MARINE CORPS. FORMER 1ST LT. PAUL KEELEY.
Keeley? Marine Corps?
GOT OUT A WHILE AGO, AFTER A...RUN OF BAD LUCK.
NEVER FELT LIKE I FINISHED THE JOB, THOUGH. IT'S WHY I CAME BACK.
MAYBE I CAN FIX SOME MISTAKES, Y'KNOW?
No. Way.
What are the fucking odds?
KEELEY (FCO): [UNINTELLIGIBLE] SAY AGAIN, SAY AGAIN, TAKING FIRE HERE!
[PAUSE]
KEELEY (FCO): -- FUCK IT -- IT AIN'T A FRIENDLY IF IT'S SHOOTING AT YOU, TANGO SEVEN. SMOKE IT!
KEELEY (FCO): --
FRIENDLY IF IT'S

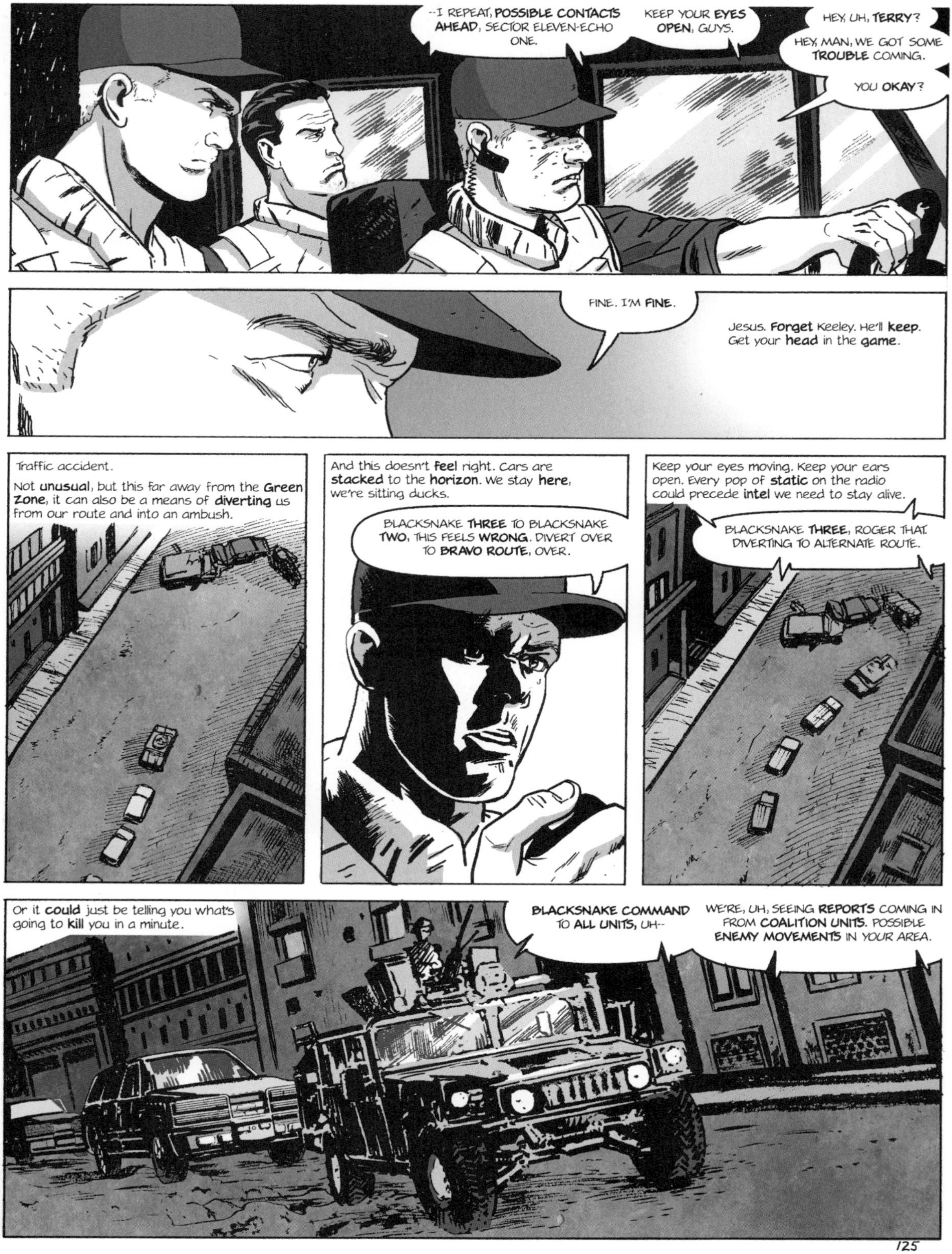
--I REPEAT, POSSIBLE CONTACTS AHEAD, SECTOR ELEVEN-ECHO ONE.
KEEP YOUR EYES OPEN, GUYS.
HEY, UH, TERRY?
HEY, MAN, WE GOT SOME TROUBLE COMING.
YOU OKAY?
FINE. I'M FINE.
Jesus. Forget Keeley. He'll keep. Get your head in the game.
Traffic accident.
Not unusual, but this far away from the Green Zone, it can also be a means of diverting us from our route and into an ambush.
And this doesn't feel right. Cars are stacked to the horizon. We stay here, we're sitting ducks.
BLACKSNAKE THREE TO BLACKSNAKE TWO, THIS FEELS WRONG. DIVERT OVER TO BRAVO ROUTE, OVER.
Keep your eyes moving. Keep your ears open. Every pop of static on the radio could precede intel we need to stay alive.
BLACKSNAKE THREE, ROGER THAT. DIVERTING TO ALTERNATE ROUTE.
Or it could just be telling you what's going to kill you in a minute.
BLACKSNAKE COMMAND TO ALL UNITS, UH--
WE'RE, UH, SEEING REPORTS COMING IN FROM COALITION UNITS. POSSIBLE ENEMY MOVEMENTS IN YOUR AREA.

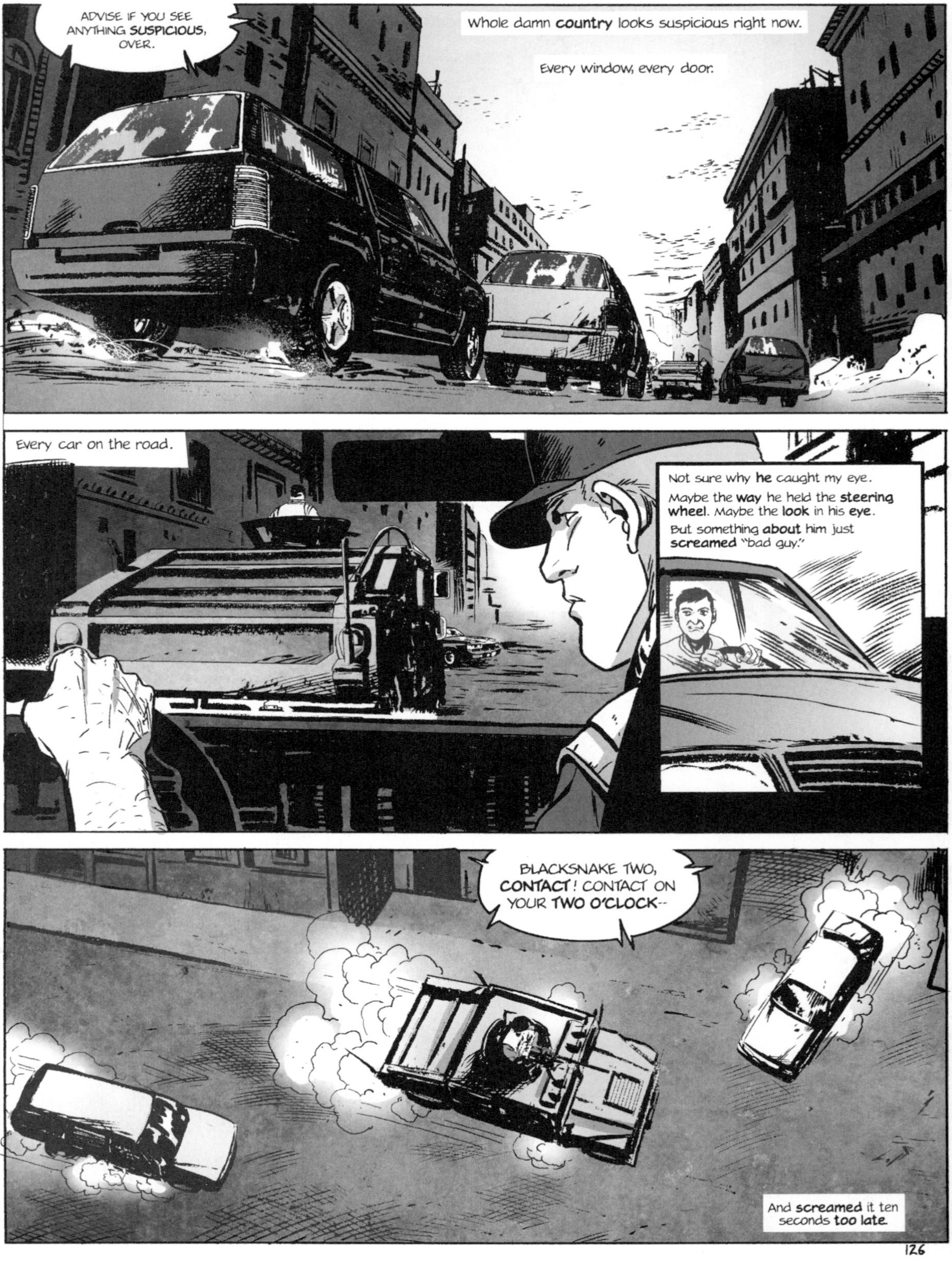
ADVISE IF YOU SEE ANYTHING SUSPICIOUS, OVER.
Whole damn country looks suspicious right now.
Every window, every door.
Every car on the road.
Not sure why he caught my eye.
Maybe the way he held the steering wheel. Maybe the look in his eye.
But something about him just screamed "bad guy."
BLACKSNAKE TWO, CONTACT! CONTACT ON YOUR TWO O'CLOCK--
And screamed it ten seconds too late.

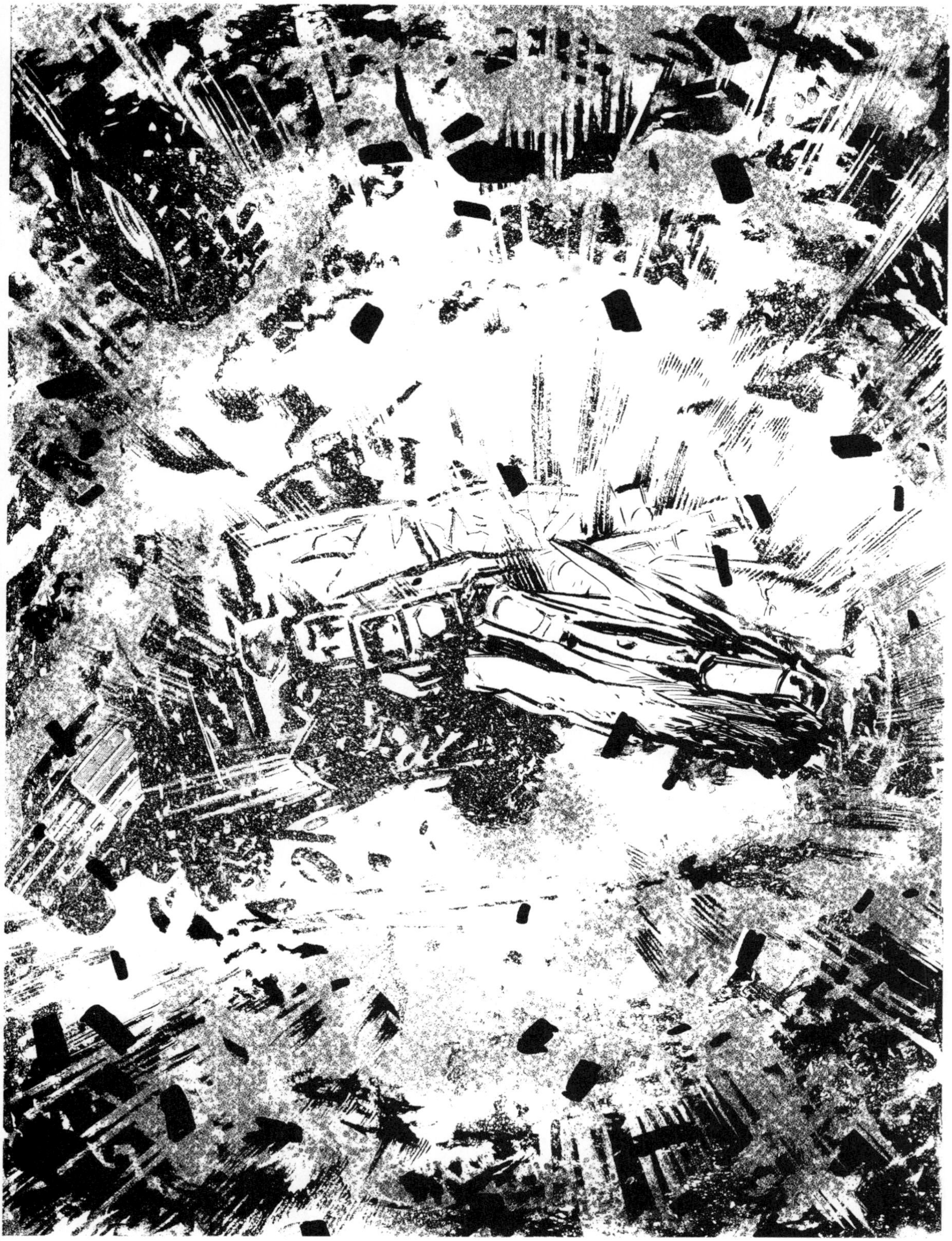

--NNNGH!

Shit--

--blast is going to crush us--

Eddie?

--crush us like a beer can--

BOBBY?

BOBBY?

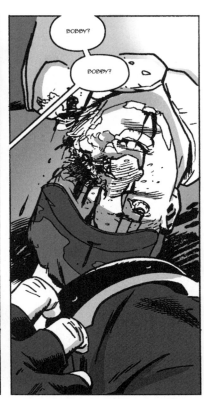

He's gone. **He's gone.**

Got to get **out** of here. We're **screwed.**

Fucking **bullet magnet**--

Get to **Eddie.** He'll be okay.

He's **always** okay.

Always the one that brings you **home.**

He's **indestructible.**

He's a fucking **rabbit's foot.**

He's--

He's--

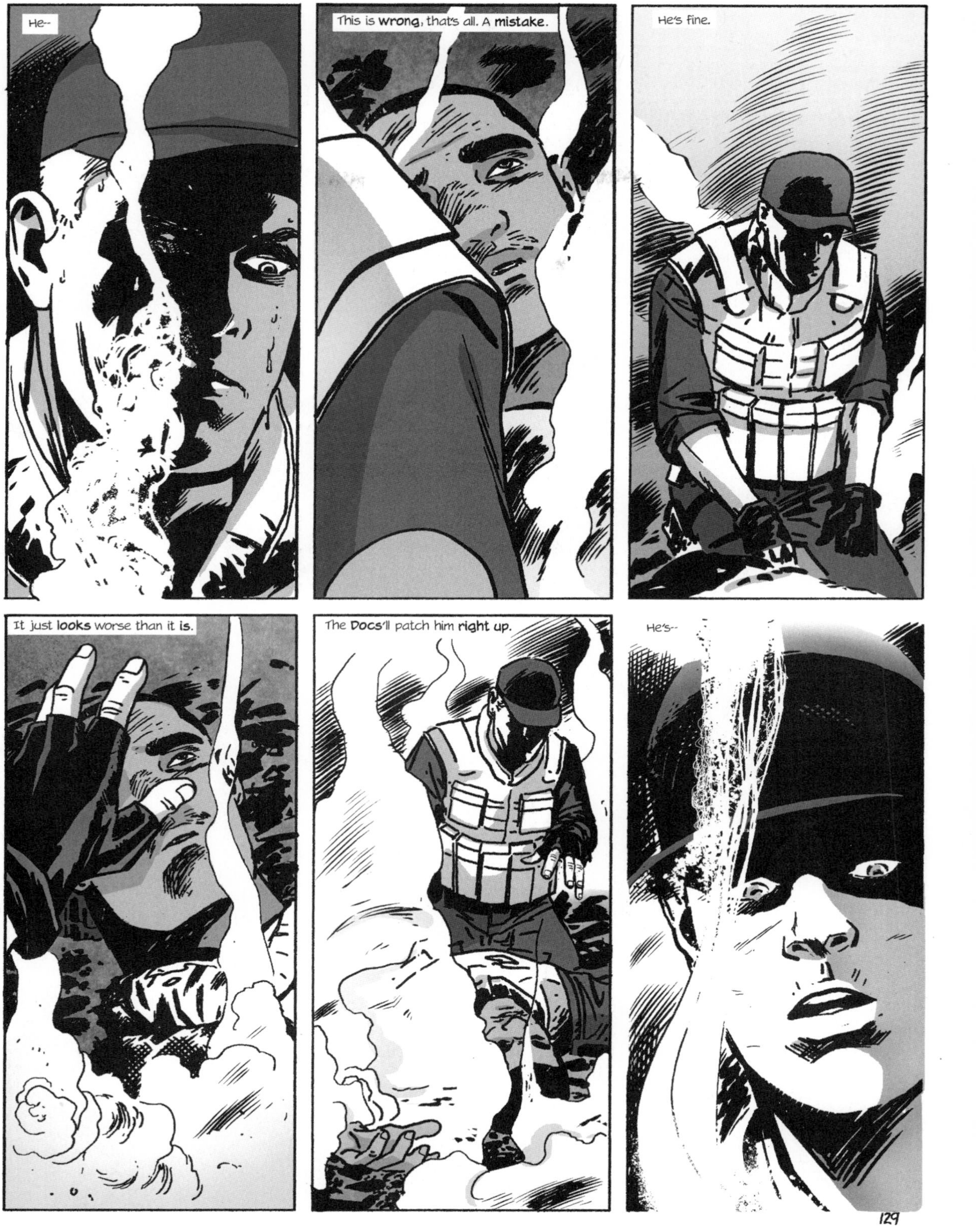
He--
This is wrong, that's all. A mistake.
He's fine.
It just looks worse than it is.
The Docs'll patch him right up.
He's--

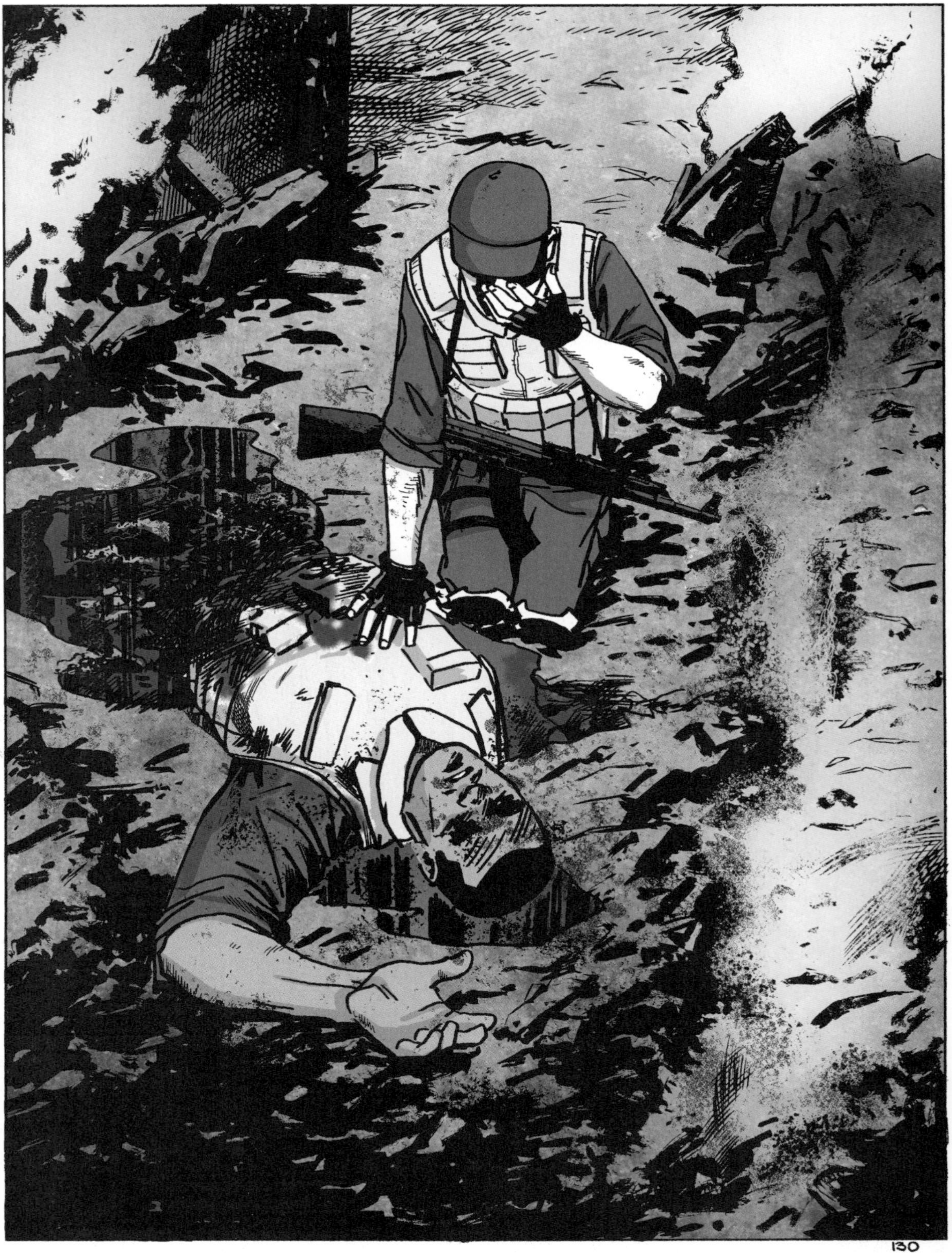

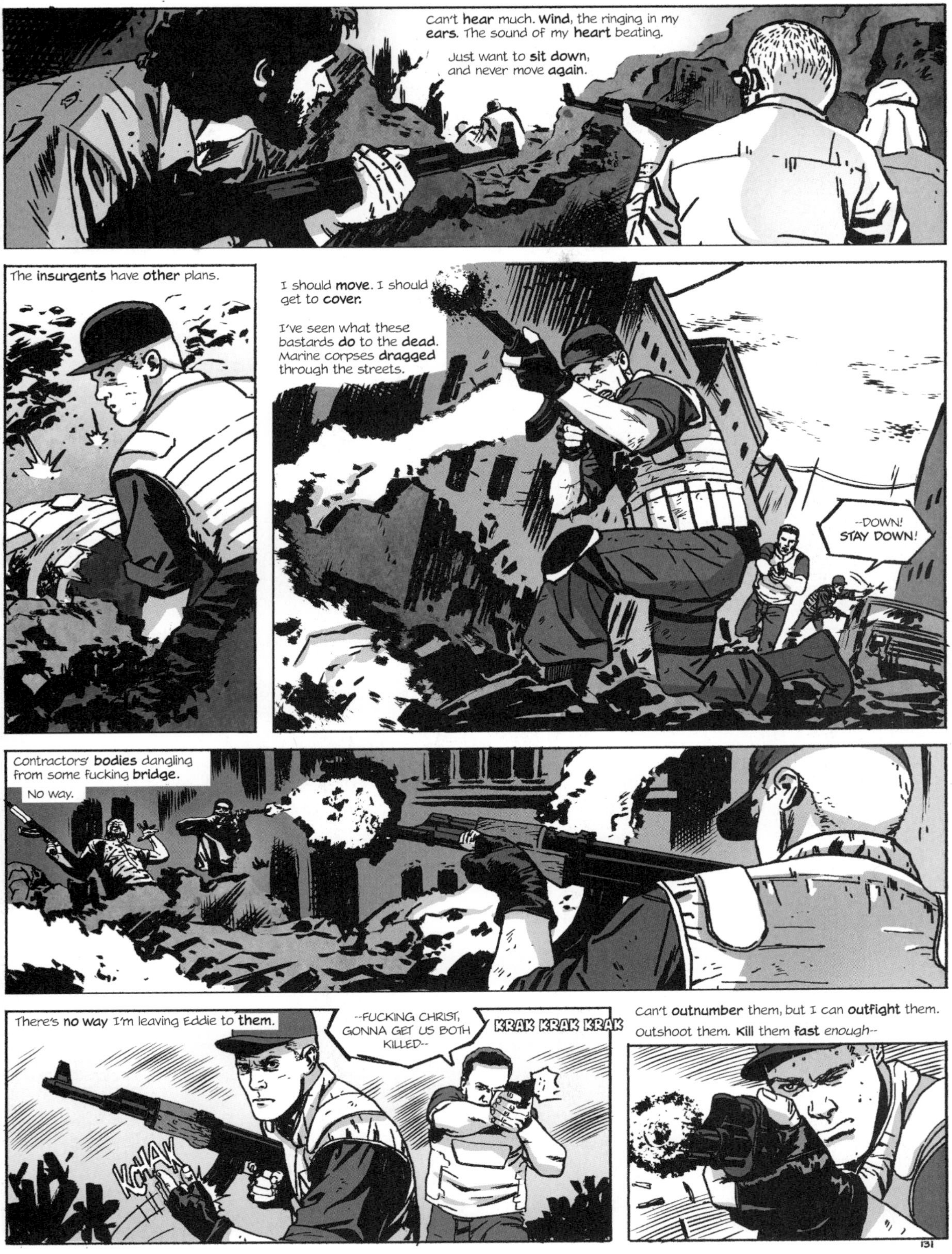

Can't hear much. Wind, the ringing in my ears. The sound of my heart beating.
Just want to sit down, and never move again.
The insurgents have other plans.
I should move. I should get to cover.
I've seen what these bastards do to the dead. Marine corpses dragged through the streets.
--DOWN! STAY DOWN!
Contractors' bodies dangling from some fucking bridge.
No way.
There's no way I'm leaving Eddie to them.
--FUCKING CHRIST, GONNA GET US BOTH KILLED--
KRAK KRAK KRAK
Can't outnumber them, but I can outfight them.
Outshoot them. Kill them fast enough--

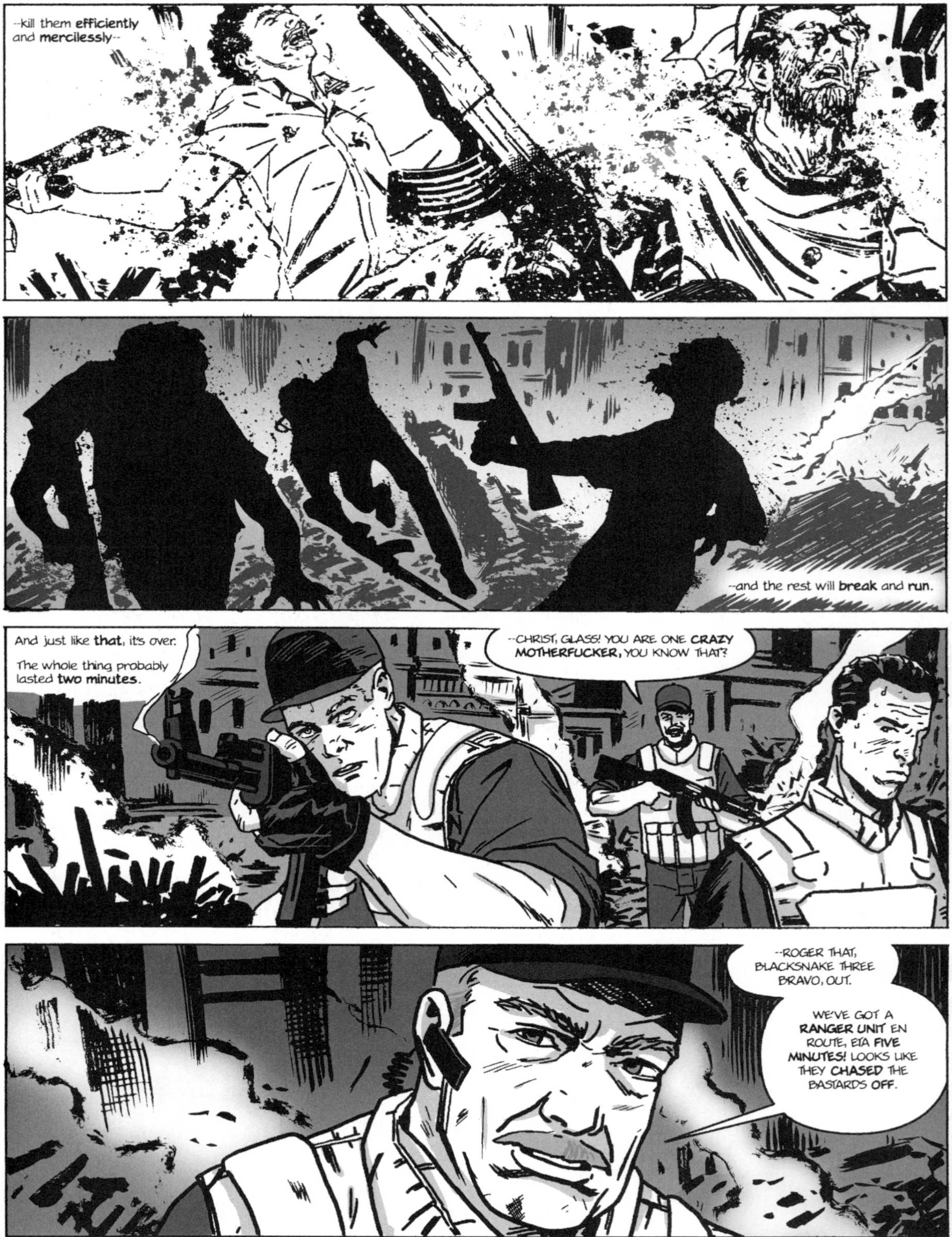
--kill them efficiently and mercilessly--
--and the rest will break and run.
And just like that, it's over.
The whole thing probably lasted two minutes.
--CHRIST, GLASS! YOU ARE ONE CRAZY MOTHERFUCKER, YOU KNOW THAT?
--ROGER THAT, BLACKSNAKE THREE BRAVO, OUT.
WE'VE GOT A RANGER UNIT EN ROUTE, ETA FIVE MINUTES! LOOKS LIKE THEY CHASED THE BASTARDS OFF.

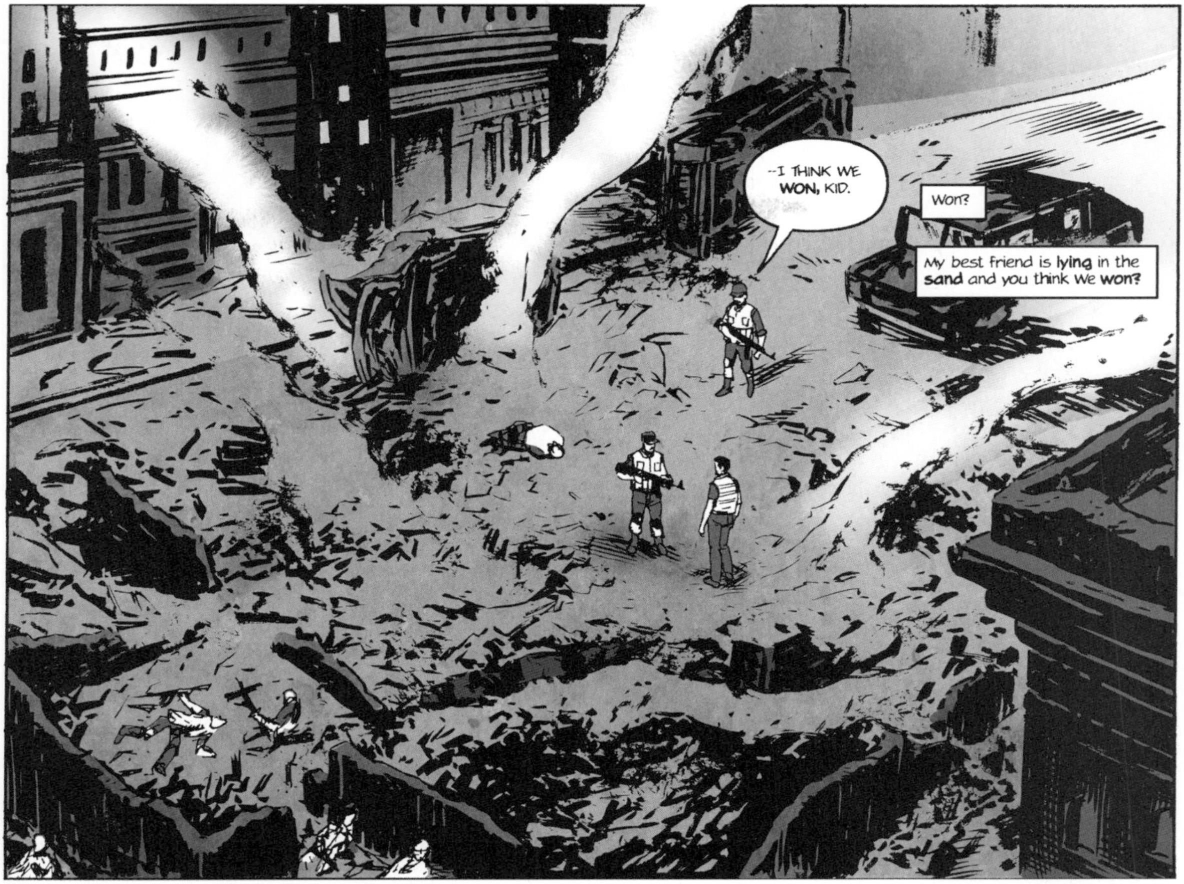
--I THINK WE WON, KID.
Won?
My best friend is lying in the sand and you think we won?

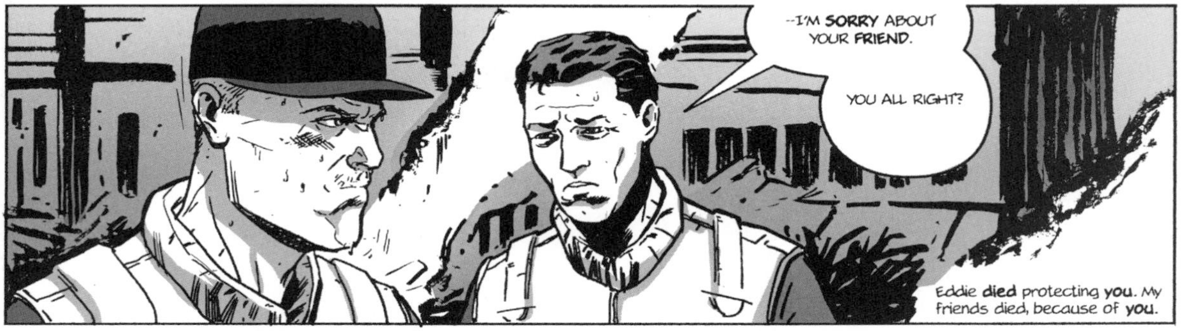
--I'M SORRY ABOUT YOUR FRIEND.
YOU ALL RIGHT?
Eddie died protecting you. My friends died, because of you.

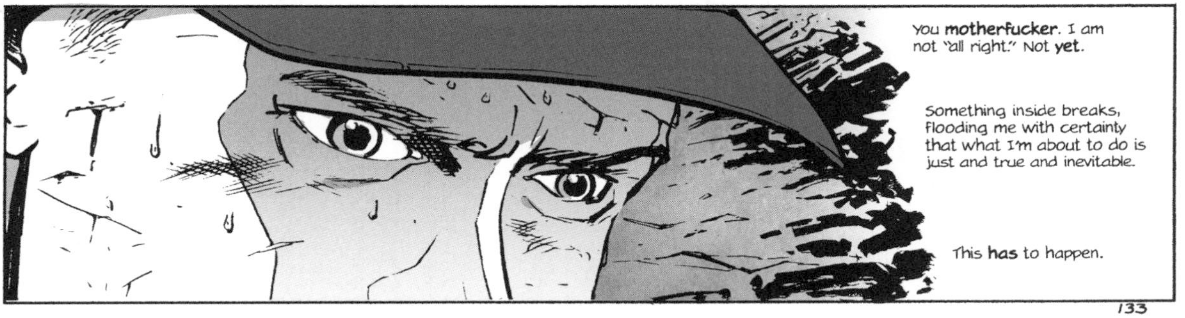
You motherfucker. I am not "all right." Not yet.
Something inside breaks, flooding me with certainty that what I'm about to do is just and true and inevitable.
This has to happen.

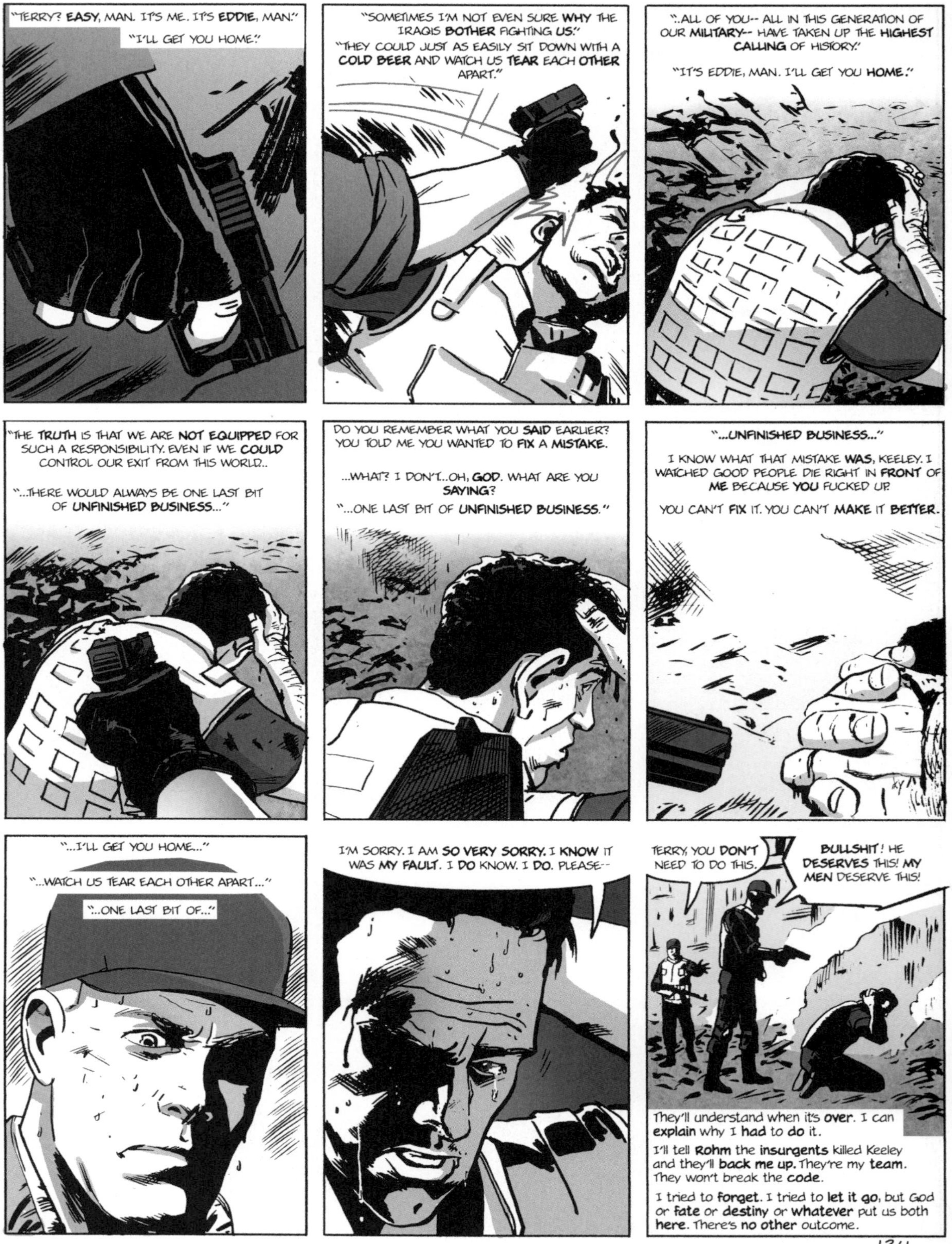

"TERRY? EASY, MAN. IT'S ME. IT'S EDDIE, MAN."
"I'LL GET YOU HOME."
"SOMETIMES I'M NOT EVEN SURE WHY THE IRAQIS BOTHER FIGHTING US."
"THEY COULD JUST AS EASILY SIT DOWN WITH A COLD BEER AND WATCH US TEAR EACH OTHER APART."
"..ALL OF YOU-- ALL IN THIS GENERATION OF OUR MILITARY-- HAVE TAKEN UP THE HIGHEST CALLING OF HISTORY."
"IT'S EDDIE, MAN. I'LL GET YOU HOME."
"THE TRUTH IS THAT WE ARE NOT EQUIPPED FOR SUCH A RESPONSIBILITY. EVEN IF WE COULD CONTROL OUR EXIT FROM THIS WORLD..
"...THERE WOULD ALWAYS BE ONE LAST BIT OF UNFINISHED BUSINESS..."
DO YOU REMEMBER WHAT YOU SAID EARLIER? YOU TOLD ME YOU WANTED TO FIX A MISTAKE.
...WHAT? I DON'T...OH, GOD. WHAT ARE YOU SAYING?
"...ONE LAST BIT OF UNFINISHED BUSINESS."
"...UNFINISHED BUSINESS..."
I KNOW WHAT THAT MISTAKE WAS, KEELEY. I WATCHED GOOD PEOPLE DIE RIGHT IN FRONT OF ME BECAUSE YOU FUCKED UP.
YOU CAN'T FIX IT. YOU CAN'T MAKE IT BETTER.
"...I'LL GET YOU HOME..."
"...WATCH US TEAR EACH OTHER APART..."
"...ONE LAST BIT OF..."
I'M SORRY. I AM SO VERY SORRY. I KNOW IT WAS MY FAULT. I DO KNOW. I DO. PLEASE--
TERRY, YOU DON'T NEED TO DO THIS.
BULLSHIT! HE DESERVES THIS! MY MEN DESERVE THIS!
They'll understand when it's over. I can explain why I had to do it.
I'll tell Rohm the insurgents killed Keeley and they'll back me up. They're my team. They won't break the code.
I tried to forget. I tried to let it go, but God or fate or destiny or whatever put us both here. There's no other outcome.

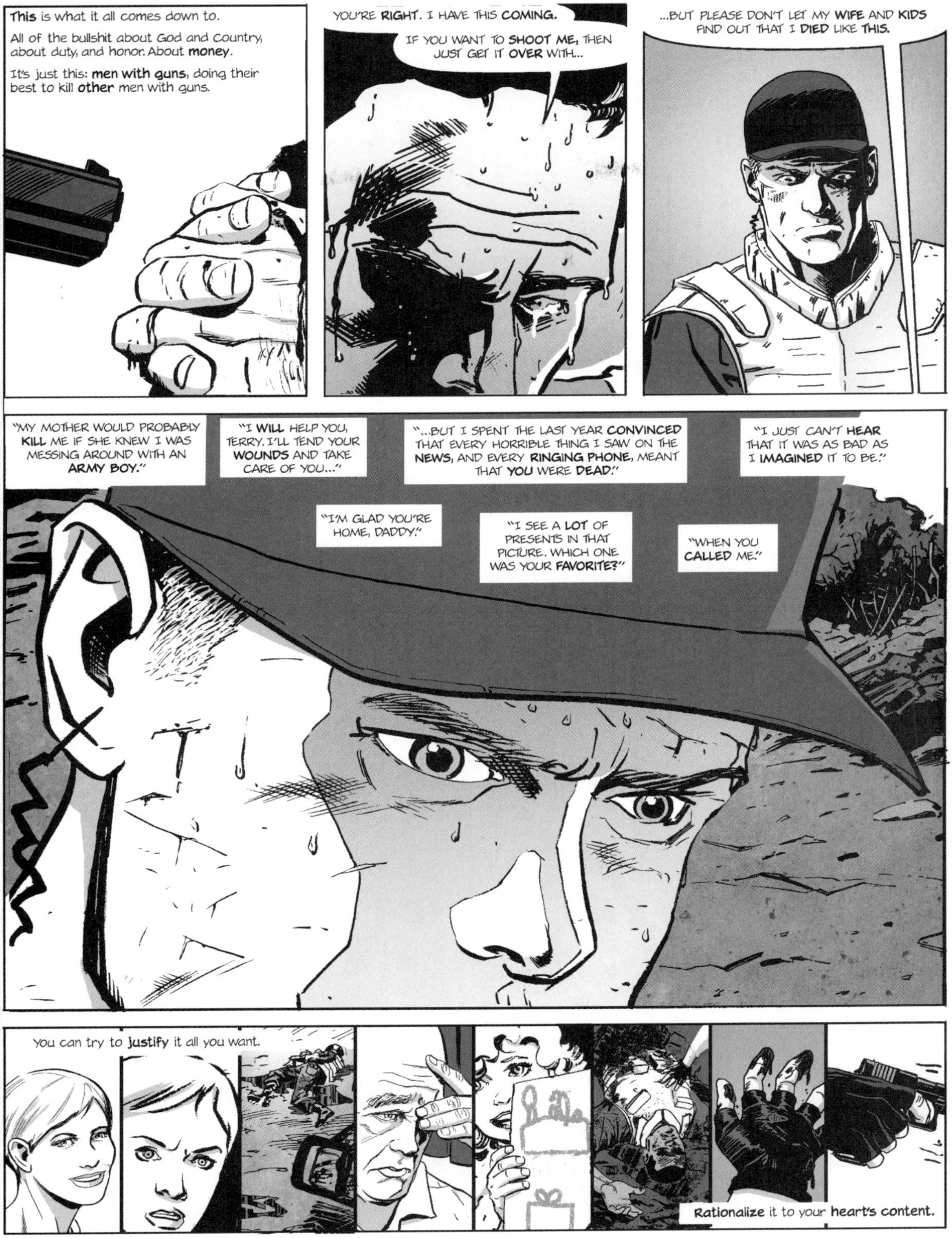
This is what it all comes down to.
All of the bullshit about God and Country, about duty, and honor. About money.
It's just this: men with guns, doing their best to kill other men with guns.
YOU'RE RIGHT. I HAVE THIS COMING.
IF YOU WANT TO SHOOT ME, THEN JUST GET IT OVER WITH...
...BUT PLEASE DON'T LET MY WIFE AND KIDS FIND OUT THAT I DIED LIKE THIS.
"MY MOTHER WOULD PROBABLY KILL ME IF SHE KNEW I WAS MESSING AROUND WITH AN ARMY BOY."
"I WILL HELP YOU, TERRY. I'LL TEND YOUR WOUNDS AND TAKE CARE OF YOU..."
"...BUT I SPENT THE LAST YEAR CONVINCED THAT EVERY HORRIBLE THING I SAW ON THE NEWS, AND EVERY RINGING PHONE, MEANT THAT YOU WERE DEAD."
"I JUST CAN'T HEAR THAT IT WAS AS BAD AS I IMAGINED IT TO BE."
"I'M GLAD YOU'RE HOME, DADDY."
"I SEE A LOT OF PRESENTS IN THAT PICTURE. WHICH ONE WAS YOUR FAVORITE?"
"WHEN YOU CALLED ME."
You can try to justify it all you want.
Rationalize it to your heart's content.

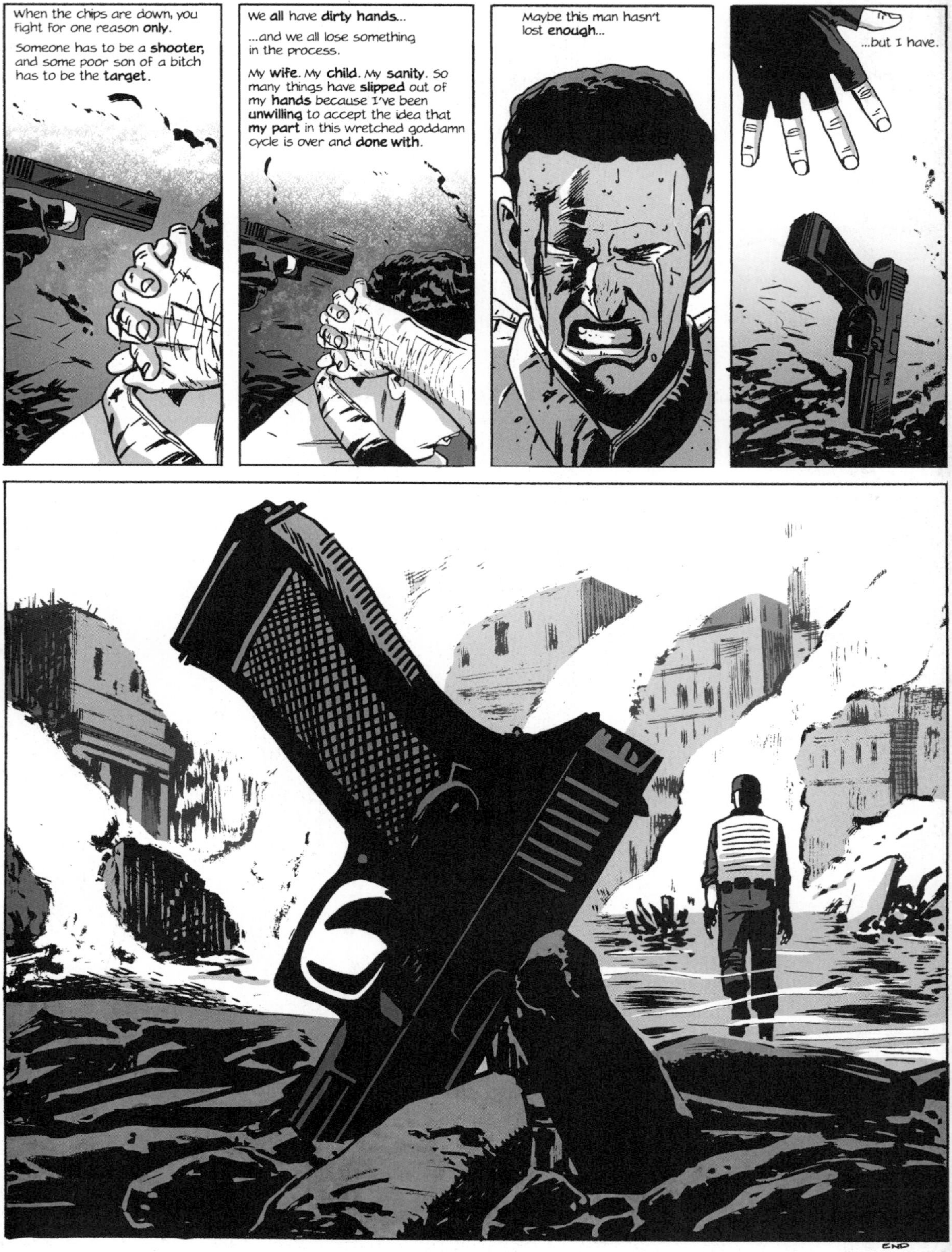
When the chips are down, you fight for one reason only.
Someone has to be a shooter, and some poor son of a bitch has to be the target.
We all have dirty hands...
...and we all lose something in the process.
My wife. My child. My sanity. So many things have slipped out of my hands because I've been unwilling to accept the idea that my part in this wretched goddamn cycle is over and done with.
Maybe this man hasn't lost enough...
...but I have.
END

Eric Trautmann is a writer and graphic designer based in coastal Washington State. After many years writing dialogue for videogames, and world-building for game franchises like *Crimson Skies*, *Perfect Dark Zero*, *Halo*, and *Gears of War*, he turned to his first love: comics.

Trautmann has co-written (with Greg Rucka) *Checkmate*, *Final Crisis: Resist* and *Action Comics* for DC as well as titles for Dynamite Entertainment. He can be found online at www.erictrautmann.us

Brandon Jerwa is best known for writing a wide variety of comics titles, such as *G.I. Joe*, *Highlander* and *Battlestar Galactica*, but he's never been content with just one creative pursuit. At any given moment, Jerwa may be producing and directing independent film projects, performing original music with his band SD6, teaching classes for aspiring writers, or serving as a cultural ambassador for the American comics industry at festivals abroad. He currently resides in Seattle, Washington.

Steve Lieber studied art at The Kubert School. His comics and illustration have been published by DC, Marvel, Dark Horse, Image, Dupuis, Scholastic and many other publishers, but he is best known for his work on *Whiteout*, a graphic novel adapted by Warner Bros. as a feature starring Kate Beckinsale.

His various projects have received nine Eisner Award nominations, and he won the Eisner for Best Limited Series for *Whiteout Volume 2: Melt*. Steve is a founding member of Periscope Studio, the largest studio of comic book artists in North America. He lives in Portland, Oregon, with his wife, the novelist Sara Ryan. http://stevelieber.com